Reimagining
the
Catholic
School

Edited by
Ned Prendergast
& Luke Monahan

VERITAS

Published 2003 by
Veritas Publications
7/8 Lower Abbey Street
Dublin 1
Email publications@veritas.ie
Website www.veritas.ie

ISBN 1 85390 662 x

A catalogue record for this book is available from the British Library.

The tapestry used on the front cover was weaved at the Reimagining the Catholic School Conference by Sr Rosaleen McCabe, a Sister of St Clare based at Harolds Cross, Dublin.

Cover design by Bill Bolger
Typesetting and layout by Veritas Publications
Printed in the Republic of Ireland by Betaprint Ltd, Dublin

Veritas books are printed on paper made from the wood pulp of managed forests. For every tree felled, at least one tree is planted, thereby renewing natural resources.

Contents

Acknowledgements

The editors wish to thank a number of people without whom this publication would not have been possible. First thanks go to all the contributors to the book whose articles arose by way of presentation to the original conference or who accepted a subsequent invitation to write on the topic.

The **Marino Trust Fund** established by the **Irish Christian Brothers** provides the seed funding for much of what happens at the Centre for Education Services. We take this opportunity to thank them for the vision they bring to the future of Irish education and for the practical support which allows initiatives such as The Catholic School – imagining the future project to be undertaken.

We were very fortunate when developing the project to have as unofficial consultants visionary people such as Tom Groome, Joe O'Keefe, Denis McLaughlin, Jim Cassin, Liz Maxwell, Theresa McCormack, Ann Walsh, Joe McCann, Stephen Deignan, and Marie Celine Clegg.

The most significant event in the life of the project to date was the landmark conference of March 2002 much of which is reflected in one form or another in this publication. We want to take this opportunity to acknowledge Martin Delaney, Maeve Mahon and Liam Lawton who devised and led so beautifully the liturgical aspects of that event; Martin Lynch who co-ordinated the technical dimensions; Geraldine Carberry, Don Herron and Maureen Mc Donagh who with the indispensable energy and professionalism of Mai Ralph managed all the administrative elements of the conference. Of great support throughout were the Marino Team at the Centre for Education Services, Br Donal Leader, Director of the Institute, the finance and facilities staff.

We were supported by many groups in terms of sponsorship, most particularly the Irish Christian Brothers. We must mention especially also the Conference of Religious of Ireland (CORI); The Association of Management of Catholic Secondary Schools (AMCSS); the De La Salle Brothers; the Loreto Sisters and the Marist Fathers. Finally we would also like to acknowledge Coillte, the ESB, Typeform Repro, EMS Copiers and CodeX Office Supplies for their generosity and support.

The Contributors

Ned Prendergast is leader of 'The Catholic School – Imagining The Future' project, based at the Centre for Education Services, Marino Institute of Education. He is development officer with the Irish Association of Pastoral Care in Education (iapce) and co-editor of *Encountering Disaffection* (iapce, 2002).

Luke Monahan is Head of the Centre for Education Services at the Marino Institute of Education, national coordinator of the Irish Association of Pastoral Care in Education and author of a range of books on educational practice, including *The Year Head, The Chaplain: A Faith Presence in The School Community,* and co-editor of *Echoes of Suicide*. He is a consultant to schools and organisations in Ireland and abroad.

Joan D. Chittister, internationally known lecturer and author, is executive director of Benetvision, a resource and research centre for contemporary spirituality in Erie, Pennsylvania. Among her books are *Passion for Life: Fragments of the Face of God* (Orbis, 1996) and *Heart of Flesh: A Feminist Spirituality for Women and Men* (Eerdmans, 1998).

Thomas Groome, a native of County Kildare, is Senior Professor of Theology and Religious Education at Boston College. His most recent books are *Educating for Life: A Spiritual Vision for Every Teacher and Parent* (Crossroads, 2000) and *What Makes Us Catholic: Eight Gifts for Life* (HarperCollins, 2002).

Carol Barry is a lecturer in Theology at the Religious Studies Department, St Patrick's College, Drumcondra, a college of Dublin City University. She has a longstanding and abiding interest in the spirituality of teaching.

Dermot A. Lane is President of Mater Dei Institute of Education and parish priest of Balally in Dublin. He is author of *Keeping Hope Alive: Stirrings in Christian Theology* (1996) and editor of *New Century New Society: Christian Perspectives* (1999).

Jacques Janssen is a professor of Cultural Psychology and Psychology of Religion at the Catholic University of Nijmegen, The Netherlands. A prolific lecturer and writer, he is very well known throughout Europe.

Liam Lawton, a priest of the Diocese of Kildare and Leighlin, is an internationally known composer of sacred music in the Celtic tradition. CDs of his music include *Ancient Ways Future Days, The Cloud's Veil; Sacred Story* and *Light The Fire.*

Maureen Gaffney, nationally known psychologist, broadcaster and author is chair of the National Economic and Social Forum. She is author of *The Way We Live Now* (Gill & Macmillan, 1996).

Joseph O'Keefe, SJ, Associate Dean of the Lynch School of Education at Boston College, is one of the best known and most prolific writers, editors and researchers on Catholic Education in the United States. He is co-editor of *The Contemporary Catholic School: Context, Identity and Diversity.*

James Norman is a lecturer in Education and Pastoral Care at the Mater Dei Institute of Education, Dublin City University, where he is head of Chaplaincy Studies. His current research is concerned with aspects of social, personal and health education in second-level schools.

Anne Codd is a Presentation sister who works with the Conference of Religious of Ireland. It was while lecturing in Parish Planning and Development at St Patrick's College, Carlow, that she developed the material presented here.

P. J. Boyle is a clinical nurse specialist (Asylum-Seekers Health Assessment) with the Northern Area Health Board, Dublin, and an occasional lecturer in the Mater Dei Institute of Education and Dublin City University. His current research is concerned with cultural competency training and education.

Joseph McCann is a Vincentian priest who is head of Religious Studies at St Patrick's College, Drumcondra, a college of Dublin City University. He is author of *Church and Organization: A Social and Theological Enquiry* (Scranton, 1993).

Noel Canavan is a senior education consultant with the Centre for Education Services at the Marino Institute of Education. He has particular responsibility for projects dealing with school culture and ethos, conflict management and leadership in the primary setting. He has been a secondary teacher and guidance counsellor for over twenty-five years.

Seamus O'Brien is a senior education consultant with the Centre for Education Services at the Marino Institute of Education. He is project leader of the Identity Project. He recently published, with Tommy Coyle, the findings of his project in *Towards an Identity and a Contribution*.

Tommy Coyle is a senior education consultant with the Centre for Education Services at the Marino Institute of Education. He is project leader of the Leadership Programme, Secondary Level and recently published, with Seamus O'Brien, the findings of his project in *Towards an Identity and a Contribution*.

Marie Celine Clegg is Director of the Loreto Education Development Office and has particular responsibility for the Trust Board of Loreto Schools. She has been a school principal and is chairperson of a number of Boards of Management. She has been president of the Association of Management of Catholic Secondary Schools.

Fiona Gallagher is a qualified catechist with specific expertise in the areas of induction and the development of Religious Education in second-level schools. She is Project Coordinator of the An Tobar Religious Education Project based in the Marino Institute of Education. The An Tobar team endeavours to respond to the professional needs of the Religious Education teacher.

Caoimhe Máirtín is Head of College at Coláiste Mhuire, Marino, a college of education for future primary teachers, affiliated to Trinity College Dublin. There are currently in excess of five-hundred students at the college.

Martin Clarke is director of the Catholic Communications Office with the Irish Bishops-Conference. Among his many roles, he is former head of the Catholic Youth Council of Ireland.

Peter McVerry is a Jesuit priest whose campaigning for and involvement with troubled young people has made him one of the most prophetic voices of Catholic Ireland.

Anne Looney worked for many years as a catechist and is now chief executive of the National Council for Curriculum and Assessment. She is well known throughout Ireland as a lecturer, writer and broadcaster on issues around Catholic education.

Brenda Power is a barrister and an award-winning journalist *(The Sunday Tribune)* and broadcaster (RTÉ), renowned for her insightful perspectives on current affairs.

Don Herron is principal of a Dublin primary school and was project officer with the Centre for Education Services at the Marino Institute of Education. He is former director of the Dublin West Education Centre. While in Marino Institute he contributed to both the Catholic school and leadership projects.

Martin Daly is principal of Catholic University School, Leeson Street, Dublin. He is a family and systems therapist and is consultant to a number of groups and organisations. He has been a contributor to the Marino Institute Leadership Programme for a number of years.

Time to Begin Again

Ned Prendergast

Though we live in a world that dreams of ending,
that always seems about to give in,
something that will not acknowledge conclusion
insists that we forever begin.
BRENDAN KENNELLY[1]

A watershed moment

Everyone agrees that we have reached a critical moment in the history of Catholic education in Ireland. Many would characterise it as a moment of 'giving in', the end of an era, a time of bereavement and loss. Highlighted strands in the unravelling of a cherished world point to the demise of the great teaching congregations and the withdrawal of religious from schools. All of this is currently set against the background of a Church grievously wounded in the wake of abuse scandals. Adding to a sense of failure, and fanned by other scandals sweeping our country, is a degree of disappointment with and questioning of the society that has emerged in Ireland. A society that Catholic schools worked so hard to build now appears to be neither civic nor moral, nor to have many hallmarks of a Christian nation. It is noted that the eclipse of a sense of God has been accompanied by an equivalent diminution in the sense of human dignity. Counterpointing all these developments is a dawning of the fact that Catholic education is now greatly enmeshed with the State's education system, with the door open to a secular future where education is market-driven, smart-targeted and commodified, and where a secular piper increasingly calls the tune. It cannot be surprising that the impact of these developments has tended to create 'a world that dreams of ending', or that for so many it has become a time of wistfulness and for wondering 'What was it all for?'.

Others, however, see the present as a challenging watershed moment, with the potential for something new and vibrant and exciting. They say that our schools are, in many ways, more Christian than they ever were and that they continue to be staffed by remarkably good and idealistic people. They view present discomforts as cathartic and liberating and as grounding us in the real world, a world in which there may be fewer Catholic schools but in which those schools will be nearer to the vision that is said to characterise and differentiate them. In a pluralist world, the argument goes, the provision of choice offers, perhaps for the first time, the possibility of real choice. From this optimist's perspective, the Education Act 1998's provision of recognition for 'the characteristic spirit' of a school and its ongoing protection of the rights of parents to choose, presents a viable legal platform for the future. Current developments leading to new trust arrangments, moreover, are seen as offering an opportunity to develop a real charter for the Catholic school into the decades ahead.

If the optimist's approach is the valid one, then the present moment is one to be grasped enthusiastially. If there is nothing like a bracing challenge to purify the motivation, then surely the time has arrived for discernment and reframing, for sifting what is important from what is accidental, for clarifying our spirituality and our purpose. It is time for a new beginning in Catholic education, time for taking the Catholic school beyond just being a cultural phenomenon, time to engage schools around a new charter and mission. It is a time, above all, to be creative and energetic, a time to listen to that which 'will not acknowledge conclusion' and which 'insists that we forever begin'.

It was into the gathering momentum of this perspective and through the generosity of the Irish Christian Brothers' Marino Trust Fund that the *Catholic School – Imagining the Future* project was set up at the Centre for Education Services at the Marino Institute of Education. Founded on the two hundredth anniversary of the first Christian Brothers' school at New Street, Waterford, in 1802, the project adopted a sapling tree as its symbol, not only because images of roots and watering and fruit-bearing were apt to its purposes, but also in order to echo the historic provenance of our origins as reflected in Normoyle's choice of 'A Tree is Planted' as the title for his biography of Edmund Rice.[2] The first initiative of the project was to hold a landmark conference on the Catholic school in the spring of 2002, the papers of which are presented in this volume.

From its initiation, the project saw its purpose as proposing a renewed role for Catholic schools which would more adequately mirror the Christian gospel. It wished to pay special attention to the 'architecture of the spirit'[3] on which the Catholic school is built, and to find methods and processes, more precise than osmosis, for passing on the torch to a new generation. It was the ambition of the new project to take up the 'hearts and minds' challenge facing Catholic schools today. If, as Donal Murray reminded us, there was 'no legally enforcable definition of the gospel spirit of freedom and love',[4] then you had to approach the matter in quite another way. Our point of departure was, as Yeats might have told us, where all the ladders started, in the 'foul rag and bone shop' of the human heart.[5] The most pertinent rag and bone shop, as we saw it in this instance (the crucial role of parents and the home is for another day) was the spirituality of the lay teacher, working away and giving his or her life to a school. It is a spirituality that has tended to be ignored or drowned out. It was our view that unless we took the challenge of the future to that arena, all the wonderful and painstaking work to set up trusts and to devise juridic persons would be pointless: we would be left with institutions that were not so much vacant as empty to the core.

Beginning with imagination
Where to begin was the question. Where do we set our foot on the ladder? The answer that came to us as we began to ponder these things, and which we believe to have been providential, was that we should begin in the realm of imagination. When we asked ourselves why we should begin in such a place we were drawn to those lines of Emily Dickinson which said that 'The Possible's slow fuse is lit / By the Imagination'.[6] We found ourselves saying that imagination is the locus of the spiritual, of transformation, of conversion, of renewal. It is where the Spirit of God fires us up, where the divine gives birth to new dreams. It is where we access the Kingdom. We told ourselves that we needed imagination to hear the voice that insists that we forever begin; we needed imagination in order to hope.

We also found 'imagining' to be such an energising and life-giving word. It evoked a vivid picture of human freedom, of moving from fear of the world to acceptance of its fluid variety. It was a word that illuminated the nature of the creativity that makes life rich and full and possible. When applied to imagining the future of Catholic education we found ourselves engaging with a concept that was focusing, releasing and invitational. Imagining the future united us in a focus beyond ourselves and released us from the things we needed to leave behind, our failures, our blockages, the extent to which we had not reached the mark. It was invitational because it presumed, screamed you might say, imagining *with* rather than imagining *for*.

Why reimagining?

Imagining the future is, of course, reimagining. It is not so much beginning as beginning again. Catholic education is something already there – we do not come out of thin air. The gospel is yesterday and today as well as tomorrow, in season and out of season. We have in our genealogy names like Nagle, Rice, Delaney, Aikenhead, McCauley, Aylward, Ball. The clay beneath our feet is sacred. It comes from places where the great congregational founders were born or walked or taught or are buried; from places like Callan and Ballygriffin, from New Street, Waterford, from Donnybrook and Harolds Cross, from Baggot Street. It comes from the monasteries and schools of the older orders of Ignatius, Benedict, Dominic, Francis. It comes from diocesan colleges and from the earth under the hedge schools. It comes from the tracks made by parents and children walking to school and from the sidelines of playgrounds where teachers trampled. It comes from the clay floors of the early schools where they gave their lives.

What enables us to renew a tradition and to light new fires is the extent to which we have been keepers of the flame.[7] Our quest is about revisiting, about a search that brings you back. The road before us and the subtle and delicate nature of our quest is suggested in the words of T. S. Eliot, which have become a kind of mantra for reimagining the Catholic school:

> We shall not cease from exploration
> And the end of all our exploring
> Will be to arrive where we started
> And know the place for the first time.[8]

Breaking a silence

How do you begin to imagine the future? Where do you start the exploration and where do you stop? We begin surely in conversation, in breaking the silence, in dialogue, in discussing who we believe ourselves to be and what it is that we believe ourselves to be trying to do. It is inevitably a wide-ranging conversation; once you start it is hard to put bounds to it. The exploratory task of reimagining is cut through with a whole series of parallel tasks and, as is so often the case, the journey turns out to be somewhat different to what you expected. 'The truth,' as Joan Chittister was to tell us, 'is always larger than the partial present'. When we begin to reimagine the Catholic school we soon find ourselves in a Church reimagining itself, in a nation reimagining itself, with teachers, parishes and education itself busy in the process of reimagining identity, roles, and the manner in which believing, belonging and participating are now to be conceived.

A Church reimagining itself in the continuing aftermath of Vatican II and the outburst of imaginary vision that was *Lumen gentium* and *Gaudium et spes*. A nation reimagining itself through the throes of globalisation and the pervasive sense of betrayal arising from being let down by economic, political and religious institutions. A teaching profession reimagining itself through the divisive dilemma of the professional versus the vocational, the voluntary versus the contractual, not to mention the challenge to develop a fresh spirituality of teaching and a new vision of pedagogy as mediation of the life-giving processes of education. Parishes reimagining themselves beyond the practice of 'leaving it all up to the school' and the attendant comedies that accompany current preparations for the sacraments. All of these issues began to creep into our conversations as we went forward and they inevitably creep, therefore, on to the pages of this book.

Being real
A great part of the challenge of the current moment arises from the wise council that we be honest and real in all that we do. Real about how preposterous a faith response may appear in the eyes of some; real about the widespread contention that belief is a private and personal matter; real about the forceful logic of the integrated or the secular.[9] Real about the fact that the staff in a Catholic school is what you find behind the staffroom door – how many teachers were recruited over that last quarter century with an active view to protecting characteristic spirit? Real about recognising that one person, be he or she principal, chaplain or RE teacher, cannot be the conscience of a school. Real about our dependence on young women teachers whose age and sex renders them among the most alienated from a patriarchal Church. Being real also says something about the demand for a gospel community overnight, when it might not have been that much of a priority in years gone by.

Being real means proceeding without illusions: illusions that we are perfect or infallible or sinless, or that we too have not been numbed and dumbed by the pervasive values of our day. The first illusion we jettison is that we begin renewal or conversion anywhere other than with ourselves. The first rag and bone shop we visit must be our own.

Being real also means engaging people in a language that is acceptable to them, in words that go as deep into the spiritual as people want to go or will allow. We are real when we begin by asking people, asking ourselves, what makes us the teachers we are, where it is that we are growing and where it

is that we are blocked. Asking what is it that we are most proud of in what
we do. Asking how we are using our talents, coping with our bereavements,
meeting our needs, especially the higher needs for fulfilment and for making
a contribution. Asking about the stories we tell ourselves, and whether these
stories are life-giving or life-draining. Being real is more about asking than
about telling; it implies a partnership approach that gives responsibility back
to people. It involves knowing that nothing else will work.

It may well be asked where the evangelisation is in all of this, where it is
that we honour the command to preach the gospel. The reply we suggest is
that while faith comes through hearing (Romans 10:17) and while our
imagining may culminate in putting on the mind of Christ (Philippians 2:5),
we must nevertheless remember that grace builds on nature and that our
relationship to the ultimate has its own drawing dynamic. We, therefore,
begin by echoing those listening words of question and invitation, which are
the first words of Christ to his disciples in the Gospel of John:

What do you seek? (John 1:38)

Being real implies that our paradigm is one that underlines the invitational
side of evangelisation, that avoids manipulation, that requests and merits
trust. It remains open to the possibility that we may be refused and is
accepting of those who choose to journey but a short distance with us along
the road that we illuminate.

The invitational paradigm we propose for reimagining the Catholic
school runs somewhat as follows:

- We invite, we do not issue a summons.
- We imagine the future *with* rather than *for*.
- We release ourselves and others from the past and share a liberating
  responsibility for the present.
- We listen to each other as we engage in conversations about what we
  seek, about the purpose of school, of education, about what it is that
  we want for young people.
- We talk of who we are and who we want to be as teachers and
  educators.
- We seek to bring our Christian heritage into dialogue with our
  deepest desires for ourselves and for others.
- We listen to the gospel with fresh ears.
- We open ourselves to be transformed by the renewal of our minds
  (Romans 12:2).
- We reimagine the Catholic school together.

A joyful task

The papers of this book come from the *Reimagining the Catholic School* conference held at City West Conference Centre, Dublin, in March 2002. The contributors include some of the most respected and original voices on Catholic education from around the world. They come from the USA, from Europe and from nearer to home. Some of the voices are prophetic, others are the voices of analysis, others still the voices of those labouring in the field or at the sensitive interstices of our society. The gathered voices address the issues that give us the categories of our reimagining – spirituality, relationships, community, engagement. They put words to our beginning again.

The teachers, parents, education officers, bishops, congregational leaders, journalists, and others who came to City West, left with hearts that were lighter than when they arrived. When we asked people what had touched them they told us that it was not only our reimagining of spirituality, relationships, community, engagement, but also the liturgies, the shared sense of community, the sacred space, the symbolic sapling tree that each took away from the final Eucharist, their each putting a stitch in Sr Rosaleen's tapestry (shown on the front cover of the book) and the fact that we were acting as if the news was good. We had begun to speak again in a language that was fresh and confident and the consequence was a renewal of the belief that we could make a difference. What we were told was that from an experiential as well as a cognitive viewpoint the experience had been one of unmitigated joy.

What worked particularly well at City West was the joy. And why shouldn't we be joyful? The people in our schools, in teaching, are such good people. We live in such interesting times. The harvest is great and the cause is worth fighting for. The message of the Catholic school is one of amazing human worth and dignity. It is good news and a challenging message. It is our happy task to tell people that the Kingdom of God is within them. Ours is the joy of attempting to speak the gospel in a new language. Ours may be the joy of seeing the light of the gospel shining in people's eyes afresh.

Why should we be afraid to bring our joyful message to a post-modern Ireland whose spiritual energy has been dissipated, whose sense of moral outrage has been neutered and whose philosophy infrequently transcends the motto that 'anything goes'. There are hungers out there for the spiritual. The wordless tug to something better will not acknowledge conclusion. There are freedoms to be purchased again. In bringing soul to our modern society we are fighting for human dignity and offering something that has to be better than the predatory greed and emptiness that encircles us.

If people left City West with joy in their hearts and a renewed sense of purpose, we hope that the content of this book will have the same effect on you. In the pages that follow we invite you to walk with us on sacred ground, to join us in making a new wineskin for new wine, in reimagining that young sapling that is the Catholic school. We hope that the journey will touch your hearts and minds, that it will give clues to tomorrow and prompts for what lies ahead, that it will light the slow fuse of the possible.

We shall not cease from exploration. It is time to begin again.

Notes

1. Kennelly, B. (1999), 'Begin' in *Begin* (Newcastle on Tyne: Bloodaxe Books).
2. Normoyle, M. C. (1975), *A Tree is Planted: The Life and Times of Edmund Rice* (Dublin: Irish Christian Brothers).
3. O'Donoghue, B. (1999), 'Westering Home' in *Here Nor There* (London: Chatto and Windus).
4. Murray, D. (2002), *The Soul of Europe* (Dublin: Veritas), p. 40.
5. Yeats, W. B. (1989), 'The Circus Animals' Desertion' in *The Collected Works of W.B. Yeats* (Dublin: Macmillan).
6. Dickinson, E. (1924), 'The Gleam of an Heroic Act' in *The Complete Poems* (Boston: Little Brown).
7. Minehan, R. (1999), *Rekindling the Flame: A Pilgrimage in the Footsteps of Brigid of Kildare* (Kildare: Solas Bríde).
8. Eliot, T. S. (1963), 'Little Gidding' in *Collected Poems 1909-1962* (London: Faber and Faber), p. 222.
9. See Humanist Philosphers' Group (2001), *Religious Schools: The Case Against* (London: British Humanists' Association).

Reimagining the Catholic School in this New Century

Joan D. Chittister, OSB

Three stories provoke today's reflections on the spiritual leadership that is required if we are to 'reimagine the Catholic School in this new century'. The first story tells about a guy who was pulled over by a State trooper. 'Sir,' the trooper said, 'you are the five thousandth person to cross this traffic counter wearing a seat belt. You have just won $5,000! What are you going to do with all that money?' 'Well,' the driver said slowly, 'I don't rightly know for sure but I suppose the first thing I oughta do is buy a driver's licence...'. So the lady sitting next to him said, 'Oh, don't pay any attention to him, Officer. He's always a smart aleck when he's drunk.' Then the guy in the back seat said, 'I told you we wouldn't get very far in a stolen car.' And finally a muffled little voice from the trunk yelled, 'Hey, buddy, are we over the border yet?' Point: reality is not always what it may seem.

The second story is about a map – a very innocent-looking kind of map – the kind that would hang on classroom walls. In the mid seventeenth century, Spanish seafarers sailed up the west coast of the Americas to what is now known as the Baja Peninsula or lower California. The cartographers of the time, aware of the Drake expeditions to the New World, and good Cartesians as well, simply drew a straight line up from the Strait of California to the strait of Juan de Fuca between Vancouver island and Washington state. Consequently, the maps that were published in 1635 show very clearly California as an island.

Now that might be only a quaint story if it were not for the fact that the missionaries of the time were using the same map to travel inland. So, given the information there, the long-time credibility of the map, let alone the prestige of its makers, the missionaries developed the first great pre-fab boat-construction project in human history. They cut their flatboats in Spain, shipped them to the Americas in pieces, and then, on the shores of Monterey, California, put them all back together again to be transported on the backs of mules to the other side of California. Then they carried those boats 12,000 feet up the Sierra Madre mountains for passage across the great strait, which, the map showed clearly, ran from the Baja to Puget Sound.

But lo and behold, the other side of those mountains was no seashore at all. It was, in fact, what is now the State of Nevada and the beginning of the great American desert. California was not an island. California was the mainland!

It would be a rather funny story except for one thing that makes it tragic: when the missionaries wrote back to tell the cartographers and the Crown that California was not an island, no one believed them. In fact, the mapmakers and the Government insisted that the map was certainly correct: it was the missionaries who were in the wrong place! What's more, in 1701, almost seventy years later, they reissued an updated version of the same map.

For fifty years then, years of the most crucial explorations of the California coastline, those maps went unchanged because someone continued to work with partial information, assumed that data from the past had the inerrancy of tradition, and then used authority to prove it.

Finally, after years and years of new reports, a few cartographers – the heretics, the radicals and the rebels, I presume – began to issue a new version. And in 1721, the last mapmaker holdout finally attached California to the mainland.

But, and this is perhaps the real tragedy, it took almost a hundred years for the gap between experience and authority to close. It took almost a hundred years for the new maps to be declared official, despite the fact that the people who were there on the site all the time knew differently from the very first day. Point: 'vision', 'imagination' is the ability to realise that the truth is always larger than the partial present.

The third story is a monastic one. Once upon a time, the story goes, a teacher travelled with great difficulty to a faraway monastery because there was an old monastic there who had a reputation for asking very piercing spiritual questions. 'Holy One,' the teacher said, 'Give me a question that will renew my soul.' 'Ah, yes, then,' the old monastic said, 'Your question is "What do they need?"'

Well, the teacher wrestled with the question for days but then got depressed, gave up and went back to the old monastic in disgust. 'Holy one,' the teacher said, 'I came here because I'm tired and depressed and dry. I didn't come here to talk about my ministry. I came to talk about my spiritual life. Please give me another question.' 'Ah, well, of course. Now I see,' the old monastic said. 'In that case, the right question for you is not "What do they need?" The right question for you is "What do they really need?"' Point: the ability to give meaning to life, the ability to reimagine what is for new times, is of the essence of spiritual leadership.

Immersion in the immediate, a sense of spiritual vision, a sense of holy imagination, the pursuit of meaning and the courage to question the seemingly unquestionable is the essence of spiritual leadership. We cannot and should not attempt to lead anyone anywhere unless we ourselves know where we are, where we are going, and from where.

In a century that has spawned Adolf Hitler, Ferdinand Marcos and Nicolae Ceausescu on one side, and Martin Luther King Jr, Dan Berrigan, Dorothy Day, Eleanor Roosevelt, Willy Birmingham, Sister Stan, Maighread Corrigan and Mahatma Gandhi on the other, the problem of spiritual leadership and the questions that underlie it have never been more urgent or more confused.

We find ourselves confronted with conflicting notions of leadership. Is it force or is it persuasion? Is it power or is it passion? What kind of leadership is really needed to save the soul of a society? Are we to be faithful followers or independent individuals? The definitions seem to shift and sway, don't they?

In highly communitarian societies it is extremely important, for instance, to foster individualism so that people do not get swallowed up in the name of the group. The pharaohs built mighty pyramids, true, but at the price of a million lives. The kings of Spain created a national treasury of South American gold, but at the price of entire Native American populations. We created a cotton and textile industry to rival Europe's, but at the price of the enslavement of a whole people back then, and a long-lingering distrust that continues into the present, and slowly simmering racism.

On the other hand, in highly individualistic societies, like our own in a post-Enlightenment West, it is just as important to foster a sense of group goals so that private interests do not usurp the common good as they often have and often do.

Last year over half of the CEOs of Fortune 500 companies, those running the global corporations that girdle the world, earned an average wage of $36 million dollars. Corporate executives take million-dollar salaries for themselves. They earn as much in an hour and half, in ninety minutes, as their employees make in a year, while their laid-off middle-class workers lose their homes to failed mortgages or, as in the case of Enron, stand to lose their entire pension plans. Those executives do not lead a community to community, although, God knows, they do indeed affect it.

Neither the 3700 juvenile offenders whom we incarcerate and then ignore in adult prisons in the Western world, nor the adults who by doing that make a mockery of rehabilitation, lead society. They only bully it.

No, leadership is not force. Leadership is the ability to see the vision beyond the reality and make a road where no road has been.

Spiritual leadership is the ability to question the present in order to show the way to the greater good, whether it is popular to pursue that good or not.

The questions of leadership are organisational ones, of course, but they are spiritual ones, too. They have something to do with the structures of a society, yes, but they have more to do with the spirit of that society and the compass of its soul.

Spiritual leadership is, as the psalmist says, the ability 'to be a light in the darkness for the upright'. And it is often a lonely, lonely task. Knowing where to go is one thing; breaking the path to it is another. And it is breaking the path that is of the essence of leadership.

It is the spiritual leader who enables us to tell one type of leadership from another, the life-giving from the death-dealing, the eternally significant from the culturally correct. Spiritual leadership is not an exercise in social isolation and religious niceties. Spirituality and spiritual leadership have something to do with critiquing the present, envisioning a better future and asking the right questions as we go.

Fortunately for us, we are a tradition rich with such people: we are, in fact, a veritable roll call of courageous figures who, in the face of the Jesus who assessed his own reality and then, contrary to its claims, envisioned fullness of life for lepers, humanity for women, freedom for those possessed by demons, and the responsibility to question, question, question authority after authority, from his first Passover in the Temple to his journey to the tomb so that the reign of God might come, committed their lives to doing the same.

Benedict of Nursia assessed his world, asked why the few controlled the many, and envisioned a whole new way of living that was the antithesis of the hierarchialism of Roman patriarchy and the basis for a whole new way of being community. Vincent de Paul and Louise de Marrillac assessed their world, asked who would help the helpless in it, and envisioned a whole new kind of security for the poor.

Mother Jones, that *émigré* from Cork, assessed her world, asked how power could be redistributed, and helped to shape a new kind of economic world where workers had the right to unionise. In fact, she was called by a US congressman 'the most dangerous woman in America', and that at the age of eighty! Tell me again how you are too old to do these things! Oscar

Romero assessed his world, asked where political legitimacy was, and lost his life to stop oppression.

Indeed, the tradition is clear: spiritual leadership is about assessing reality, about reclaiming the cosmic vision, and about being courageous enough to ask the right questions along the way. Clearly, if we want to be spiritual leaders, we, too, must wonder whether today, now, here, our Catholic schools are asking what today's students really need. We must ask if we are really steeping today's students in the stench of this world's total reality. We must ask ourselves if we are really using the right maps to lead them on their gospel way.

How can we possibly be the spiritual leaders that such a tradition has a right to expect and that we purport to be, by virtue of our very vocation to the process of human growth, unless we are using the right maps, or at least have the courage to ask for another one when old ones stop working, as did the missionary teachers before us.

If Catholic education is really 'education that makes a difference', that 'leads the way', we have to enable students to assess their world, both its raging possibilities and its limitless brutalities, as well as simply to function in it. They must leave us able and willing to envision something better for the world than power and profit at any cost. They must have the skills to question its assumptions about Darwinian economics and biological stereotypes rather than simply accept them. They must have the commitment to question its social axioms rather than simply comply with them.

The data are in and the data are clear: there have been thirty-six student killings in US schools, let alone on US streets, in the last eighteen months. Three weeks ago the Josephson Institute of Ethics released a survey of over 15,000 highschool students that finds that 47 per cent of highschoolers and 22 per cent of middleschool boys have brought guns to school. And half of those when they were drunk! Here in Ireland, every year, as many teenagers have died from drug abuse in the Republic as died in each of those same years in the North from sectarian violence. How long then, in a society dealing with teen alcoholism, before the guns are here too? Indeed, our children, the marginalised and mercilessly ignored, have been infected with frenzy and meaninglessness.

But from Piaget to Wallace, from Kohlberg to Gilligan, from Smetana to Harvard's Robert Brooks, developmental psychologists, social domain theorists and now resiliency researchers have all warned that the development of moral maturity and emotional strength is not a matter of class exercises or verbal learnings or even peer group analyses of hypothetical social situations. The fact is that children, they all point out, simply cannot rise to another level of moral development unless they see it modelled in someone else, in parents, in teachers, in, as Julius Segal calls them, 'charismatic adults'. Obviously, for that to happen, if teachers truly want a better life for the next generation, this generation of adults, of Christians, of teachers, you and I, have the obligation to assess our world first, proclaim the vision ourselves, and ask a few questions of our own.

No uncertainty of yours and mine will forgive us for failing to do so. No whimpering 'economics is not my field', no demure 'I don't get involved in politics', no pious 'I'm sure that God will lead the Church in the way it is meant to go' will satisfy our spiritual responsibility now any more than it did for those who sat by while someone else engineered slavery or colonialism, the Crusades or the Inquisition, the Holocaust or the killing fields of Cambodia.

Massive social change, today's only social certainty when devoid of spiritual imagination, leads to social chaos; social chaos leads to confusion, and confusion leads, social psychologists tell us, to alienation. It is a sorry state. Alienation is that feeling of rootlessness and disorientation of soul that comes with a loss of social bearings and fixed values and immutable standards and clear consensus on the things that count. It is a direction without destination, a voyage without values.

When everything is in flux, but old institutions and yesterday's leaders lend their energy only to resist rather than to light the way down the new road, when standards become uncertain and integrity blurs because more energy is being put into rebuilding the age that is dying instead of, as Boethius implies, giving soul to the age that is coming to life, we get out of touch with what matters, with what really matters!

The alienated distance themselves, certainly psychologically, often even physically, commonly spiritually. They ignore or they withdraw from what they do not understand and cannot control for fear of its unknown demands on them. They hide in a citizenship that deteriorates, at best, into a kind of patriotic civility and a religion that becomes, at most, a checklist of customs, a pious nest, a spiritual Jacuzzi, all of which are weak and puny and unacceptable substitutes for the gospel life.

But constant change and total chaos and complete confusion and deep, deep alienation is the very nature of life in a world aspin in technological change, adrift in space, and engulfed in the globalisation of industry, economics, politics, race and even religion.

Obviously, then, the questions must begin: Will they really clone people? And, if so, so what? Will they really replace workers with robots, and if so, so what? Will they really engineer food in laboratories, and if so, so what for countries in new famine and for countries that do not have laboratories in which to engineer food and whose only export income comes from food production?

What will happen to the technological have-nots in the world who are already a century behind, and whose 'development' has already been destroyed by our 'developed' technology? Those are the kind of questions that must plague the Christian soul today. That's the stuff of spiritual leadership. That's the task for teachers in Catholic schools now if we want to reimagine Catholic schools from concentration on catechism to the justice of Jesus, if those schools are really to 'make a difference', if we are really to 'have faith in the future', if teachers are really to 'lead the way' into this new century, but, most of all, into this gospel.

It's not the catechism answers we teach them to give; it's the moral questions we teach them to ask that are the index, the measure, of spiritual leadership now. So what shall we teach about reality, what vision shall we give, what questions shall we ask, what map shall we ourselves use this time to chart the unknown: one drawn from past realities or one hard-gotten by walking new and unknown territory ourselves? It is precisely ambiguity, in other words, that is the very geography of leadership.

Tutors are for times of light; we have need for leaders now.

What you model, what you value, what you question and where you lead through your curricula, your textbooks and your own personal commitments in life will be the values, the visions and the answers we get in the next generation. The map you use to explore this new world will be the path by which the next world walks.

So the question for spiritual leaders in Catholic schools today must become: 'On what roads should we lead them now?'

The answer to that question, I contend, has been clear for two thousand years. We must lead them down the roads of the one who said, 'I am the Way.' We must lead them down the road to Egypt, where Joseph and Mary, refugees from the dictator Herod, sought political asylum. We must take them into a world where today's fourteen million refugees and twenty-five million displaced persons live in squalor and starvation, fear and destitution.

We must teach them to ask of a country created by immigrants (mine) and whose émigrés were accepted everywhere worldwide (yours) why the borders of our countries are tight against immigrants now while countries far poorer, far more crowded, are far more open to them than we are.

While forests were coming down on behalf of Western economic interests and farmlands were drying up under a punctured ozone layer, the global population increased from 2.5 billion in 1950 to six billion in 1999, a 300 per cent increase in population in fifty years. Now those people are swarming across the borders of the world, following the garbage cans of the world looking for water, food and work. Ask them, as you map their way through history, how it was that in the early 1940s Christian countries drove caravans and sent boatloads of Jews – anchored on the shores of Miami, knocking desperately on our borders – back to European concentration camps, and still sends boatload after boatload back to other deadly and dangerous places yet today. Ask them in the name of Jesus Who is the Way what that has to do with being Christian?

Lead them down the road to Galilee where Jesus walked day after day, healing the sick, feeding the hungry, defending the poor. Show them the ten million children on their own streets, the streets of their own world, who wait without social support services in the richest countries in the world, in the richest period in history.

Help them to see the working poor, those millions of the world population everywhere who are working low-paying jobs for part-time pay, or, worse, who work two jobs with no benefits, no compensation, no paid vacations, no day-care services, no pensions and less than full-time pay. Teach them to ask what they will do in their day to heal this.

Lead them up the road to Tabor to the mountaintop where Jesus appears to the apostles, not with Nathan the priest or with David the king, the institution men of Israel, but with the prophets Moses and Elijah; with Moses, a liberator of peoples, and Elijah whom King Ahab called 'that troublemaker of Israel'.

Take them up the road to Tabor, indeed, and teach them to question aloud how it is that Jesus did not allow the apostles to stay there in contemplative content or intellectual disinterest but led them instead straight back down to the bottom of the mountain, to the dirty towns and throngs of hurting peoples below who were waiting to be healed.

Teach them to ask, for instance, whether or not the fact that the West has not sent healing medicine to the hordes of people with Aids in Africa might not just be a new kind of racism...

Teach them to ask, while the Celtic Tiger roars, whether or not, in our lust for money in the West, the fact that one-fifth of the world's population lives in abject poverty and two-thirds of those are women; the fact that both North American and European Union Development Aid going to low-income countries has fallen from 75 per cent to 51 per cent in the last ten years; the fact that more women die in India from pregnancy complications in a week than die for that reason in the whole of Europe for an entire year, in the light of those things, whether or not human greed is just as dangerous as human weapons.

Teach them to ask whether or not we are really peaceful people if we are not at the same time economically just people.

By all means, lead them to the top of Tabor, but take them to the bottom of Tabor as well, where, now as then, the poor wait for the disciples of Jesus who claim to 'lead' the way, to cast out demons on their behalf. Lead them down the road to Samaria to the place where Jesus, the Jewish man, spoke deep, deep theology to a Samaritan woman, announced to her first that he was the Messiah and then sent her to evangelise an entire city.

Lead them to where all the women of the world wait today at wells gone dry for them to become visible, to have their questions heard, to have their answers listened to, to hear a word of theology that ennobles them, too, and to be sent, as the Samaritan woman was, to evangelise the cities where, as scripture says so clearly, 'Because of her thousands were converted that day'.

Teach them to ask why in the light of Samaria it can possibly be that women are forbidden to ask for the fullness of the spiritual life. Teach them to ask how it is that one sex can take upon itself the right to define what God wants of the other one.

Teach them to ask what kind of God it is that would give women a mind, a soul, a baptism and a call, and then forbid them to answer it when a sacramental Church is in danger of losing the sacraments.

Those who seek to silence the questions of women at dry wells yet today seek, whether they realise it or not, to silence, too, the Hail Mary, the Magnificat, the woman in the rich man's house, Mary Magdalen at the tomb, Jesus himself at this well, and the feminine voice of God, which said, 'Let us make them in our image. Male and female let us make them.'

Most of all, teach them not to despair. After all, the disciples who were with Jesus that day didn't want him talking to a woman either. 'Send her away,' they said. 'She is following after us.' But, scripture says, he did not. He would not. Teach them, like Jesus, to silence the silencing.

Lead them down the road to Jerusalem, the centre of the synagogue, the centre of the State. Lead them to scrutinise our own centres of power in a world where far too few of the privileged, the comfortable, or the powerful, cry out for those fifty-seven million people in the European Union without enough to eat, cry out for those five million without shelter, for those seventeen million whose homes are rotting, and for those millions everywhere whose breathing is threatened by smog and pollution, while we in the West argue and debate clean-air legislation, and renege on global environmental treaties, and cut child-care funds for those whose lives are being eaten up by economic disparity, by those who preach 'progress, progress, progress' for themselves but put no faces on the bottom lines of their graphs.

The poor in Ireland have €84 of disposable income per week compared to the rich who have €1,125 of disposable income per week.

How is it that we can put half the budget of the Western world into wartime preparations in peacetime and plead that we don't have money enough in our countries to meet human needs. Indeed, the streets of our societies run red with the blood of our own children. We have taught them violence well. But how will we ever be able to convince them that our violence is good but their violence is bad, while nations, our allies, develop weapon system after weapon system for the powerful to use against the desperate and unarmed? And we say nothing and we never object. Instead, we argue, 'That's not our problem. I have nothing to do with that.' Remind them that it was on the road to Jerusalem that Jesus told the Pharisees 'Stop these ones from shouting' and 'Even the stones will cry out'. Teach them that crying out for the other is, in the end, what spiritual leadership is all about.

Finally, lead them down the road to Emmaus. Lead them to where community happens as it did for the disciples on the road in the 'breaking of the bread', where no one is outcast and no one is without value and no one is excluded from the feast that is humanity.

Spiritual leadership demands that in this world of power and profit, sexism and economic domination, we bring them to see what reality really is. We lead them to envision a better way, and we teach them to question the things that obstruct its coming. We must show them in our own lives the kind of courageous persistence it takes to wrest the gospel from the caricature of old maps and bring it to new life in new ways that protect both the born and the unborn child, and that recognise that abortion on demand is not just a woman's decision. It is the decision of every one of us who fails to pursue the honest questions 'What is life?', 'What is human?', 'What is human life?' in an age of clones. It is the decision of every one of us who allows one last sexist trick on women by those who will pay for abortions, but will not pay for the daycare and food stamps and educational monies it would take to raise the children that are conceived.

We must lead them to speak for all the nobodies that nobody wants to be, so that the poor do not have to add grovelling to poverty in the next generation. We must call them to give human dignity to the gay and lesbian community, so that no more people are beaten, reviled or crippled physically or emotionally or economically in the next generation because we tolerated hate in the name of religion in ours. We must show them how to respect all the brown and black and red and yellow 'others', all the cripples and the lepers and the outcasts and the women who swarm this time to us for acceptance, for community, for equality, and for the safe, warm touch of the Christ whom we say lives in us.

The philosopher Chuang Tzu says, 'How shall I talk of the sea to a frog that has never left its pond?' How can we expect of them what we fail to be ourselves?

What you are, your students will be. What you have the courage to question, they will learn to question, too. Spiritual leadership demands, in other words, that you yourself take them where there are no roads and leave a path.

When we teach them the doctrine of 'free will' we must teach them that the other side of free will is responsibility, that we are all agents, not spectators. As Camus said, 'The saints of our times are those who refuse to be either its executioners or its victims.' We must teach them, in other words, that time changes nothing, people do. And we must teach it with our lives.

You are what will or will not make Catholic education different. Pity the Church that does not think and its teachers who are not thinkers themselves. Pity the children who are taught to recite the past but forbidden to examine the present or, worse, to imagine a different future.

Pity the country left with the children who are forbidden to think by teachers who fail to show them how to think.

When I was a young Catholic schoolteacher we suddenly realised that we had ghettoised ourselves to the point that we were teaching from 'Catholic' arithmetic books and 'Catholic' history books and 'Catholic' geography books and even 'Catholic' spellers (whatever in heaven's name they were!).

But I have come these years to think it would be a great new act of spiritual leadership, totally consonant with a hundred years of papal encyclicals on social justice, if there were indeed a Catholic arithmetic that concentrated not on the splitting of apple pies to teach fractions but on the distribution of the food of the world to others.

It would be a good idea to have a Catholic geography that taught who was taking whose resources and at what cost to them. It would require great spiritual leadership to write a Catholic history that taught the sins against conscience of the authoritarian systems. And it could be real teaching if we had a Catholic science that taught the full humanity of women and a Catholic economics that taught the sinfulness of the ill-gotten gains of sweatshops' new industrial slavery. And, oh yes, by the way, let's finally get a Catholic speller that spells 'male' and 'female' E-q-u-a-l in the languages of both State and Church so that we have it at our disposal for the building of the reign of God everywhere, in politics and international economics and law, in all the seminaries and synods and sacristies of the world.

Maybe, then, we would be doing twice as well as we are now.

Oh, yes, we've come a long, long road since Hiroshima and Vatican II, but without you it is only one short thought back to the dangers of the cold war, internalised racism, theologised sexism and the intellectual boundaries of Vatican I.

You are Catholic school teachers.

You are the shapers of the real future of both Church and State. Decide which Church, which State you want, and teach it, be it, lead it. Then what you begin to reimagine, they will be able to imagine in full.

What is spiritual leadership? It is the commitment, the courage, the questions it will take to make the prophetic normative, not to get power but to do good.

What is your curriculum? Ceaseless focus on real issues, and a vision for the gospel.

Where is your school? Everywhere.

What is your task? To honour the questions of those for whom old maps do not show the way and old answers do not persuade; to teach students that precisely when people do not want them to ask questions, that is exactly when they must.

Teach them that when we do not allow questions, we do both Church and State irreparable harm. We deny the Holy Spirit; we turn the State into a gulag and the Church into a cult. Worst of all, we ourselves make suspect the very quality of thought in the Catholic school.

The task of the teacher, the Christian teacher, must be to determine not what is the world that is politically convenient for us today, but what is the world we are called to leave behind.

At one time, Irish educators gave us missionaries of the catechism. I'm asking you now to give us missionaries of conscience. I'm asking you to call the country, call the world's students, to the gospel.

I'm begging you, if you really want to be spiritual leaders, leave behind a cold, clear sense of reality, leave behind a vision of the better, leave behind a memory of the unremitting courage to ask the hard, the necessary questions.

And whatever you do, do not give up. Persist. Have faith. And when your most sublime ideas meet the greatest resistance, remember that today's heresy is tomorrow's social dogma. So it was when Galileo questioned the nature of the universe. So it was when Luther asked for the publication of the scriptures in the vernacular. So it was when the black woman Sojourner Truth demanded the end to slavery. So it was when Elizabeth Cady Stanton and the Pankhursts went on a hunger strike for a woman's right to vote. So it was when John Courtney Murray argued for freedom of conscience, and so it was when Martin Luther King Jr wanted to integrate busses! So it was when people wanted nothing more than communion in the hand.

Can you honestly say that those questions should not have been asked?

Indeed, teach them to question. Teach them to question intellectual isolationism, spiritual exclusionism, cultural imperialism and sexual reductionism. For all our sakes, teach them to think. The integrity of the Church, the existence of the globe, and, without doubt, 'faith in the future', depend on your leading the way. For the sake of the children, for the sake of the Church, reimagine a role for the Catholic school beyond standard brand Catholicity and equal to the Christian gospel.

THE SPIRITUAL CORE

Forging in the Smithy of the Teacher's Soul:
The best hope for Irish education

Thomas Groome

At the end of *Portrait of the Artist as a Young Man*, James Joyce has Stephen Dedalus make this entry under 26 April: 'Mother is putting my new secondhand clothes in order. She prays now, she says, that I may learn in my own life and away from home and friends what the heart is and what it feels. Welcome, O Life. I go to encounter for the millionth time the reality of experience and to forge in the smithy of my soul the uncreated conscience of my race'.

There is ample evidence that the 'reality of experience' at this time poses a deep crisis for Ireland and for Irish education. It surely feels like we are 'away from home and friends' – or at least from the Ireland that we used to know. And precisely because education is so significant in forging the 'conscience of [our] race', this is an urgent time for educators to turn to 'what the heart is, and what it feels'. For there is much riding on how we negotiate our way through this time of seismic shifts and transitions. Irish education is likely at a make-or-break point, when the socio-cultural forces at work could prove terribly destructive or lend a lease of new life. Indeed, the Chinese are wise to spell crisis as 'dangerous opportunity'.

I believe that the outcome depends on what we manage 'to forge in the smithy' of our own souls as educators. For years I've said that 'the heart of education is the heart of the educator'. Like never before, the future of Irish education, and particularly of what is done by the designation 'Catholic', depends on the spirituality of its educators – 'what the heart is, and what it feels'.

I'm convinced, too, that the raw material is already present – 'uncreated' – yet waiting to be 'forged'. Further, I'm confident that we can delve again into the depth structures of the Celtic spirit and of Catholic Christianity, drawing forth from those old rivers the living waters that which will bring new life. And some of those deep streams of faith may appear new to us, or more likely as old truths that we need to know 'again, for the first time' (Eliot) or as if 'secondhand clothes'. Forging in the smithy of our souls, as educators, the spiritual resources to craft well the conscience of our race; this is the urgent task of our time. Only by grounding ourselves again on such a rock can 'hope and history rhyme' (Heaney) for Irish education.

Before proceeding, let us remind ourselves of the caution needed for 'Reimagining the Catholic School', the theme of our conference. Whenever a community of faith attempts to define its own particularity, it must studiously avoid all traces of sectarianism. By this I mean a defensive and divisive attitude that separates us from all 'others', from anyone who is not 'one of ourselves'. That 'religious' people can define themselves over-against others is patently but too often tragically true. Most of the wars of this time, and of every time since the dawn of history, have been legitimated if not caused by sectarian religion; surely Ireland knows this well.

When Catholic Christians attempt to state their particular identity, we must keep before us the doctrine of our faith – nay the dogma – of the universality of God's love, thus binding us to live in harmony and love with all 'others'. This core conviction of our faith gives us a bondedness with all God's people. Why would my commitment to Catholic Christian faith ever do anything but turn me toward all 'others' with love and a sense of solidarity? In particular and in the context of this conversation, let us remember our bondedness with all baptised Christians as co-members of the Body of Christ. With our Protestant brothers and sisters we share a common faith in the Triune God, in Jesus as our Saviour and Liberator, in the scriptures as 'God's word' to our lives, in the Church as God's sacrament of salvation, in our common creeds, in our shared baptism and so on. Our commitment to Catholic Christian faith should never do anything other than unite us with all the motley crew that is the Body of Christ, as Vatican II so forcefully reminded.

And yet, though our faith always turns us toward the neighbour in love, we remember that Catholicism is a particular way of being religious and being Christian. Even as we must remember the wisdom of Jesus that 'In my Father's house there are many mansions' (John 14:2), we affirm anew that the Catholic Christian community is our home within God's family. Further, our Catholic tradition still lends its own 'spiritual philosophy' for education, as it has done for nigh two thousand years. So let us proceed with great ecumenical sensitivity, even as we reflect upon our own particularity and its implications for how we might craft 'Catholic' education in post-modern Ireland.

Building on a rock

Chapter 7 of Matthew's Gospel is a great example of Jesus the Teacher at work, engaging people's lives with some of the core themes of his gospel. He begins by urging disciples not to judge others, cautioning that we can easily miss the plank in our own eye for the splinter in the neighbour's – for us here, an ecumenical sentiment. Then he summarises 'the whole law and the prophets' with his version of the golden rule: 'Do unto others as you would have them do to you'. Thereafter he warns about the narrowness of the gate that leads to life, the danger of false prophets and how to recognise them (by their bad fruits), and what it takes to be a true disciple – not simply talking the talk but walking the walk. Jesus ends his collage of teachings with the following reflection. He says, 'Everyone who hears these words of mine and acts on them will be like a wise person who built their house upon a rock. The rain fell, the floods came, and the winds blew and buffeted the house. But it did not collapse; it was set solidly on rock.' Whereas whoever hears Jesus' words and does not act on them, they have built on sand. When the storm comes – and he makes the storm sound inevitable – their house will collapse for sure (See Matthew 7:24-27).

In this light, we should ask 'What might be the rock foundation for Irish education that identifies itself as Catholic?' What would lend a reliable base so that no matter what students encounter in life, their education will be a rock that can weather any storm? That modern Irish education has done eminently well by way of technical rationality is its reputation around the world, and justifiably so. But on what basis can we educate 'the conscience of the race' in these post-modern times. We could speak of such foundations as a philosophy. However, when a philosophy is prompted and embraced out of faith conviction, and becomes operative in people's vocation – in this case, of educators – then I suggest that our foundation is spiritual.

There are myriad descriptions and definitions of spirituality. For here, and echoing the Matthew text, I propose that Christian spirituality is simply 'faith at work'. In other words, spirituality is one's faith convictions that become operative in lifestyle and vocation. Consistent with a classic Catholic understanding, spirituality is what we 'do' from and with a faith perspective. So, when Catholic educators allow their faith commitments to shape the whole curriculum – what and how, who and why they teach – then their teaching becomes their 'faith at work' and its foundation is their own spirituality, 'what the heart is, and what it feels'.

It seems self-evident to say that any education named as 'Catholic' should reflect the core convictions of Catholic faith, should rise out of the deep structures of Catholic Christianity. How else would it qualify as 'Catholic'? But if we hear the advice of Jesus, such faith cannot be rhetoric that we mouth or publish as the mission statement of our school. It must become operative throughout the curriculum. And for this existential realisation, we can only look to our own good selves, to the people who carry it on. If such faith is not our own and made evident in every aspect of our educating, then we build on sand. Whereas, the rock foundation for Catholic education will be its teachers putting their faith into practice, not just outside of their classroom but within it – throughout the curriculum.

Not a new proposal
To say that Catholic education must be built on the rock of educators' own spirituality is not a novel proposal; in fact, this has been the sentiment since the beginning of the Church. When the Risen Christ assembled the remnants of his community on a hillside in Galilee, he gave them the great commission to 'go make disciples' among all peoples (See Matthew 28:16-20). Essential to this mandate was to 'teach them to observe all that I commanded you' – in other words, to live as disciples. And Jesus made an extraordinary promise to the first teachers and to those ever after: 'I will be with you always, until the end of time'. So, they were to go and educate, motivated by their faith conviction; they were to put this faith into practice and encourage new disciples to do likewise; and they were to work as if the Risen Christ is a constant and empowering presence. Surely we can say that, from the beginning, the Church's educating had a spiritual foundation – disciples putting their faith to work to 'forge' the soul of others.

Indeed, all education, at its best, is a spiritual activity in that it reaches into the deep heart's core (Yeats) of people and changes them in life-giving ways. It ever invites them toward new horizons – to reach beyond themselves in life-long growth, and ever more. In other words, the best of education fosters the human desire for the Transcendent. It was this recognition that prompted the great philosopher Alfred North Whitehead to insist: 'We can be content with no less than the old summary of educational ideal which has been current at any time from the dawn of our civilisation. The essence of all education is that it be religious'.

Whitehead was only representing the better understanding of education that had endured throughout the history of Western civilisation. Beginning some 2500 years before, Plato described the function of the teacher as 'to turn the soul' of the student toward 'the true, the good, and the beautiful'. Such soul-turning demands the soul of both teacher and student – a spiritual enterprise. If true of general education, then surely Catholic education, reflecting the commitments of Christian faith and sponsored by a Catholic community, should find its foundations in the spirituality of its participants.

Recall that a great debate arose in the early Christian centuries as to whether or not the Church should be involved in education at all – beyond its own self-interest of catechesis. One side argued that the Christian community's only educational work is to teach the faith, and should not be involved in general education. Why should the Church bother with teaching people reading, 'riting, 'rithmatic, and rhetoric? In the great battle cry of Tertullian, a leading exponent of this view, 'Jerusalem has no need of Athens'. In other words, it is enough to teach the gospel and sacred scriptures; don't bother with the 'learning of the pagans'.

Wiser voices prevailed, however, insisting that the Church's faith was precisely what required it to educate in a holistic way; that all education, in the cherished phrase of Clement of Alexandria (writing *circa* 200), 'is a work of salvation'. In other words, the Church's function of carrying on the mission and ministry of Jesus requires that it attend to the 'salvation' of the whole person, and thus to their education. This latter position won the day.

Ever since then, the Catholic community has made education one of its primary functions in the world. Its first formal schools were sponsored by communities of monks, beginning, let us remember, right here in the Celtic Church and then in the Benedictine monasteries. Thereafter came the cathedral schools of the Middle Ages, which led on to the founding of the great universities – Paris, Oxford, Cambridge, Padua, Pisa, Salamanca, Lisbon, and many others. These grand seats of learning were all sponsored and staffed by the Church and accredited by papal charter. Then, as Catholicism spread into mission lands, its commitment to education went too – into every culture and country. We might say, without exaggeration, that the Catholic Church has been the single most significant agent of education in the history of the world.

Now, for most of the past two thousand years, Catholic education was carried on by vowed religious of some kind – monks, sisters, and brothers – who committed themselves to it as a ministry of salvation, educating because of and out of their spirituality. The success of post-modern Ireland is much indebted to the work of those great 'religious' educators. Now, in an age when Irish education is shifting from the hands of vowed religious to laity, the question becomes, 'Can we still build Irish education on such a spiritual foundation?' Surely we can and must say 'yes'.

We can say yes because, as Vatican II raised up in Catholic consciousness, every Christian is called to holiness: 'all the faithful of Christ of whatever rank or status are called to the fullness of the Christian life'. So, spirituality

is not for an élite few – 'the religious' – but for all the baptised. And so much
progress has been made since the Council toward an inclusive spirituality.
Sure, the spirituality of our laity will not be the same as that of vowed
religious, but with opportunity for spiritual growth, lay teachers and
administrators can lend a solid spiritual foundation to Catholic education in
Ireland today.

And we must say yes to a lay spirituality as the foundation for Catholic
education. In Ireland, as elsewhere throughout the Western world, the
number of vowed religious and priests working in schools has dropped
dramatically. So, with the vast majority of faculty and staff being lay people,
we simply must foster their spirituality as the foundation of the education
that goes on there; otherwise, we will not be sponsoring Catholic schools.
For without a Catholic spirituality as the basis, no school should represent
itself to the world as Catholic.

When Clement referred to education as 'a work of salvation' he was
placing it squarely within the Church's ministry. Over the years, it became
integral to the Church's description of its work as *'cura animarum'* – the care
of souls. In a deep sense, the intent of Catholic education is always 'to forge
in the smithy of [the] soul' the character and convictions that will be 'the
conscience of the race'. Now, as educators, we haven't spoken much of
'soul' lately, and for good reason. 'Soul' had become limited to what
Descartes called 'the ghost in the machine of the body', and its salvation
confined to an afterlife – getting souls into heaven. But in the broader and
richer Christian tradition, 'soul' referred to the whole person, and 'salvation'
was not confined to the afterlife but included human welfare in this one.

When Catholic education enables people to have a life as well as to make
a living, when it gives them a sense of worthwhile purpose, when it enables
them to make meaning out of life, to choose and maintain their priorities,
when it nurtures them in respect, reverence and responsibility, as well as
teaching the other 'four Rs', when it encourages people to grow in 'right
relationship' with God, self, others and creation, when it fosters the full
development of their talents and gifts, when it nurtures them in values and
virtues that are life-giving for self and others – in sum, when it educates for
life for all – then it is truly 'saving souls'. And such education must engage
the souls of both teachers and students!

Allowing faith to work
If we are to move beyond pious rhetoric, then spirituality must permeate the
whole curriculum of Catholic education – what and why, how and who we
teach. In gist, it invites teachers to bring their own souls and their deep-
heart's core convictions in faith to the teaching task, and likewise that they

engage the souls of their students, reaching into their 'deep heart's core' as persons.

A spiritual foundation invites educators consciously to put their faith to work within their vocation; often they may do so without a lot of explicit God-talk. I'm thinking of a history teacher I had during my secondary school years here in Ireland at Belcamp College, Fr Paul Byrne – we called him 'Muscles'. He rarely mentioned God when teaching history, and yet he likely taught us more than the religion teachers about living our faith, about being good and honest people, caring for others. A lot of it he did simply by how he related with us; you just knew that Muscles cared about you and about the world, and about how we were going to live in it. Without ever sounding preachy, we had no doubt about his values and commitments; we knew intuitively what mattered most to Muscles, how he made sense out of life, found purpose and meaning. In a word, he shared his soul with us. Every good teacher does as much.

And his teaching style was crafted to engage our souls in that he drew us in as active learners about the stuff that matters most in life. His questioning was rarely simple recall of what he'd taught, but invited what we thought and felt and were coming to see for ourselves. Nigh forty years later, I still remember a class on the Irish rebellion of Easter 1916 that he crafted around a poem by W. B. Yeats – 'The Rose Tree'. I sensed even then that the poetry was a way of drawing us in. By the time we got through, we knew much more than the data of that event; we had grappled with some of the great questions of life, had argued about values and meaning; far more than learning about 'the Rebellion', we had learned from it for our own lives. Muscles had gotten into our souls – and the bit of poetry helped.

Years ago, St Augustine wrote about 'the teacher within' each person, proposing that when we learn something, the 'real' teacher is not the teacher on the outside but inside. And Augustine explained that the 'teacher within' is the divine presence at the core of the person, our own souls. He insisted that the teacher – the one outside – must recognise this divine capacity of students to be active learners and deliberately craft the teaching/learning dynamic to engage their souls. This he contrasted to treating students as passive receptacles of what the teacher already knows – what Freire called 'banking education'. With rhetorical flourish, Augustine mused, 'for what parents would be so ridiculous as to send their child to school to learn what the teacher thinks'. In other words, send them to learn to think for themselves; education should honour their own souls.

Parker Palmer has revived this Augustinian proposal of late, and writes of it as the teacher within the teacher awakening the teacher within the student. Though Palmer uses little overtly spiritual language, it is clear that he intends teachers consciously to work out of their own souls, and that they draw students into the conversation of education in ways that deeply engage their souls. The amazing thing is that Palmer's primary audience is public school teachers in the United States, working in a system that excludes teaching for or from any particular faith. Surely his proposal should find ready resonance in the hearts of Irish educators who teach in schools specifically designated as Catholic.

An affirmation and celebration of life

The faith that should be put to work in Catholic education is not simply the personal faith of the individual educator – though this is essential – but a faith that reflects the deep structures of Catholic Christianity. For what else is Catholic education but an education that reflects the foundational convictions of Catholicism. Following on, Catholic educators must take these deep rivers of faith that define Catholicism and allow them to become operative commitments throughout their vocation – put them to work in their teaching. To explicate a bit, let us take the example of how Catholic Christianity understands 'the person' and reflect briefly on what such an anthropology might mean for educators who let it shape their vocation.

The heading above summarises the core of a Catholic outlook on the person – a total affirmation and celebration of our 'human condition'. And why? Here we could tell a long-winded story of great conversations and debates about original sin, about nature and grace, about the meaning of Jesus for human history, indeed about many of the central themes of Christian faith, but we can only summarise.

The enduring Catholic position is that people are made originally 'in God's own image and likeness' (Genesis 1:27); that we are alive by the very life-breath of God (Genesis 2:7); and that our divine life is never lost – even after 'the Fall' (Genesis 3). Beyond these great mythic stories – that are profoundly true if not literally so – the greatest affirmation of the human condition is the Christian conviction that in Jesus Christ, God came among us as one of ourselves. What could be a greater sign of affirmation for our human condition? Further, by his life, death, and resurrection Jesus has elevated the human family as 'sons and daughters of God' (Galatians 3:26), making us 'like a new creation' (2 Corinthians 5:17).

These affirmations from creation, incarnation and salvation in Jesus notwithstanding, the fact remains – with evidence within and all around us – that ours is a 'broken' condition, that we are terribly capable of sin. And yet, on the scales that weighs whether we are essentially good or evil, the Catholic position tilts distinctly toward the good. Our disposition toward goodness outweighs its opposite; our original grace outweighs our original sinfulness. So, rather than seeing ourselves as totally corrupt – as the great Protestant reformer John Calvin argued – we are essentially good, and this in our unity as body/soul persons. For this reason, our human life should be embraced and cherished as a great gift; foolish we are if we don't enjoy and celebrate its every day.

Such an anthropology demands that we treat all people with dignity and equality; they are entitled to as much by divine copyright. Further, given our essential goodness, and that our divine spark is never quenched, we are capable of receiving and being empowered by God's grace. In fact, our human condition is a covenant with God, with us being graced to become partners in the realisation of God's reign. God chooses to work through human efforts – in Aquinas' famous phrase, 'grace works through nature' – for the well-being of all. This means that by God's grace and our own good efforts we can participate in God's work of salvation, we can be real players in history, helping to make and keep life human for oneself and others.

For the educator
Let us imagine what such an understanding of the person might mean as Catholic teachers and administrators take this perspective, make it their own, and put it to work in their educating. First, pause and recognise an obvious point: teachers' attitudes toward students are most significant for how and what they teach. If I walk into my classroom at the beginning of a year presuming that 'these kids are trouble' – last year's teacher warned me – then I will surely treat them that way, and, be assured, they won't disappoint my low expectations.

On the other hand, if I enter into any teaching/learning event with a positive anthropology – something like the one just outlined and proposed by the deep structures of Catholic faith – then the pedagogy that ensues will surely be more for life. Even the social sciences assure us that students are more likely to live up to high expectations, and to live down to low ones. Think of all the great movies we've seen about teachers – *Dead Poet's Society, Mr Holland's Opus, Blackboard Jungle, To Sir With Love* (I'm dating myself now). All, in one way or another, portray an educator who refused to accept the negative anthropology they found in place and insisted on practising a positive one instead. It can make a world of difference to education.

So, imagine for yourself some import for your pedagogy if you accept something akin to a Catholic anthropology; what would it mean to put such faith to work – as your spirituality? To stimulate your imagining, let me make a few suggestions.

- Celebrate and educate the whole person. You may well be their math teacher, but for God's sake and for theirs, don't limit yourself to 'only' teaching math. Regardless of what your explicit curriculum might be, you will have ample opportunity to affirm their gifts and talents, to foster their values and virtues, to shape their outlook on life. You will be able to encourage them to claim their rights and responsibilities – the two must go together. In other words, and perhaps more through the implicit curriculum, you will be able to educate them as whole persons – besides teaching them math. And why would you settle for less, if you are a Catholic educator?

- Engage students as active participants. Teach in a way that encourages them to become agents in their own education. Engage their 'teacher within', as Augustine called it, or more precisely their souls. As you do so, you will educate them for life for all – in ways that favour life for themselves and others; and you will enable them to become life-long learners. What a gift for life!

- Create a respectful and challenging environment. Every participant in Catholic education is entitled to be treated with the utmost respect. Never should they encounter discrimination on any basis; never should they experience 'put-down' or diminishment of their personhood. On the contrary, they should always be made to feel welcome and included, appreciated and affirmed.

- Real respect also includes a challenge to 'reach beyond their grasp' for their own excellence, to do the best they can – given their talents and opportunities. The best of education stretches people, never allowing them to settle for personal mediocrity. Every gift should be mentored to the full. And the combination of a respectful and challenging environment is most effective for character formation. We become the best people we can be when we experience both affirmation and invitation.

- Always hold out hope of becoming 'fully alive to the glory of God'. Think back to the great teachers you've had in your own life – the Muscles Byrnes you've encountered. Note how they were determined to resist a social fatalism about their students, to insist that they could rise above negative influences – whatever they might be – and alter their own destiny for life. As Catholic Christians we have always rejected – at least officially – the theology of predestination. No one is ever determined by personal disposition, cultural influences or social circumstances to 'turn out' a certain way. Powerful influences notwithstanding, we always remain agents in our own becoming, and good education should enhance our abilities to choose for life.

St Irenaeus, writing *circa* 175, proposed that 'the glory of God is the human person fully alive'. He was echoing the sentiment of Jesus: 'I came that you might have life, and have it to the full' (John 10:10). In other words, the more people grow and develop into their full potential, the more God is glorified. Surely Catholic educators should hold out to all the hope of such fullness of life, and mentor that hope into realisation. If we do, then our work takes on a priestly hue, for indeed it gives glory to God.

To conclude

In my presentation to the participants at the 'Reimagining the Catholic School' conference, we went on to review some more of the core convictions of Catholic faith – like sacramentality, communality, spirituality and justice – raising them up and proposing what they might mean for the spirituality of Catholic educators. In my book *Educating for Life* I lay out eight deep structures of Catholic identity and their implications for the vocation of Catholic educators – teachers, administrators and parents.

Given the history of Ireland and its traditional Catholicity – so deep to its identity – it would seem that now is the time to reclaim the depth structures of Catholic Christianity as the spirituality that grounds its Catholic education. And those deep core convictions need never aid and abet sectarianism; in fact, they should help to heal the traces of such that endures. At its best, Catholic Christianity can provide a rich spiritual foundation for educators, prompting them to educate for life for all. Whether or not that happens depends on what gets forged in the smithy of the teacher's own soul; only from a life-giving spirituality can we forge anew the 'conscience of [our] race'.

And for those who would lament that it may be too late to draw upon such foundations, let me offer you a *seanfhocal* I learned here as a child; my friends tell me that this is an Ulster Irish version: *'Is furus aibhleog a fhadú'* – 'A quenched coal is easily rekindled'.

Spirituality and the Educator:
Cherishing and challenging the spirituality of the educator

Carol Barry

The main purpose, and my concern in writing this paper, is firstly to explore the connection and the vital relevance of spirituality for the educator, and secondly to indicate why, for the sake of both the educator and the student, it is so important to make this significant connection.

At the outset I would like to say that my own awareness and conviction concerning the need to cherish and challenge the spirituality of the educator has arisen and developed from three sources: (1) twenty years of involvement in our schools as a member of a retreat team, working with both students and teachers; (2) studies in the area of spirituality and education; (3) the pleasure and privilege of lecturing (and above all listening) to student teachers as they speak of their own experiences and their deep-felt needs, fears and anxieties.

During a superb course on 'Spirituality and Education' with Dr Aostere Johnson at St Michael's College, Vermont, USA, Parker Palmer's wonderful book *The Courage To Teach* came to my attention. It was with great joy that I read this book, which articulates in such an inspiring way so much of what I have personally come to understand about spirituality and its significance for educators. I will draw on Palmer's insights throughout this paper, but first I believe that in order to approach our subject matter we need to clarify briefly what we mean by 'spirituality' and to whom we are referring when we speak of 'the educator'.

Spirituality

Ronald Rolheiser rightly refers to the fact that although today there are books on spirituality everywhere, there are still some major misunderstandings about the concept. Chief among these is the idea that 'spirituality is somehow exotic, esoteric, and not something that issues forth from the bread and butter of ordinary life... so rarely is spirituality understood as referring to something vital and non-negotiable lying at the heart of our lives'. Joan Chittister defines it thus: 'Spirituality speaks for interpretation. It is more than churchgoing. It is the way in which we express a living faith in a real world. It is the sum total of attitudes and actions that define our faith'. Joanne Wolski Conn offers a specifically Christian definition when she says: 'Christian spirituality involves the human capacity of self-transcendent knowledge, love and commitment as it is actualised through the experience of God, in Jesus, by the gift of the spirit... Christian spirituality includes every dimension of human life'. Spiritual questions are true human questions irrespective of whether people align themselves to specific religious traditions/institutions. Sandra Schneider contends that there exists a deep hunger, 'a profound and authentic desire of twentieth-/twenty-first-century humanity for the wholeness in the midst of fragmentation, for community in the face of isolation and loneliness, for liberating transcendences, for the meaning in life, for values that endure'. Her own understanding of spirituality is 'the experience of consciously striving to integrate one's life not in terms of isolation and self-absorption, but in self-transcendence, towards the ultimate value one perceives'.

Whenever we think about or seek to understand questions such as 'What is the meaning of life?', 'Why do we get up in the morning?', 'Why did we decide to be teachers?', 'Why do we stay teaching?', 'What engages us? Drives us?', 'Have we a vision of life, for life, of the human person?', 'What are our values; what is the ultimate value we perceive?', 'Do we live lives of faith that speak for integration?' – whenever we ponder or are forced to ponder these truly human questions, we consequently find ourselves caught up with spiritual questions. The longings that Parker Palmer speaks of in his definition of spirituality resonate with the murmurings of teachers I have listened to: 'By spiritual I mean the diverse ways we answer the heart's longing to be connected to the largeness of life – a longing that admits love and work, especially the work called teaching'.

'The educator'

Steven Glazer believes that 'by letting all phenomena – all our experience – be our teachers, school is never out. Education never stops, learning never stops. We learn from our experience, our awareness, our bodies. We greet life: we meet life face to face'. To allow life to be our educator, however, requires openness, and indeed the very desire to learn, for we can, as Glazer reminds us, 'deny or expose, we have the choice of learning or forgetting... we can choose to grow or not'.

Accepting the above truth however, we are normally referring to parents and significant adults as well as members of the teaching profession when we refer to educators. While acknowledging parents/guardians as the primary educators of their children, the need for collaboration between parents and the teaching profession in the education of children, and the fact that the content of this paper is relevant for parents too, I am primarily addressing those involved in the teaching profession (be it in primary, secondary or third-level educational institutions) when I speak of educators. And I do so only because of the context of the specific conference this paper is written for and the workshops involved.

In view of our definitions of spirituality I believe the issues we will address are relevant for all teachers, irrespective of their given subject, for, as Parker Palmer states, 'Spirituality – the human quest for connectedness – is not something that needs to be brought into or "added to" the curriculum. It is at the heart of every subject we teach, where it waits to be brought forth'.

To cherish – to challenge!

Parker Palmer believes we will never transform education if we fail to cherish and challenge – the human heart is the source of good teaching. He also reminds us that most people become teachers 'for reasons of the heart, animated by a passion for some subject and for helping others to learn'. Palmer observes that many teachers lose heart for many different reasons as the years go by, and he goes on to ask: 'How can we take heart in teaching once more so that we can, as good teachers always do, give our heart to our students? How can we who teach reclaim our hearts, for the sake of our students, ourselves, and educational reform?'

'For the sake of our students'

Jesus made it clear that he came 'so that they might have life and have it more abundantly' (John 10:10). In the Gospels we see the word become flesh as Jesus brought life to the minds, hearts, spirit and bodies of those who encountered his life. Teachers have, I believe, the privilege to bring life to their students, or the power to sap the life from their students' self-esteem, their very spirit. (I often use the symbol of an old-fashioned candle-snuffer to illustrate this point!) As teachers, we can 'snuff' the light in our students' souls or help their own 'light' – their talents, capabilities, virtues, and so on – flare to life.

I think most people will admit that when they look back on their educational experiences they remember (at times with great clarity) the teachers who inspired them, who helped them develop a love for certain subjects, for example History, English, Art and Music teachers who encouraged them and nurtured their budding talents. They will use words such as 'patient', 'enthusiastic', 'friendly', and 'kind', to refer to those influential teachers of fond remembrances. Equally, sadly, people remember (with equally great clarity) teachers who instilled fear, dislike of given subjects, who belittled by sarcasm or the harsh word their students' sense of self-esteem. At times, as I have come to realise, the 'words' of teachers have had a lasting (crippling even) effect on their students, long after the sting of a slap had passed away. Words used to describe these less-than-fond remembrances of such teachers include 'harsh', 'sarcastic', 'fearful', 'depressive', and 'gloomy'.

I have listened to numerous people of diverse backgrounds, ages and educational experiences and concur with Palmer: 'Teaching, like any truly human activity, emerges from our inwardness, for better or worse. As I teach, I project the condition of my soul, onto my students, my subjects and our way of being together'. Our teaching – how we teach – in other words the manner of our teaching, reflects our innermost selves. As the psychologist Gordan Allport states, 'What is actually taught turns out in the long run as being less important than the manner of teaching – often we remember a person because of their goodness and sincerity and example long after we have forgotten what they actually said and taught'. Professional competency, good methodology and sound peopleogy is not being dismissed as irrelevant or unimportant here; rather, the following insights are being highlighted for the sake of our students, yes, but also for the sake of our teachers:

- Teaching holds a mirror to the soul.
- Willingness to look into that mirror to see the self it reflects is needed.
- Courage is required to acknowledge how the quality of my selfhood forms – or deforms – the way I relate to my students, my subjects, my colleagues and my world.

'For the sake of our educators'

Every career brings its own drawbacks and joy; teachers, too, have days when it all makes sense that you chose your given career, and days when you question the sanity of your choice! In our staffrooms, we can quickly identify people who still love teaching, have a passion for their subjects and indeed love their pupils, even after a few decades of teaching. Sadly, we can also, if we are honest, find people in our staffrooms showing early signs of burnout, disinterest, even apathy towards subject matters and, worse still, towards students. And some of these teachers have not even completed one decade of teaching! Reasons for 'loss of heart' when it comes to teaching are varied and complex and ultimately tied up with all areas of the teacher's life, for 'Teaching and learning, done well, are done not by disembodied intellects but by whole persons whose minds cannot be disconnected from feeling and spirit, from heart and soul'. To state the obvious (yet the obvious can be forgotten), teachers are people, people who have their own personal joys, concerns, needs, anxieties, health issues, family problems, and so on. At the same time they are engaged in the education of the young, a highly significant and deeply influential role. There is currently also the problem, as Palmer points out, that 'Teacher bashing has become a popular sport. Panic-stricken by the demands of our day, we need scapegoats for the problems we cannot solve and sins we cannot bear'. There can be the tendency for some people to blame teachers for being unable to cure social ills that no one knows how to treat; we insist that they instantly adopt whatever 'solution' has most recently been concocted by our national panacea machine; and, in the process, we demoralise, even paralyse the very teachers who could help us find our way.

Palmer goes on to remind us, prophetically, I believe: 'In our rush to reform education, we have forgotten a simple truth; reform will never be achieved by renewing appropriations, re-structuring schools, re-writing curricula, and revising texts if we continue to demean and dishearten the human resource called the teacher on whom so much depends'. The teacher, not the video, not the teaching aids, not the latest technology is, was and always will be the greatest resource for the child in the school. Technique and methodology have their place, but 'technique is what teachers use until the real teacher arrives'. And that means a person, a whole person, conscious and growing daily more aware of their own 'inner landscape', must turn up; in other words, a spiritually-awakened pilgrim.

'Teacher, what about you?'

A few years ago, whilst directing a 'reflection day' for teachers, a young male primary school teacher of about thirty shared this experience. He had prepared well a religion lesson during which his class would imaginatively engage with some Gospel stories; he had beautiful teaching aids that day, including colourful candles and flowers. As part of the exercise the children had to remain very quiet and imagine themselves in the Gospel story in order to 'hear' what Jesus was saying to them. To his delight all went well, even the 'messers' stayed quiet, did not pinch anyone, no distractions! Bliss! The children even respectfully listened to each other's sharings from their quiet moments.

Delighted with such a 'successful' lesson, he turned to clear up and get ready for the next lesson when, to his horror, a little girl up front said, 'Teacher, what about you, what did Jesus say to you?' When he turned to her, he said, he could not manage a professional bluff, there was something in her eyes as she stared at him waiting for his reply that penetrated his heart. He had not entered into the exercise, was not even sure if he believed in Jesus, never mind prayed to him or sought to hear from him; in his life, silent reflection was an alien experience! He told us he eventually tried to fob her off with the excuse that he had to 'keep an eye on the class, and therefore could not listen to Jesus'. However, with the doggedness of an inspired seven-year-old she reminded him, 'You said Jesus would say something to everyone in the class!'

As he continued his story he related to us how he could only look at her and apologise that he was not 'listening'. A certain look came into her eyes, 'a disappointed look' – this shook him. He felt pinned to the spot, a place of deep discomfort where somehow he felt 'false', his sense of personal identity and integrity challenged by this seven-year-old girl in a way no parent, priest, teacher had ever managed. Consequently, he decided to attend voluntarily the reflection/retreat day organised for staff of his school. Calling himself a 'lapsed Catholic' who took his obligation to teach religion as a primary school teacher seriously and very professionally, he admitted that as an adult he had never explored or reflected on any deep, meaningful life questions. He believed if he was to have any genuine sense of integrity as he stood before his class he at least needed to find the questions that are worth living, worth 'wrapping' your life around' as Palmer puts it, even if he never found certain answers.

'The "Who" question'
Parker Palmer raises a very significant question, one that indeed should be central to any discussion on what constitutes good teaching. This question is one that the teacher in our story would now concur is worth asking, and that is more challenging to us than the traditional educational questions: 'What do we teach?', 'How do we teach?', 'Why do we teach?'

This question that educators need to ask, to reflect on and to find answers to in order to evoke their own spirituality is simply, 'Who is the self that teaches?' Educators need to explore their inner life, to go on the inner journey, even as they daily walk the linear journey of birth to death. Why? Firstly, because the more familiar they are with their inner terrain, the more sure-footed their teaching – and living – becomes. Secondly, whoever our students may be, whatever subjects, ultimately we teach who we are. A person is taught, a person teaches. Palmer says, 'When I hear teachers ask whether they can take their spirituality into the classroom with them, I wonder what the option is – as long as we take ourselves into the classroom, we take our spirituality with us… If we do not live good questions, and live them in a way that is life-given, our own deformations will permeate the work we do and contribute to the deformation of the students whose lives we touch'.

'Fruitful solitude'

Joan Chittister in her book *Wisdom Distilled from the Daily* speaks of the wisdom of St Benedict's rule, which affirmed the importance of a balanced life; a life in which work, prayer and holy leisure are equally afforded respect and time; where silence, solitude and contemplation, understood as the pursuit of meaning, are valued not as a luxury but as a necessity for health and personal growth. 'Life without silent space is not life at all – no life is to be so busy that there is no time to take stock of it. No day is to be so full of business that the gospel does not intrude. No schedule is to be so tight that there is no room for reflection on whether what is being done is worth doing at all. No work should be so all-consuming that nothing else can ever get in – not my husband, not my wife, not my hobbies, not my friends, not nature, not reading, not prayer. How shall we ever put on the mind of Christ if we never take time to determine what the mind of Christ was then and is now, for me.'

Bendictine spirituality is a call to mindfulness, a call that teachers in their very humanity need to answer; for many are tired, but as Chittister points out, at times 'the fact is that it is our souls, not our bodies that are tired. The fact is that we are so over-stimulated and so under-energised that the same old things stay simply the same old things, always. The sense of excitement that comes with newness and freshness is gone. Only contemplation, the recognition of meaning in life, can possibly bring that kind of energy back. But that means we have to take time, make time for ourselves for holy reading and gentle awareness and deep reflection. In contemplation we stretch our understanding so that our hearts can come to peace'.

In order to cherish their own hearts teachers (like all people) need to create some space for silence in what can be hectic lifestyles. John O'Donohue expresses this wisdom so beautifully when he refers to Meister Eckhard's point: 'There is a place in the soul that neither space, nor time, nor flesh can touch. This is the eternal place within us. It would be a lovely gift to yourself to go there often – to be nourished, strengthened, renewed. The deepest things that you need are not elsewhere… a fruitful solitude without silence and space is inconceivable… real friendship and holiness enables a person to frequently visit the hearth of his/her own solitude…'.

'Inner eviction'

I believe John O'Donohue speaks great wisdom when he warns: 'There is a great sinister eviction taking place; people's lives are being dragged outwards all the time. The inner world of the soul is suffering a great eviction from the landlord forces of advertising and external social reality. This outer exile really impoverishes us. One of the reasons why so many people are suffering from stress is not that they are doing stressful things but that they allow so little time for silence'.

Personal responsibility

Each person and each teacher has to take responsibility for his or her own personal development, live deeply in their own questions, and challenge, cherish and nourish in ways they believe right for themselves, their own spirituality. As we have said, we need to do this both for our own sakes as well as for the sake of the students whose lives we touch. We need to remember, as Charles Healy reminds us in his excellent article on 'The Spirituality of the Religious Educator': 'Institutions reform slowly, and as long as we wait, depending on "them" to do the job for us – forgetting that institutions are also "us" – we merely postpone reform and continue the slow slide to cynicism that characterises too many teaching careers. There is an alternative to waiting: we can reclaim our belief in the power of inwardness to transform our work and our lives'.

Charles Healy also reminds us of what provides and sustains a spirit of hope, purpose and perserverance along with the faith-filled vision that is so necessary for an educator:

- A faith-filled perspective – God can and does work through us and is with us in our work. We need to be open to the power of God's spirit at work in us; we are not on our own.
- Importance of prayer – it is an abiding attitude that seeks to deepen and nourish the awareness of God and God's love and the actual workings of God's love in our lives.
- Sustaining hope – drawing consolation and strength from seemingly small events. Maintaining a sense of awe and wonder. Realising that often we can only plant, and leave the harvesting to a time or place or manner we may never know. We can only do our best and leave the rest to God. Realising that there is a great meaning and significance to our work and efforts.
- Love – as the foundation of our spirituality (1 John 10:4). It is no exaggeration to say that every religious educator is called to signify Christ's loving presence in this world to every child and student he or she teaches.

Donald C. Wesley affirms that 'believing in someone is a concern of the spirit and it matters in the classroom'. For teachers to believe in their students and to encourage their discovery of hidden talents, indeed their sense of self, teachers need to believe in their own selves, to value and treasure their own abilities and gifts. In so doing they are on the road to being an inspiring teacher and, as Wesley says, 'inspired teaching, the kind that encompasses the spiritual, is not only seen, but also felt and experienced'. And that last point I believe we all know to be true.

Institutional responsibility?

Yes, we are all responsible for our personal development. However, in conclusion I would like to at least acknowledge a few questions raised by Palmer; to provide the answers is beyond my capabilities and subject matter for another paper. But the questions are worth asking, especially of third-level educational institutions:

- How can educational institutions sustain and deepen the selfhood from which good teaching comes?
- How can educational institutions support the teacher's inner life, and should they be expected to do so?
- To educate is to guide students on an inner journey towards more truthful ways of seeing and living in the world. How can schools perform their mission without encouraging the guides to do the same?

As Palmer himself believes, 'the most important step towards evoking the spirit in education is to bring teachers together to talk, not about curriculum, technique, budget or politics, but about the deeper questions of our lives. Only if we can do this with one another – in ways that honour both the importance of our questions and the diversity with which we hold them – will we be able to do it for our students, who need our companionship on their journeys'. Based on my own experience of talking with and listening to teachers, and the insights gained from the students I have the honour of lecturing on this very subject of 'Spirituality and the Educator', I wholeheartedly agree with this last suggestion. Teachers, if they so desire, deserve the opportunity in 'solitude and in community' to explore the spiritual dimension of a teacher's life.

'Only a handful of flour... a little oil' (1 Kings 17:7-6)
Elijah the prophet, led by spirit, once asked a widow woman to give him some water and some bread. She had come to the end of her own resources and was baking the last cake of bread for herself and her son in preparation for death. She felt she had nothing left to give, yet in obedience to the prophetic request she offered the little she had and in her willingness to give was able to provide for Elijah, and she was abundantly blessed with divine provision for the future – her 'jar of flour did not go empty, nor the jug of oil run dry, as the Lord had foretold'. As educators, with many people drawing on our resources, it can at times be a painful experience to be asked to give once more of ourselves to our students, our subjects, our colleagues and our schools. Yet these can be graced moments in which we remember to draw on our greatest resource. As the Teacher reminds us: 'The Holy Spirit that the Father will send in my name... will teach you everything and remind you of all that I told you... remain in me as I remain in you... whoever remains in me, with me in them, bears fruit in plenty, for cut off from me you do nothing... it is to the glory of my Father that you should bear much fruit'. The call is 'to stay', to stay 'until you are clothed with the power from on high'.

Bibliography
Bausch, William, *The Yellow Brick Road* (Dublin: The Columba Press, 1999).
Chittister, Joan, *Wisdom Distilled from the Daily* (San Francisco: Harper, 1991).
Educational Leadership, 56:4 (Dec 1998 – Jan 1999). All articles related to Spirituality and Education.
Glazer, Steven (ed.), *The Heart of Learning, A New Consciousness Reader* (New York: Penguin Putnam, 1999).
Guinan, Michael, *To be Human before God: Insights from Biblical Spirituality* (Collegeville: Liturgical Press, 1994).
Healy, Charles, 'The Spirituality of the Religious Educator' in *Emerging Issues in Education*, Durka, G. and Smith, J. (eds), (New York: Paulist Press, 1979).
Kelsey, Morton, 'Educating Children Spiritually and Psychologically' in *Religious Education*, vol. 4 (Fall 1994).
Palmer, Parker J., *The Courage to Teach* (San Francisco: Jossey-Bass, 1998).
Rolheiser, Ronald, *Seeking Spirituality* (London: Hodder & Staughton, 1998).
Wicks, Robert J., *Availability* (New York: Paulist Press, 1999).

Imagination in the Service of Catholic Education
Homily Text – Readings:
2 Corinthians 5:5-20; Matthew 9:14-17

Dermot A. Lane

Coming at the end of a most stimulating and provocative two days together, I am conscious that there is little left to be said at this stage that has not already been said, and said far more eloquently than I can sum up in this homily.

And yet the Word of God, the Good News of Jesus Christ is, as always, fresh and challenging, like a two-edged sword activating our Christian memories and stretching our religious imaginations.

Who could fail to be struck by those two very vivid images invoked by Jesus in the Gospel that we have just heard (Matthew 9:14-17)? The image of the unshrunk piece of cloth being sewn on to the old garment, which subsequently tears away, symbolises some of the issues being experienced in our Church today. Likewise, the image of the new wine, that is, the messianic wine, being put into old wine skins which then burst and are destroyed, captures many of the tensions that we have been hearing about over the last two days.

Furthermore, these two striking images take on a particular significance when placed in the context of our first reading (2 Corinthians 5:5-20), which reminds us that the old has passed away and the new has come: 'If anyone is in Christ, there is a new creation' (2 Corinthians 5:17).We need all the time to continue to explore what is distinctively new about the Christian message and this is best done through the exercise of imagination.

What is most significant about these wisdom sayings of Jesus is that they were issued at a time and in a context similar to what is happening in the life of the Catholic Church today. Jesus was seeking to reform Judaism, just as the promptings of the Spirit coming to us from the Second Vatican Council and subsequent developments have been seeking to reform the Church today.

At present the new wine of Vatican II all too often is being put into old wine skins and, as we know, the old wine skins are frequently bursting all around us because they are unable to contain the new wine.

The new wine from Vatican II includes the call to lay ministry, according primacy to adult faith formation within Religious Education, recognising the radical equality of all who are baptised in Christ, taking seriously the summons to work towards Christian unity, respecting the value of other religious traditions, effecting a dialogue between faith and culture, and developing the link between Christian faith and action for justice in Church and society.

This new wine of Vatican II, and developments since Vatican II, is in need of a new religious imagination. A new imaginative framework, a new kind of template is required, if we are to assimilate and appropriate this vision of Vatican II. And so the theme of this conference, 'Reimagining the Catholic School', is timely and urgent.

However, the creative exercise of imagination will only succeed if it is connected to the work of memory. If we forget the past, if we ignore tradition, if we neglect history, then we are doomed not only to repeat history but also to continue to make the same mistakes of the past in the present.

The memory I have in mind here is not the memory of nostalgia or sentimentality or a hankering after so-called 'good old days', which we now know were not so good. Instead, it is the particular memory of Jesus: the prophetic, liberating and healing memory of Jesus released into the world through his saving death and resurrection and the outpouring of his Spirit. This is the vision that animates Christian faith.

If that memory of Jesus is to live again and to be realised once again among his disciples, then it needs a new imagination. Imagination lives out of memory and it is memory that activates imagination.

It was our own Patrick Kavanagh who captured this most fundamental but neglected truth when he wrote in one of his poems:

> On the stem
> Of memory, imaginations flourish.
> (Why Sorrow)

Our Catholic imagination can and will flourish on the foundation of the historical memory of Jesus: the memory of his mission and ministry for the coming reign of God, his liberating death and resurrection, and the outpouring of his transforming Spirit at Pentecost.

Imagination divorced from memory quickly becomes incredible and reduced to mere fantasy. Imagination yoked to memory, especially the historical memory of Jesus as the Christ, will be both prophetic and empowering, disturbing and liberating, healing and redemptive.

One of the more imaginative descriptions of the Catholic school is to see it as 'a community of memory', that is, a community dedicated to keeping the prophetic memory of Jesus alive imaginatively in the twenty-first century. Only those who do not appreciate the place of memory within Judaism, and the very specific, quasi-sacramental meaning of memory within the Jewish imagination, will find it difficult to accept this description of the Catholic school at the beginning of the twenty-first century. For the Jew, to remember is to reactivate and reactualise the past in the present in a way that transforms lives.

An important part of the role of the Catholic school, therefore, is to keep the prophetic, liberating and healing memory of Jesus alive. Catholic teachers, and in particular religious educators, are called to be bearers of the memory of Jesus. As bearers of the memory of Jesus they will also be agents of hope in a world that has become aimless, apathetic and empty for too many young people today.

If that is how we are to reimagine the Catholic school, then we must also begin to reimagine the Catholic parish, and that, it seems to me, is one of the many important things that Anne Looney, the CEO of the NCCA, is hinting at in her wide-ranging paper.

The good work already going on in Catholic schools, and it needs to be acknowledged more explicitly that there is good work going on, is not always succeeding simply because it is not receiving the pastoral support it deserves within the local parish community. I make this observation and criticism as one working in a parish and who knows only too well how much we fail to support local Catholic schools. It has always been a part of Catholic thinking that the school cannot assume sole responsibility for the faith formation of pupils. Rather, this is a task to be shared by home, school and parish working in tandem.

A further feature in reimagining the Catholic school is connected to the understanding of Catholic identity and Catholic education today. For too many people Catholic education has become synonymous with sectarianism. This misunderstanding and misrepresentation of Catholic education is often based on a pre-Vatican II experience of Catholic education. It needs to be remembered that the Second Vatican Council reshaped Catholic identity and education and that this reshaping formally committed the Catholic Church to working with other Churches in promoting Christian unity.

Consequently, ecumenism is not an optional extra within Catholic schools but rather an essential element within the school mission. Likewise, to be Catholic today requires that we be inter-religious, especially in the light of the emerging multicultural reality of the new Ireland: ecumenism and interfaith dialogue are integral elements of the Catholic school and should be inscribed in the Mission Statements of Catholic schools. The Catholic school that is not ecumenical, that is, which does not recognise and respect the ecclesial character of other Christian Churches, is not truly Catholic. Likewise, the Catholic school that fails to value the elements of truth and grace within the other world religions is not in tune with the teaching of the Second Vatican Council and the significant developments that have taken place in the Catholic Church since then in the area of interfaith dialogue.

Other essential characteristics within the reimagining of the Catholic school include the presence of a prophetic voice on behalf of the poor within society and the promotion of a faith that performs justice in the name of the coming Reign of God. Once again, these are not just optional extras. They are explicit aspects of the social teaching of the Catholic Church and, therefore, should be visible marks of a Catholic school in the twenty-first century.

Also central to the imagination influencing the Catholic school is the paschal character of Christian identity. The centrepiece of Catholic existence is the presence of the crucified and risen Christ helping us to come to grips with the cruciform character of human experience. There is a very important sense in which it must be said that for the Christian 'the fire and rose are one' and that the object of Christian hope is 'a bright darkness'.

A further ingredient of the Catholic imagination is the vision that formation in faith cannot be divorced from the content of faith. Catholic faith is always a faith that exists in critical conversation with reason and, therefore, is never a purely private faith. Catholic Religious Education in schools is an interdisciplinary affair, being grounded in educational theory and practice, and closely but critically connected to the reigning culture.

An additional feature of the Catholic imagination which is important for the future of schools concerns the way we understand education. The Catholic school must resist the increasing temptation to reduce education to a function of the economy and a utility of the marketplace. Education is about opening minds to the lifelong search for a wisdom that is deeper than information, for an understanding of life that goes beyond knowledge, for an appreciation of the dignity of the other that is respectful of difference. There is a tendency to reduce education to training, knowledge to skills, and understanding to an accumulation of information. This approach to education may succeed in the short term but it shortchanges young people in the long term. Of course, skills and information are important, but they do not prepare pupils for the inevitability of personal failure, tragedy and loss, as well as the success, joy and responsibility that comes with freedom.

And finally, the Catholic imagination within our schools must make room for the existence of the symbolic and sacramental dimensions of life. We live in a universe that is charged with the grandeur of God and a sacramental presence. Within the sacramental order of existence, pride of place must be given to the Eucharist, that location where memory and imagination interact most creatively within the Catholic community. If the Eucharist is about bringing Christian memory and imagination together, and I believe it is, then perhaps we also need to reimagine the way we celebrate the Eucharist in greater fidelity to the command of Christ at the Last Supper: 'Do this in memory of me'.

If we are to be faithful to this commandment of Jesus at the Last Supper, then greater account must be taken of the meal-ministry of the historical Jesus, the Passover context of the Last Supper, and the washing of the feet which followed the institution of the Eucharist. In other words, the organic unity that exists between the meal-ministry of the historical Jesus, the institution of the Eucharist at the Last Supper, the context of the Jewish Passover, and the dramatic action of the washing of the feet, need to inform more clearly and visibly the way we celebrate the Eucharist.

In conclusion we can say with confidence that memory and imagination are important pillars in the reconstruction of Catholic education and Catholic schools for the twenty-first century. To that extent we must thank Marino Institute of Education for gathering us together and, in particular, for provoking us to reimagine the Catholic school for tomorrow in this new way.

Re-engaging the Adolescent Religious Imagination

Jacques Janssen

'Our time is one of religious decline. The once enduring vitality of the religious is in decay. The masses have become either superstitious or gullible, or even indifferent to religion. Society's elites are agnostic or sceptical, and its political leaders are hypocrites. Youth is in open conflict with established society and with the authorities of the past. They experiment with Eastern religions and techniques of meditation. The greater part of mankind is affected by the decay of the times'. There is no doubt that Europe's religious landscape is in turmoil and will change dramatically in the coming decades. The differences between young and old are great, and clearly indicate a decline in the importance of traditional, institutional religion. Today even the core believers amongst the young have ideas and practices that differ fundamentally from those of the older generation and that are greatly at odds with official prescriptions.

However, the pessimistic description of culture and the state of religion that I opened with, actually comes from the Annals of the famous Roman historian Cornelius Tacitus. When he wrote these words, late in the first century AD, he was referring to the state of the ancient Hellenistic world at that time, almost two thousand years ago. Religion has been in one crisis or another in whichever era you choose to study, while young people all over the world experiment with ideas and practices that deviate from those prescribed by the official Churches. Religious socialisation is a risky enterprise from the very beginning. The young very often choose to go their own way. Very often this takes them in directions that their predecessors may regret or even deplore. Another couple of quotes, now from a famous poem: 'Rarely does human worth rise through the branches' and 'from sweet seed may come forth bitter'. Parents and teachers know this from daily experience. Despite their best efforts, the young don't follow in their footsteps. These quotations are also from long ago. Their author is the 'poeta christianissimus', as Boccaccio honourably called him, Dante Alighieri, on his way from hell to paradise, 701 years ago.

It is a source of hope and comfort to know that we are not the first generation to find ourselves in trouble. However, our responsibilities and problems don't simply disappear when we relate them to the responsibilities and problems of other people in other times. Every era faces its own crisis. The crisis of today is a crisis of belongingness. In Europe, the numbers of Church members and churchgoers, as well as several others indicators of institutional religiosity, are in steady decline. 'What instruments we have agree' that religion as an institution is fading. Since the 1970s, the Netherlands, the country I live in, has taken the lead in this process. In 1945, 40 per cent of the Dutch population were Catholics. Today this percentage has halved, and by 2025 the figure will have fallen further to around 15 per cent. In 1945, 15 per cent of the people were not members of any Church. Today, the figure exceeds 60 per cent, and it is predicted to rise to 70 per cent by 2020. If we also take into consideration the fact that all across Europe, the younger generation scores substantially lower on almost every indicator of religious behaviour than older people, we can deduce that Dutch youth has reached the peak of secularisation. In the European Values Study of 1990, 53 per cent of Dutch youths were reported to be non-Church members. At that time, this was indeed the highest percentage in Western Europe. Churches are losing contact with the younger generation. In the years to come, the results of this mutual estrangement will become more and more visible in participation and opinion indexes. In each of the various countries of Europe, this process has taken a specific turn due to the different national histories. In countries such as Italy and Ireland, the Church can still count on a solid majority. But even in these countries, decline is setting in. As we will see, the outlook for religion in the Netherlands is actually more favourable in some respects than in many other countries, despite it being the country with the lowest rate of Church membership.

The pessimistic forecasts of contemporary sociologists and historians need to be taken seriously. Let us first try to understand what they mean. They view the decline of the Church as the latest phase in an ongoing process of secularisation. The Church is no longer the leading institution in Europe. It has very little influence left, whether it be in science, politics, social affairs, daily life, or in issues of life and death. People are educated and free; they can make their own decisions. They can no longer be manipulated by fears and threats about a hereafter. They live their own lives for their own sakes, in the here and now. The philosophers of enlightenment and disenchantment, such as Arthur Schopenhauer and Max Weber, seem to have been proved right in the end.

But there is more to life than can be grasped by a sociological theory on secularisation. Firstly, at the very time when people are turning their backs on Churches, there has been no growth in humanistic, agnostic or atheistic institutions. These institutions are in crisis too. Democratic socialism, which in the sixties was an inspiring political movement for many young people, has lost its galvanising force. The several parties find it difficult to get across the difference they make, especially when they are in government. The end of ideology, announced by Daniel Bell in the 1950s, seems irrevocable. Politics is nowadays a pragmatic way of balancing different interests. Scepticism functions, as it did in Tacitus' time, as an attitudinal alternative to idealism. Secondly, at the very time when people are turning their backs on Churches, re-enchantment is setting in. A New Age has been proclaimed, and a rapidly and steadily growing number of people are becoming interested in a cornucopia of religious products. Hymns, holy oils, books and meditative techniques from all over the world are being bought and sold in abundance, to enrich and spiritualise the homes we live in. Is this enlightenment? What enlightenment? As François-Renée de Chateaubriand put it in 1802, in *Génie du christianisme*: 'When people do believe in nothing, they are close to believing anything; they will have diviners where they once had prophets, sortilege where they once had religious ceremonies and they will open up the haunts of sorcerers when they close down the temples of the Lord'. In the Netherlands, the secularised country *par excellence*, all kinds of religions are prospering, while their adherents are dedicated and active. The country is home to the leading experimental garden of religiosity in Europe. It would take a book to describe its religious flora.

We live in paradoxical times. While the historians and the sociologists tamp down the ground that God is buried under, biologists and psychologists point to the genetic and neuropsychological basis of religion. People cannot live without myths and rites. Even when religion is sociologically invisible it is at the same time deeply rooted psychologically. God won't go away. In a very recent Dutch survey it was shown that there is no difference in the occurrence of mystical and religious experiences between Church members and non-Church members.

How should we understand this paradoxical situation? I think that the main cultural process that has brought about this state of affairs can be summed up as the fragmentation of self and culture. For many centuries, cultures remained geographically bound. But today, you can find people from all over the world living side by side in any European town. In the old days, people's selves were adapted to the one-dimensional world in which they lived. Today the self is no longer taken for granted. Its has become a problem that people have to solve themselves. There are no longer any readymade solutions. People live their lives as multiple, dialogical selves moving through flexible cultural environments. The self has become a complex combination of bits and pieces from several cultures; culture is scattered in several selves. Flexibility has become a requirement in all domains of life.

People no longer have a job for life. In fact, young people don't actually like the idea of a job for life. Temping agencies are booming, and the young are eager to join them. People want flexibility in their personal relationships too. The age at which young people have their first sexual experience is falling, whereas the average age at which people sanctify their relationships in matrimony is steadily increasing. In fact, many are opting for new kinds of provisional contracts to formalise their relationships. Meanwhile more and more marriages are ending in divorce, mostly followed by remarriage. In politics, people change their allegiances from party to party, while only a very few – and a steadily decreasing number for that matter – actually want to become party members. Our democracies tend to become democracies of spectators. Even youth culture is no longer a clear-cut phenomenon. Many youngsters prefer to surf on the edges of conflicting youth cultures and not to submerge themselves in any particular one of them. They want to be themselves, not just part of a subculture. In the seventies, if you had asked a male punk 'What is being a punk all about? How did you become one?', he would have told you at great length how he became a punk, about what being a punk meant to him and what punk culture was all about. In those days punks still lived in tribes. Recently I posed the same question to a punk, adorned with chains and a genuine Mohawk haircut. His answer was: 'No, I'm not a punk, I'm Pete!'. Then he told me that he had put together his own outfit, and that only afterwards did he realise that it did happen to resemble the clothes worn by those people popularly known as 'punks'. Even where fashion and youth culture seem to mould the outfits and opinions of the young inch by inch, they still perceive themselves as self-made and want to present themselves as such, with a personal name rather than a generic one.

People invent or reinvent institutions or behavioural patterns to gain some basic stability in an unstable world. 'Subcultural style-surfing' has become a way of life. It seems a contradiction in terms to talk of 'stabilising instability', but that's exactly what people want to do. Earlier on I mentioned temping agencies: a very intelligent institutional invention. Young people prefer not to tie themselves to a fixed job. They want to be free. But they need to work to be able to live up to the standards of their subculture. The temping agency has the answer: it stabilises their need for instability. In politics, the young prefer to support single-issue pressure groups, such as Amnesty International and Greenpeace, rather than political parties. In the field of religion, a consumerist attitude prevails: the young tend to make up their own religions. They take elements from various religions, constructing a personal necklace from all kinds of beads, both indigenous and exotic, held together by the thin thread of their biography. The young prefer to experience and experiment, in religion as with everything else. The idea of reincarnation is a typical example of post-modern religious reinvention. Traditionally within our Christian culture there has been widespread belief in the resurrection of the flesh. Today more and more people, even Christians, believe in reincarnation. Why? Why is this belief so popular? Technically, I would say that both beliefs are equally complicated and equally hard to prove scientifically. So there is no rational explanation for this change in attitude. But there is a cultural and emotional explanation. The Resurrection is connected with the Last Judgement, which will be handed down, once and for all, for each individual. It is a one-take affair, carved out of stone above the entrances of our churches, completely inflexible. By definition, reincarnation offers flexibility. It offers you another chance, eventually, over and over again. That's why it suits the spiritual identity of modern peoples. Faced with modernity and post-modernity, the Church falters. The children of the dark are more inventive and more alert: the temping agency and the Internet offer new ways to bring people together. Pastoral care cannot simply reject them. New institutional inventions such as 'rent a priest' and 'hire a minister' are too easily ridiculed and dismissed. Pastoral care will soon have to become increasingly attuned to the needs of the individual. I do see the potential pitfalls in this, but we should also recognise the possibilities and the necessities. Yet there is some hope. Some days ago I learned that in the new habits of the Franciscan friars a pocket is sewed into the garment for the mobile telephone. And last week the Pope sent his first e-mail!

Whatever its merits, there is a tendency in several cultural domains, especially amongst the young, to construct provisional, revocable, temporary and individual patterns of home-spun ideas. Social scientists use words like 'bricolage', 'patchwork', 'zap culture' and 'meander culture' to characterise today's culture. We could call modern man a 'Meanderthal', always looking for new combinations; twisting and turning, always claiming to be master of his own life. But is the fact that people are making up their own religions, creating unique combinations of elements from different traditions in their own minds, really such a new thing? I think not. The phenomenon of individualisation has already been documented long ago, ever since the beginnings of the Renaissance. Once again we see an old source foreshadowing a modern or even post-modern cultural process. As said the famous Roman emperor and stoic, Marcus Aurelius, said in his Meditations: 'he who has seen present things, has seen all, both everything which has taken place from all eternity and everything which will be for time without end. [...] There is nothing new; all things are both familiar and short-lived'. But hidden in similarity there is always a difference. Individualism is no longer the privilege of a well-educated and well-to-do minority, as it was before. In our time it has become everybody's responsibility to be an individual. This presents an opportunity for many, but a burden for others, who just pretend to be individuals or even collapse under the cultural burden of the age.

When I presented this characterisation of modern culture and youth culture in April this year at the CEEC congress in Rome, some Italian participants assured me that in Italy things are completely different. Directly after my lecture the congress went by bus to the Vatican to meet the Pope. On the way I saw a billboard that summarised my lecture in one sentence and in Italian. It read: CAMBIA LAVORO PRIMA CHE LUI CAMBI TE. That is: 'Change your job before your job changes you'. Back in the congress hall I rephrased this slogan: change your religion before your religion changes you; change your husband before your husband changes you. Now they understood, and an old Italian father came to me after the discussion and assured me that he had recognised the Italian youth in my presentation.

This is the culture we are part of, whether we like it or not. I'm not saying that we have to accept it uncritically. It is full of paradoxes. Think of the many lookalikes you see in the street, all claiming originality. How original can we and should we be? Is modern youth culture nothing more than a complete and utter sham, albeit a fashionable one? Perhaps. But let whoever casts the first stone show caution. We cannot choose the times we live in, yet these times affect us all. And those of us who still live in the old, stable and predictable world have to be wary of the future, to look out for our children and grandchildren. The times they are a-changing.

The main question is whether Christianity is still credible, still a sensible option in these modern, or rather post-modern, times. As the Flemish exegete Peter Schmidt puts it in his wonderful book about the image of Christ throughout the centuries: 'It really has become difficult to imagine that billions of galaxies, which are billions of years old, and stars that died as black holes millions of years ago, are attuned to the salvation of humankind. [...] Neither can we picture anything concrete when it is said that all of this has been created in and through Christ'. Let me rephrase Schmidt's thesis in psychological and cultural terms. It really has become difficult to imagine that we, the people of this time, floating, temporarily and loosely organised multiple selves, lost in space in an ever-changing multicultural context, have a Father in heaven who cares for us, that He knows our names and calls to us personally, that He sent his Son, Jesus Christ, to die for us, and to deliver us, multiple selves grasping in a multiple cultural context.

The facts show that Christianity remains an option for young people and that many of them are interested in religious issues. If you want to see this in practice, I suggest you visit Taizé, in the French department of Burgundy, situated in between Cluny and Cîteaux, where the roots of Western monastic life can be found. The Taizé monastery was founded by Frère Roger Schutz in 1940 as an ecumenical brotherhood. Since the sixties, young people from all over Europe have been drawn there. Thousands of them gather there each year to meet, to sing and to pray. Since 1977, in a number of major European cities, annual ecumenical meetings have been organised in December: last year for example, 80,000 young people gathered in Barcelona. When I visited Taizé, I was struck by the excitement and spontaneity of so many young people. It was like the exciting, sparkling atmosphere in the schoolyard when the school term finishes and the holidays begin. The services are held in a temporary church building, a huge extending hall. Young people don't feel at home in traditional, permanent, concrete buildings. Frère Schutz understands them very well and consciously rejected the idea of building a big new church. The tent-like construction of Taizé coordinates the uncoordinated religious feelings of today's youth: a multicoloured mass gathered around the small community of monks, wrapped in white habits. At the end of the season the monks stay, while the young people go off in all directions, sharing a memory. No one knows how important it will prove to be, and nobody knows how long they will share it. As far as I know, no research has been done into this phenomenon. My guess would be that the Taizé brethren would not support the idea of carrying out such research anyway. They share what they have with anyone who wants to share it. They do so unconditionally, without demands, and without expecting anything in return. They carefully organise a seemingly unorganised meeting place, providing the conditions for an unconditional encounter, using what Frère Schutz has called 'la dynamique du provisoire', that is, 'the dynamics of the provisional'.

Young people like to be part of a crowd: at pop concerts, in Taizé. Just think of the two million young people who visited Rome last year. The Pope, 'a superstar in his eighties' as a liberal Dutch newspaper described him, had to fly to be able to see the whole crowd. Young people like these kinds of gatherings, that is, gatherings that leave them to be themselves. Gatherings where they can be invisible, hidden in a huge crowd. So the young are indeed attracted by religious symbols, but they keep their distance, hiding in crowds and hiding within themselves, the religiosity of many of them survives in the catacombs of the self, not daring to come out.

Let me illustrate this by referring to research my colleagues and I carried out into the prayer practices of modern youths, because prayer is 'hot'. From previous, European research we know that when the interviewer introduces the word 'God', this has an intimidating effect on youngsters. When asked straight out whether they often pray to God, only 11 per cent of Dutch youths said yes, while 42 per cent of Dutch people over sixty did so. But when asked whether they have moments of prayer or contemplation, 61 per cent of youths answered affirmatively. And this time there was no substantial difference between this figure and the figure for the elderly (68 per cent). The same pattern is evident in every country in Europe. However, in our research, we asked young people an open-ended question on how they actually pray. Without any prompting 44 per cent of those questioned said their prayers have a direction and 68 per cent of them said their prayers were directed towards 'God'. So, asking a question does not always produce the answer, whereas not asking the question sometimes does. The advice famously given by Polonius to his servant Reynaldo in Shakespeare's *Hamlet* certainly applies here: 'by indirections find directions out'. This is a very important piece of advice for modern educators. I will elaborate on this later.

Let me return to the prayer practices of Dutch youths. Prayer turned out to be a widespread and important individualised ritual for the young. While only 39 per cent of Dutch youths said that they were members of a Church, 82 per cent said that they prayed, at least sometimes. In the European studies I mentioned earlier, Dutch youths came at the bottom of a table of sixteen countries with regard to Church membership. However, they came in third place in terms of prayer, below only Ireland and Italy. So even in countries where institutional religion is in decline, many young people say that they pray. The prototypical prayer said by youths goes as follows: faced with negative problems affecting others, they ask or hope for something, or they meditate. They direct their prayers to God, looking for emotional relief. They do this at night, lying in bed, with their eyes closed and hands clasped. Several aspects of this praying practice can be found in traditional praying: most people pray when in trouble, most people pray to God and most ask for relief and for the strength to face life. However, both time and place are exceptional: young people preferably pray at night, in bed. Today's busy and hectic lifestyles leave no time for silence and meditation. In bed, people are finally on their own, and find an opportunity to reflect upon the day, alone and in silence. The paramount reality of everyday life is interrupted. In between active thought and deep sleep, brain activity declines to a mode of passive receptivity, which prepares one to 'turn inwards' and meditate upon the contradictions of daily life. Our findings on prayer can also be interpreted as showing an individualised, do-it-yourself form of confession. People use prayer to cope with feelings of guilt, grief, disappointment and deficiency. New resolutions and plans can be made. So prayer has an important psychological function in the construction of identity. As St Augustine said, it is not meant to instruct God but to construct oneself: 'ut ipsa [referring to 'mens', that is, soul] construatur' not 'ut Deus instruatur'. We have to change ourselves, not God. In psychological terms, prayer can be described as a mechanism for making up an inventory of daily events, to give meaning to them and learn to accept the inevitable or to change what can be changed.

When we asked the young who this God was that they had mentioned, they used all sorts of words and metaphors. It seems that they constructed their own definitions on the spot. A Belgian panel study by Hutsebaut and Verhoeven found no correlation between the definitions of God that young people gave at the age of twelve, and those they gave at the age of fifteen. It seems that, like our respondents, they lack a common stock of words and metaphors. In a Dutch study, youngsters were unable to give answers to the well-known Vergote/Tamayo questionnaire on the image of God because they thought the items were no longer suitable to describe God. Traditional images of God have lost their credibility. Instead, young people prefer a vague and abstract, self-made representation of God. They devoutly practise the mission set out in 'An American Prayer' by rock star Jim Morrison: 'Let's reinvent the gods'.

For St Augustine, the construction of identity was of course the construction of a religious identity. I'm not suggesting that all of the young have this intention. Their prayer can be criticised from a religious point of view. But as personal meditation, straight from the heart, seeking contact, it is a sincere beginning and we should not ignore it. One of our respondents assessed these prayers as follows: 'I pray to God, in whom I don't believe, to help my friend who believes that He will help him, if He exists'. This is really post-modern praying. Oliviero Toscani, designer of the Benetton ad campaigns, recently edited a small prayer book that was published in a number of different languages. His job involves capturing the spirit of the times. The book contains the prayers of young people from all over the world. These prayers are sincere, coming straight from the heart. But the God to whom the young pray is mysterious, rather absent and seldom viewed as a father. As the Dutch writer Frans Kellendonk expressed it, God fills an emptiness they experience. But they have trouble finding the words to describe their feelings. The French journal *Esprit* described the religious situation of our times as 'les temps des religions sans Dieu', the age of religions without God. The formulation is negative and in plural. Perhaps it largely explains why Buddhism is gaining such popularity in Western society. However, in a book on Christian mysticism, Bruno Borchert stressed the religious dimension to today's atheism: 'It does not arise out of scepticism and indifference but out of a loss of faith in old images and an inability to find new ones. This lack of contact with God can prove to be a good breeding ground for a fresh form of mysticism'.

The French sociologist Danièle Hervieu-Léger recently characterised modern believers as pilgrims. Their worship is voluntary, autonomous, temporary, individual, mobile and occasional. Traditional believers on the other hand worship out of a sense of duty, at fixed times and places, in groups and regularly. The American psychologist Daniel Batson described the modern believer as a seeker, a 'quest-believer', while he characterised the traditional believer as an 'intrinsic believer'. In his remarkable essay *'Credo di credere'*, 'I believe that I believe', the Italian philosopher Gianni Vattimo interprets the Christian message as a transcription of a weak ontology. In fact, he recovered the faith he had as a youth, once this faith had been purified by secularisation and was no longer based on strict convictions.

In summary, we can say that the young include more believers than 'belongers', more quest-believers than intrinsic believers, that they tend to subscribe to a weak ontology, hesitantly moving to an uncertain point X, a metaphor that Vattimo borrows from, of all people, Nietzsche. The young are eager to believe but evidently reluctant to belong. They want to search, but are they ready to find and engage themselves? Well, there is the rub. Batson, arguing from a psychological point of view, sees the quest-believer as being more tolerant, more open-minded and more social-minded. 'Quest is best' is his famous conclusion. Psychologically, the older intrinsic 'belongers' seem to be at a disadvantage to the young. But sociologically the situation is reversed. In Batson's words: 'While at an individual level, intrinsic religiosity is not related to induced tolerance and increased sensitivity to the needs of others, religious institutions, primarily backed by intrinsic believers, really are concerned about the downtrodden in society and helping in several ways'. Young believers are reluctant to belong and their participation in societal and volunteer activities is low and inconsistent. Their contribution to the social capital of society is low. If this is just an effect of age, then we may expect a change in the long run. Once they grow older, they will start to participate. However, if this is a generational effect, and there are indications that it is, then the problem will get worse in the future.

Let me summarise, then conclude and thereby open the discussion. Firstly, as I have explained, God will not go away; the young are interested in religion. There really is a precious treasure within. But today's religiosity is fragile and vulnerable. It certainly lacks the determination and militancy that the Catholic Church has exuded throughout the centuries, and occasionally still does. Peter Schmidt, the Flemish exegete I mentioned earlier, concludes his book on the image of Christ by stating that Christ has been as powerless for two centuries as he was during his life and on the cross. His image has been fragmented into bits and pieces, all over the world; he has become the icon of God's absence. Christ is no longer the possession of one single Church or denomination. He unites people in their longing for meaning, their longing for God. Schmidt concludes that, even living in an emancipated world, it really is possible to believe, if one's belief is based upon Christ's original powerlessness. Schmidt's vision bears out Vattimo's philosophy of weak ontology. Both works eloquently summarise what we can learn from today's young people. They don't like power, history, institutions or grand narratives. They have no vested interest, just biography and themselves, just weak personal narratives. We can learn from their unselfish, critical attitude towards the Church as an institution. Church history shows several examples of very debatable policy; and the Church is also making history today. I'm not sure that the next generations will be positive about the Church politics of our days. So I really understand the young when they hesitate to join the club.

However, my second and concluding remark is: how can we help the young to connect their deep and genuine feelings with social and religious reality? How do we relate biography to history? I'm not here to provide the right answers, just (hopefully) to pose the right questions and to suggest some answers. And here they are. First of all, there is an enormous lack of religious knowledge amongst the young. Once again, this is a timeless phenomenon. In his well-known study on magic, Keith Thomas refers to a medieval survey on people's religious knowledge. The results are shocking. When asked about the Trinity, one interviewee said: 'I know the father and the son because I tend their sheep, but that third fellow I've never heard of'. You may laugh, but try conducting the experiment yourselves, back home. Ask your own students what Easter is about or who St Paul is. Ask and prepare for a shock. One of my colleagues did so, and subsequently desperately advised God to let it rain for forty days and nights and then start all over again. As far as I know, God rejected the idea. It is our responsibility to instruct and inform the young. Schools and universities have a huge task ahead of them.

Secondly, knowledge is necessary, but is not enough in itself. It is very important for young people to develop personal relationships with teachers. One teacher can be sufficient. To my regret, hardly any research has been done on this subject. But we all know from our own experiences how important some of our old teachers were for our own biographies.

Thirdly, it is our task to captivate the young, not to capture them. Don't try to imitate them. Be yourself and maintain a distance. Youth is, as Marcel Pagnol strikingly said, 'un temps des secrets', a time of secrecy. Anton van Duinkerken, once a famous Catholic and writer in the Netherlands, referred in his memoirs to an experience he once had at school. For several days, the class had been analysing an intricate love poem by a Dutch poet. Then one of the pupils asked the teacher whether the girl the poem was written for could actually have understood such a complex piece of work. Well, said the teacher, the poet was hoping that one day she would come and ask him about it. That, in a nutshell, is our role: to create interest and wait. Don't push it: little plants grow by themselves. Just irrigate and wait. In education, so said the German writer Lichtenberg, nothing is more important than 'das Ungefähr'. That is, it has to be done incidentally, not expressly; approximately, on a wing and a prayer. By providing the opportunity, as the brothers at Taizé do, using 'la dynamique du provisoire', finding out directions by indirections. And then, one day, they will come and ask you. It is indeed difficult for us to leave the young in peace. We desperately want to understand them. My stay in Taizé was short. The first time, since I study and observe youth, I felt like an intruder, remembering T.S. Eliot's poem: 'If you came this way, … You would have to put off sense and notion. You are not here to verify, instruct yourself, inform curiosity; or carry report. You are here to kneel where prayer has been valid…'. I did the right thing and took the road to Cîteaux, to find my own peace…

Fourthly and finally, the Belgian cardinal Godfried Danneels recently spoke of the return of an old longing in people, the longing for beauty: 'The introduction to the numerous models of beauty in churches, museums, music, literature and theatre is a path to God that is seldom followed'. I can speak from experience. Driven by a personal need, drying up in today's rational, agnostic university system, I remembered an old school teacher from more than twenty years ago who had introduced me to Dante Alighieri's *Divina Commedia*. For four years I sacrificed almost all of my free time in order to translate the first part, Hell. It was a hell of a job, but more than worthwhile. I found a companion for life and rediscovered my Christian roots. Now many people share my enthusiasm. I regularly lecture on Dante, and the Gregorian choir 'Karolus Magnus' I sing in have recently released a double CD *La Divina Commedia Gregoriana* (http://listen.to/karolus-magnus). When I lecture and perform I notice many young people in the audience. I pretend not to see them and just do my thing, leading them from hell, through purgatory, to paradise. Paradise is far away and I'm in no hurry to get there. The same can be said of the young people. For the time being we are just on our way.

New Song in an Ancient Land

Liam Lawton

For the past few years I have been led on a path of discovery – a path that has taken me, as it were, back through the past to help me towards the future. I speak of the influence of my tradition – the spirituality of early Christian Ireland – on my quest to rediscover the beauty and richness of such a tradition in our liturgy and worship. As a composer and performer of sacred music, being rooted in a particular tradition has enabled me to appreciate the richness and diversity of other faiths and other traditions. However, we have still much to do and to learn so that the ageless beauty of our Irish spirituality and customs will not fall into oblivion.

We live in a country that has a glorious heritage of folk music, haunting melodies and songs that are slowly being forgotten. But where are the spiritual songs that have clothed themselves in this musical richness? Why is it that Africans, Asians and Central Americans have allowed the gospel to take root in their folk music but we in Ireland have for the most part avoided such an occasion, as if Christ had never rejoiced in seeing children piping or dancing in the streets.

We live in a country that, as elsewhere in the West, has witnessed a continuous decline in levels of church attendance, yet ironically the majority of people claim to believe in God and accept the fact of Christ. But where are the words and music that might yet allow those on the fringes of the Church or those who have rejected the trappings of organised religion to deepen their faith and praise their Creator?

Our country, by virtue of its Celtic influences and history, had at the core of early Christian evangelising the affirmation that in Jesus, God took on matter, became part of the world, lit up the ordinary with holiness and did not despise the secular, which he came to save. But where are the liturgies that allow the sacred to touch and transform the whole fabric of society rather than just the religious pieces?

The Celts, like the ancient Jews, are our spiritual ancestors. Both, in different ways, recognised that the spirit of God was simply docile. The Jewish psalmist wrote of how, when everything seemed proper, it was God's will to 'share my mountain refuge'. The Celtic monks, knowing the same restlessness and provocation that issues from the Creator, depicted the Holy Spirit as a dove and a wild goose. But where in our contemporary devotions are there glimpses that God, in the twenty-first century, can be expected to surprise, contradict, upset or rile us in order that the kingdom may come?

I believe that within our education system we can begin to address these imbalances. When we come together in faith and prayer, in worship, we can dare to believe that when we take our blessings, our hopes and worries to the Lord, he may direct us and console us, and lead us into the future.

When we come together to worship, the celebration of liturgy seeks to lead the school community away from self-centredness towards love of God and neighbour. For this reason it plays a vital role in the religious formation of young people, as well as preparing them for the liturgical life of the Church.

According to the Northern Ireland Directive for Catholic Schools, 'the source of a school's worshipping spirit is Christ and his Church. Every form of worship within the school community expresses this truth. Worship brings into focus the "raison d'être" of the school, namely the spread of God's kingdom. It sensitises the worshipping community to the presence or absence of kingdom values in our world. In this respect worship seeks to integrate faith and culture. This involves a total response of body, mind, emotions and will. Teachers and students engage in a range of experiences of prayer and liturgy expressed through movement, music, symbol, image, ritual, imagination and language' (page 25).

Catechism and liturgy are profoundly related. Both have their roots in the mystery of life touched by a gracious God. Catechetical preparation for good liturgical participation is not just a matter of understanding the gestures and actions. While not in any way undermining the importance of solid Catholic doctrine and worship, familiarity with scripture and other such knowledge, what cannot be underestimated is the fact that it is the catechist who will create the conditions that will either encourage or discourage the faithful from accepting, or not, the Christian message.

Sometimes people may come with great insight and creativity but are 'taught' how to conform and at times 'crushed' in their desire to explore other possibilities. I remember once, in my valiant effort to be creative, being asked by the person in charge, 'Yes, fine, but why can't you be like everyone else and do as they are doing?' Such voices can continue to ring in the ears of those who may not have the confidence to see beyond the narrow limitations of others.

The book of Revelation reminds us that 'the spirit comes to make all things new' (Rev. 21:5), thus as liturgical catechists we need to revisit this reading many times in our service of our young. How arrogant to presume that the Spirit communicates through the adult only, or even within the sanctuary area of the Church.

It is easy to persuade ourselves that 'I am not creative' and to live within the limits set by an education philosophy that places boundaries on individual creativity. It can be a safe place to stay! Often when I offer workshops to teachers for Confirmation or First Communion preparation, I will invariably ask the question, 'So, how many people will keep returning to the same ideas, same music and same formulas, year after year?' If there is honesty in the group, many answer 'yes, we do'.

We may ask 'Why change if something works?' But my response is that surely this begins to limit the creative imagination of the people/pupils we are serving, and rather than encouraging the growth of the Spirit, it imposes and becomes restrictive. The same can be said for any group that gathers for liturgical worship on a yearly or continuous basis outside of the school setting.

Being creative is about allowing people to make choices, and central to such action is effective encouragement, enabling and empowering others to believe in themselves. Of course, in order to foster the creative imagination of others we need to be aware of our own innate creativity. The more we trust our own gifts, the more we can help others to take the risk and examine their own potential.

For me, one of the greatest languages of communication and creativity is the language of music. It is part of the world of all young people – a force that binds, heals and unites. To ignore such a fact would be to our detriment. To reach the place of our youth, we need to be able to speak their language and enter 'their world'. Thus when we come into our worship and liturgical spaces, imposing liturgy that is not relevant or outmoded can, in fact, be a destructive force in the life of the young Christian.

Music and song can give a much richer meaning and help contextualise the message of the gospel in the world of today. Complementing this will be visual imagery, symbols, mime, dance and movement, and all forms of art.

In my own work I have sought to contemporise some of the more positive and beautiful aspects of our own culture, rooting religious experience in the faith story of our people, reflecting on the history of past generations. Such a faith journey has been complimented by the great interest in the secular world in all things Irish.

Though some may view this as commercial cynicism, I have been able to tap into a wealth of hidden talent in all parts of the country, which, when harnessed, can truly reflect the divine imagination of the Spirit at work.

For far too long we have ignored or underestimated the great riches within our people, who have waited patiently to be invited to participate, though sadly some have left because there was no place for them. Only recently I had the privilege of working in a rural school in Limerick only to be amazed at what had been achieved and encouraged by the teachers and which translated beautifully into the liturgical space. Such action only happens where there is courage, vision and support, coupled with adequate resources. The sacraments of the Church allow us to express our relationship with God in the context of our daily lives. Thus the liturgical catechesis needs to help us to express this life with all its difficulties and blessings in worship and ritual. Perhaps the most important aspect is an enriching, probing, creative exploration of those basic life experiences: birth and death, health and sickness, richness and poverty, love and sin, freedom and slavery, togetherness and loneliness, service and selfishness, peace and anxiety, joy and sorrow, growth and diminishment, creativity and destructiveness. Good liturgical catechesis must be broad ranged and dig deeply into significant human experiences that in their depths open out to mystery and hope. The best preparation for liturgy is a holistic approach added to biblical background that allows for a creative appreciation of life's mysteries.

Such appreciation is achieved, I believe, by a creative openness to the richness of natural, cultural and biblical symbolism. This openness will tend to more imaginative, expressive and poetic expression rather than one that becomes conceptual and analytical. The need for rich symbolism is all important. Proper liturgical catechesis encourages all that is creative, poetic, imaginative. Our people/pupils have been blessed with many talents and with creativity, and we as teachers and ministers must direct and help our children to harness their gifts, and so invite them into a sacred space where they can embellish our worship with their imagination and gifts.

Each faith community, each parish, each school has its own story that should be celebrated when the faithful gather to worship. Part of this story means acknowledging the past, gathering in the present and praying into the future as a community. Here we share unique experiences that will not be part of the experience of any other community, and so the need for liturgical and ritual expression will vary.

In my own work as a composer I return constantly to the faith story of our people and use this as a means of catechesis. It has been my experience that when people become aware of the richness of their own tradition and when faith is grounded in the actual experiences, worship becomes more tangible and meaningful. When I am invited to participate and express my personal gifts and attributes, I then cannot say that there is no place for me.

Within the school year there are many opportunities to explore creativity. It is not some rare, esoteric gift enjoyed by a few people such as artists, craftspeople, musicians, authors, dancers or the like. Rather, it is something that comes with being alive, sensitive, questioning, open to the prompting and workings of the Spirit of God – where we are willing to learn from the past and explore the future. To be creative is to call the gifts of others forth. It is about co-creating with the Spirit rather than conforming to the easy option.

It is too easy to say that people don't sing – we have to examine the reasons why, and now I believe people don't sing in liturgy because we, in positions of responsibility, have failed them. We have not provided the necessary supports and resources that allow people to express themselves in ways befitting to their life experiences. Our liturgical spaces should be places where people experience a sense of belonging and comfort. Very often the opposite is their experience.

I began to write and compose because somewhere, sometime, someone believed in me. Without such support I probably would have ended up frustrated and unhappy. I owe much to those who encouraged my creative spirit. However, all of us can be the conduit of God's creative spirit by empowering others to find their own God-given gifts. Only then will we be ready to sing a new song in an ancient land.

A CARING COMMUNITY

At the Heart it's Relationships

Maureen Gaffney

This audience is full of eminent educationalists and religious leaders. I am neither. What I am bringing here today is a psychological perspective, some ideas about how I see the role of schools, how they should or could envisage themselves in terms of helping young people to develop a sense of what is required in relationships. When I was preparing the paper I thought about all of the elements that we know are crucial to relationships. We know that intimacy is a key part of making relationships work; we know that equality – as between men and women and equality between people in general – is a key part of what makes relationships work; we know commitment is important; we know managing anger is important; we know that forgiveness is important.

Catholic education has probably changed since my adolescence time, but what I immediately remember of my own education are all the rules and regulations about intimacy, all the rules and regulations about commitment. What was missing was an education in how to understand and achieve those kinds of things in relationships. What actually stops us from being intimate in relationships? What are the stages of intimacy? What prevents us from forgiving each other? Why, despite our best efforts, do we get angry with others? What is it that makes it so difficult for people to treat each other equally? How do you reconcile your own and another person's interests? How do you build and sustain commitment in a relationship?

The question I pose for you today is this: What is the added value, if any, that the Catholic school brings to all of those relationship issues? How exactly should a Catholic school help young people to form fulfilled, happy and responsible relationships?

I set out a very broad framework within which such an agenda might be approached. In my view:

- The broader mission of schools is help youngsters to become more and more themselves – to achieve psychological authenticity.
- The desire to be authentic – to be fully and uniquely yourself – finds a particular resonance in young people.
- A crucial part of authenticity is to develop a coherent sense of self.
- Relationships are an essential part of self-knowledge. We come to know ourselves as we are known, through our relationship with others.
- How we know ourselves in relationships is an essential part of moral development.
- The great challenge for schools is to reconnect moral teaching with the reality of the issues and dilemmas young people face in their day-to-day relationships.

The desire to be authentic – the desire to be fully and uniquely yourself – I think is a mission that young people would immediately identify with and can be enthusiastic about, because that is their business. We all want to become more and more ourselves – but it is particularly urgent in adolescence, when you don't even know if ever you will achieve any kind of stable sense of self. A crucial part of becoming authentically yourself is to develop a coherent sense of who you are, to become aware of, understand and gather up all the bits of you into something that makes sense to you. Relationships are an essential part of that self-knowledge. We come to know ourselves as we are known through our relationship with others. We process internally all of the experiences we had in relationships – with parents, siblings, friends, teachers and so on – and out of that we begin to see patterns that we weave into a sense of self, of personal identity. So we don't go away to a mountain for forty days and think 'Who am I?' The answer to that question comes from our experiences in relationships, and the great challenge for schools is to reconnect moral teaching with the reality of the issues and the dilemmas that young people face in their day-to-day relationships.

Psychological authenticity

The psychologist Carl Jung believed that the deep desire and energy of life is to become more and more yourself. I recast that slightly as the deep desire to become authentically yourself, to find some understanding and expression of who you really are. In Shakespeare's great injunction: to thine own self be true. While this desire is present at all stages of the lifecycle, it is of the utmost urgency at critical transition points in life, and most particularly in adolescence, as young people cross the great divide between childhood and adulthood.

Let me start with the dictionary definition of authentic: (1) of undisputed origin or authorship; (2) accurate in representing the facts, trustworthy, reliable; (3) a duly executed deed or document; (4) from the Latin, *authenticus*, coming from the author, and from the Greek *authentikos*, meaning one who acts independently.

In psychological terms, then, we might define authenticity as being unique, 'of undisputed origin or authorship'; true to yourself, implying a lack of self-deception; insight, duly arrived at, of the origins and interplay of forces in your personality; trustworthy; reliable in how you represent yourself to others, implying a relationship with others as a component of authenticity; and finally, being the 'author' of your self, being responsible for yourself, and acting with independence and freedom.

It may be more accurate to describe 'being authentic' as a process rather than an achieved state. The process of becoming authentic can be understood as the process of self-actualisation, self-realisation or self-development, which though interpreted in widely different ways, implies an expansion of consciousness, psychological growth and maturation. This process of self-realisation can happen at different levels and can be guided by models of psychological development – and, of course, by different models of religious belief. In addition, these models are themselves shaped by prevailing cultural values.

The social and cultural context

Schools must be concerned with what psychological authenticity means at a particular cultural juncture. I have discussed this in more depth in an article that was published in *Doctrine and Life* in 2000. There I argued that the issue of psychological authenticity must be understood in the context of what I believe to be the dominant cultural conflict in modern society. It is this: in the conflict between the desire for personal happiness and the desire to be in relationship with others (at an individual or societal level), the balance now seems precariously weighted in favour of self.

In very summary form, I believe that at every level of our functioning in Western societies, we are increasingly confronted with the problem of disconnection: from our authentic sense of self; from intimacy with others in personal relationships; from our fellow citizens.

The ethos of individualism

One way to understand the current balance or imbalance between the desire for personal happiness and the desire for relationship with others is under the rubric of individualism, the prevailing, dominant ethos that over-arches virtually every point of conflict, ambivalence and choice in the culture. Individualism has become the benchmark of modernity at a societal level, and of self-development and maturity at an individual level. Individualism, at a sociological and psychological level, carries with it a culture fostering individual rights rather than externally mandated obligation; self-expression, autonomy, freedom of choice and action rather than self or societal control; personal worth based on personal achievement rather than from prescribed authority roles.

When I say 'rather than' I do not mean to imply that it is a straight either/or. Rather, in a dilemma, or in uncertain situations, there is external and internal pressure to resolve the issue in question in favour of the prevailing ethos. Neither do I mean to imply that the values of individualism are inherently wrong. On the contrary, I strongly believe that much of the gains in modern, free societies derive from the growth and expansion of individualism.

My point is that individualism has been too narrowly defined. It rests on an overly circumscribed base of understanding as to what it means to be a full human being, and it is dominated by an over-focus on personal autonomy rather than connectedness in relationships. Over the course of his work, Jung came to see the goal of self-development over the entire lifespan as what he called 'individuation', that is, the process of becoming more and more yourself. Individuals always exist in relation to others – in relationships that may be current or in the past, external in the world or internalised. Thus, the self cannot be understood or realised in an authentic way except in relationship to others. So, perhaps, we should more properly talk, not of 'self' but of 'self-in-relation', as many feminist psychologists do.

Model of self

The process of individuation – of becoming more and more yourself – also has to rest, explicitly or implicitly, on a model of self, a kind of road map. What is the scope of self-development? What are the different bits of self that have to be understood and integrated? Of course, any model of self can only be an approximation of the complexity and diversity that is implicit in trying to describe any human being. Imagined in diagrammatic terms, there are three broad areas of self – the unconscious, the conscious ego and what we might call the higher self. At the bottom of the imagined diagram is the unconscious, the origins of self – the raw material of our genetic base and early learning experiences in our families. The great achievement of Freud, at the beginning of the last century, was to discover the lasting and profound effect of this unconscious realm, particularly the sexual and aggressive drives, on psychological functioning. Evolutionary biology will undoubtedly have more to add. Over the past thirty years, psychological research strongly suggests that our biological need for attachment is a powerful influence on behaviour and that our early experiences of attachment have much more long-lasting and profound effects than were once thought.

At the middle level is our ordinary field of consciousness, within which the ego resides. Our experience of the self is mostly at this level, that is, the sensations and experiences of body, feelings and mind that float in and out of consciousness. We are also intermittently aware of internal dialogue, of 'voices within' – the severe critic, the consoler, the slave-driver, the supporter, the eternal optimist. These voices are not just the rehearsals and post-mortems attending social interaction but represent how we have made internal what was once external. For example, attachment research indicates that children seem to internalise both sides of the relationship with parents – not just their own subjective experiences but the emotions and attitudes of the parent as well. So both sides of a relationship are – to varying degrees – unconsciously internalised and become part of the self.

The dynamic of that part of self – the ego – or its basic energy is striving for achievement, control and mastery of the world. The process of socialisation at home and at school is mainly the consolidation and strengthening of the ego.

It is hardly surprising then that notions of self-development or authenticity are very often located at this level. Most of the expansion of consciousness that has taken place in the modern journey towards individuality is at this ego level. It is reflected in a widespread psychological sophistication, unimaginable even twenty years ago. The downside is that the whole notion of self-development or authenticity has, to some extent, become trapped at this level.

But, occasionally, despite the dominance of the ego, we know that something from another realm of the self breaks through, in what the psychologist Maslow called 'peak experiences'. These are the experiences of intense emotion – positive or negative – that shift us into a different level of awareness. At moments of great joy as well as great sadness, at points of great communion, as well as points of intense disconnection, there is a sense that there are deeper truths under the surface; a realisation that the conscious ego striving for all we desire – success, affirmation, power, closeness – brings with it neither the meaning, coherence, bonding or sense of direction that we desire. We become conscious, even briefly, of another realm of the self – an experience of ourselves as 'more than' what we know.

That 'other realm' is the third or top part of the imagined diagram of self, the realm of higher consciousness, the source of higher intuitions and inspirations – artistic, philosophical, ethical, religious and spiritual experience. This realm of self might be termed 'spiritual', but spiritual very broadly defined as the possessing of higher values. What we might call a 'higher self', that is, an intuitive sense that despite all the change and fragmentation in ourselves, there is an internal unifying force that gives coherence to all the diverse elements of our self. We are only fleetingly aware of this 'higher self' but the result is an experience of personal and existential authenticity: 'This is the whole of me. I am more than my successes, more than my failures. Here I stand'.

Jung also conceived of a connection between the self and what he called a collective unconscious; theologians call it God. I will leave that aspect to my elders and betters. Again, in everyday terms, this sense of connection to a spiritual force or God may be experienced as a kind of spiritual intuition, prompted by 'peak experiences' of intense emotion. This intuition may be expressed in a very sense of the presence of God, or no more definitively than a sense that 'out there, somewhere, is a force that gives meaning to all this'.

Implications for self-development

If we think of the self in this more complex way, self-development, becoming authentic also becomes more complex – and more interesting. For example, the unresolved unconscious conflicts of our early life have a way of following us into and undermining our more cherished conscious images of self. Similarly, the search for higher values can become entangled with the ego's appetites and neediness – for power, self-aggrandisement and intolerance of others' experience. Thus, authentic self-development will necessarily have to address all elements of the self. Put another way, it is only by experiencing the self at all the different levels that the experience of an authentic sense of self and others is possible.

Spiritual hunger

Authentic self-development can also only happen if we are aware and engaged with the third realm of self – the search for the deeper values that shape our desires and who we can become – and each individual has a unique combination and understanding of these deeper values. Freud at the end of the nineteenth century faced the challenge of discovering, treating, and increasing individual and public awareness of the unconscious realm of self. I would argue that the challenge now, at the beginning of the twenty-first century, is the parallel 'discovery' and nurturing of the spiritual dimension of self, and for schools the development of appropriate structures and supports to reflect that dimension in the young person's personal functioning.

In adolescence, there is an increasing interiority, a search for deeper meaning. Striving for the desired success, control, affirmation, power and control of the adult world, the adolescent response is often a sense of disappointment, a feeling of emptiness. The adolescent asks for the first time the prototypical question: 'Is this all there is?' – a question that continues to reverberate at every key transition in adult life. Buried beneath that question are deeper but often poorly understood desires: for more meaning in life, more coherence, more unity, more direction – what might be called a psychological experience of spiritual hunger.

At this historical juncture, in affluent Western societies, with organised religion in decline, at least in its recognisable form, many commentators note a vacuum, a spiritual hunger. Psychology can indeed provide an arena within which individuals can experience themselves at a deeper emotional level, and provide a framework of meaning for the decisions and dilemmas that confront them. But it cannot by itself provide a spiritual awakening. Rather, psychological self-understanding is best seen as a critical component of authenticity and appears increasingly to be the preferred starting point in Western cultures.

Thus, it seems inevitable that schools and religious leaders will have to deepen their understanding of psychological development and integrate that understanding into their canon of beliefs in a meaningful way. I believe that the relevance of organised religion – and maybe faith schools – in the new century will be significantly determined by how effectively they are perceived as helping individuals to a fuller understanding of self and personal experiences, and via that understanding, helping them to a better resolution of the moral dilemmas that are located in daily experiences of relationships.

Reconnecting authenticity with the reality of the issues and dilemmas young people face in their day-to-day relationships
What are the relationship issues for young people? Just reflect on a thirteen-year-old and a nineteen-year-old. When else in the human lifecycle, apart from infancy, would six years make such a difference? At the end of the six years, the young person must be able to answer the question: Who am I? To do that, four monumental tasks have to be confronted: (1) The young person must fashion a sense of individual uniqueness ('This is me'); (2) while at the same time finding a satisfying place in the peer group and then in the larger society ('This is where I belong'); (3) while also keeping some continuity

with the old self of childhood ('This is the way I always was'); and finally (4) while forging a sexual identity.

Because this process of change is so dramatic, families and schools have to engage with it in a very personal way and are occasionally rocked to their foundations, not so much by the big crises in relation to drugs, crime, sex, but by their weaknesses being exposed in the process.

Why is that? Because an adolescent forging a new identity involves re-engaging again with issues like: Who cares about me? Whom can I turn to? Will I be supported or abandoned? What is my potential? What are my weaknesses and strengths? What really matters to me? And all those questions involve the young person re-examining relationship with parents, and with teachers, especially in terms of what they expect of you.

Many argue that young people have become more confrontational, more difficult, and harder to manage. But the mistake is for parents and schools to take fright, to be so shocked by the first stirrings of rebellion, that they do not understand that this need for independence and autonomy has an equally powerful counterforce – the continued need for closeness and support right up to the twenties. All the psychological evidence shows that parents and schools remain crucial in young people's lives, that they continue to exert very significant influence on them if they manage to stay emotionally close to them. And this is even more true of vulnerable young people.

When young people confront us – as parents or as teachers – it should not be a cue for frightened withdrawal or authoritarian control. Better to hear the confrontation not as 'I reject you' but as 'How about not making assumptions about me? I'm different than I was. I want my needs to be taken into account too'.

Is it more difficult for young people now? Yes and no. There are more opportunities, of course, but also more pressures. There is no hiding place for failure. There is a huge emphasis on independence, autonomy and personal freedom. Young people have so much external independence (money, free time, freedom in where they go, when they come in, etc.) in comparison to the last generation, that it is easy to forget their continuing need for a safe haven, for emotional closeness and reassurance, for the calm centre.

What is it like to be an adolescent? What does the world feel like for them day to day? Where were they? At home, they spend the largest time in bedrooms (waking and sleeping time). So there's lots of solitary withdrawal. They spend a startlingly small amount of time with family. One study showed that only 5 per cent of their total time is spent alone with parent(s), which translated into twenty minutes with mother and five minutes per day with father alone. Rivalry with siblings over resources, privileges and physical space is a cause of much discontent.

Parents might be horrified (or reassured) by the finding that friction and conflict are endemic in family life with adolescents. When with their family, adolescents' negative thoughts outnumber their positive thoughts by about ten to one. When asked to say what they were thinking when interacting with parents, adolescents tend to report thoughts like 'How pig-headed my parents are' or 'God, how incompetent my mum is' or 'What a (expletive deleted) my father is' or 'I HATE my sister' or 'Why are my parents making such a bloody fuss?' They feel tense about how their parents eat, dress, talk. They feel stuck with having to pay attention to these irritating habits over which they have no control – a tension only rivalled by how irritating they find their teachers' habits.

Adolescents spend nearly a third of their time at school. But there is no direct evidence for how much actual 'face time' they spend with teachers and other school staff. The window of opportunity for talking, listening, influencing, is very narrow. What is the experience of school like? Many adolescents are concentrating for less than half the time they spend in class. They often feel bored, sad, irritable. But they like group presentations and discussions. Most of all, they love those teachers who succeed in pulling them into a subject by their own enthusiasm.

Young people spend a lot of time feeling alienated from what they are doing. Their personal goals are not in harmony with what they are doing. A big task of adolescence is to learn to enjoy what you have to do. Parents and schools have a crucial role in that regard: to help them to clarify goals, give them meaningful feedback, give them hope and reassurance. Just think of the number of times an adolescent has to be somewhere – in class, at church. Who defines where he goes? Who defines what she has to do? what kind of mood he is expected to be in? whether she is listened to? Adolescents experience such control as a loss of inner freedom as well as external freedom. The worst conflicts erupt about issues that involve what teenagers call 'show' – keeping domestic order, keeping up appearances, what the neighbours will think, etc. For them, concern about such externalities is a hypocritical evasion of what is really important, namely, their inner feelings.

Adolescents feel more extremely than adults. They show less concentration than adults, less energy. They are less willing or able to mobilise their energy. They feel this negative way much more often when they are with adults, in places structured by adults (classroom, church, part-time job) than when they are with friends.

They are more moody than adults, less anchored in the middle ground. They are more likely to experience euphoria, to catch a glimpse of the world that is nearly perfect. But they also experience more despair. They are very vulnerable to unexpected events. Adolescents can be upset by what appear to parents and teachers to be apparently trivial things. Even a misplaced word can threaten a teenager's precarious sense of self.

What about experiences with friends? Adolescents experience time with friends as the most positive part of their lives. They feel free, happy to be where they are and doing what they are doing, open, involved, positive. Why? Because they are talking about themselves, about issues that really matter to them. They get comfort and support from each other about the things that are driving them crazy. As they get older, self-disclosure becomes very important.

What is being alone like? If they can't structure their time, they are prey to loneliness, to worrying and brooding about the things that have gone wrong for them. They brood about how they look. They feel lonely because they are not with a good friend, or a romantic partner. They worry about their image: 'Did I look like an idiot?' They wonder what they will do next weekend. They daydream. And if they can structure positive daydreams, or solve the problem they were thinking about, they feel much better when they rejoin company.

How can schools connect up to this adolescent agenda?
How can schools take the raw material of adolescent experience and help the young person to shape it into an authentic sense of self and a coherent moral framework? A good start is to structure moral education around those very experiences. Ask yourselves: what do we, as educators, know about the experience of feeling overwhelmed? not personally connected to what we are doing? What do we know about making stupid mistakes caused by lack of experience? about being disappointed? about being disillusioned? about the experience of unrequited love? about loneliness? about being frustrated beyond endurance by the intransigence of authority? about the feeling that life is passing you by? about the experience of having extraordinary hopes for the future and ourselves? Do we even remember that experience?

Engaging authentically with such an agenda would be a revolutionary act for schools. It would allow truthfulness in discussions between educators and young people. It would require openness about the nature of adult experience and a respect for different views. It would require active listening. It would require both adults and young people to give an account of their own experiences – and that is the basis for accountability for decisions and actions.

Think again of the issues that preoccupy adolescents. Behind the detail of the squabbles with parents, the heartache about friends, the rivalry with others, is the most basic psychological dilemma – the relation of self to others. To what extent am I the same as, or connected with others, and to what extent am I self-sufficient, different and separate from others?

The task for schools now is to develop a critical awareness in young people that the mission of becoming personally authentic, more and more yourself, is intimately connected with being authentically in relationships. So, we have to help them reframe their personal dilemmas into moral choices in a way that makes sense to them:

- Being autonomous versus being in connection with others.
- Having freedom from interference versus making a commitment.
- Living by the rules of fair exchange versus making an act of trust.
- Being in control versus opening up communication.
- Having rights versus taking responsibility.

The challenge I lay out for schools is to help young people to develop a spirituality of relationships, grounded in the reality of their lives and their own uniqueness, a spirituality that is without the comforts of easy answers.

It is a spirituality that has to be, of necessity, full of feeling. Since the language of the spirit is beyond words for most of us, except for poets. I will end with a quote from one of my favourites – the great American poet Robert Lowell. In many ways, he seems the most unlikely source of spiritual sustenance. Lowell experienced extraordinary pain and losses in his own life: being unwanted by his mother; the agonising break-up of his marriages; the failed attempts at reconciliations; the crippling depression he suffered; the emotional distance from his father; the inevitable disappointments in life; the fear of dying. Young people can identify with at least some of those personal crises.

But they can also identify with his great passions and enthusiasms. As a young man, Lowell had also embraced his poetry as a quest for the sublime, writing poems of blazing passion and religious vision, elegantly and formally structured by formal plot and rhyme. He wanted to make life happen, to create poems that were exquisitely made objects.

Yet in later life, confronted by the frailties in his own life, he abandons the fiery certainty and vision of his early work; instead, he 'prays for the grace of accuracy' as he writes of the 'sacramental instants' of daily life.

It is the last poem he ever wrote, 'Epilogue', that I love the most. In this poem, he harks back to what used to work for him. He rails, temporarily, against the inadequacy of words to capture the truth of what happens, to make something of his life 'paralysed by fact'. Temporarily, he despairs. 'All's misalliance' he says. Akin to the 'I just can't stand this anymore' or 'It's all gone wrong for me' experience that so often besets adolescents.

Those blessed structures, plot and rhyme –
why are they no help to me now
I want to make
something imagined, not recalled?
I hear the noise of my own voice:
The painter's vision is not a lens,
it trembles to caress the light.
But sometimes everything I write
with the threadbare art of my eye
seems a snapshot,
lurid, rapid, garish, grouped,
heightened from life,
yet paralysed by fact.
All's misalliance.

But he returns with the most celebratory of lines: 'Yet why not say what happened?' In this final poem, Lowell knows with 'the grace of accuracy' that the miracle of life is the truth of what happens, not the way it might have been, or the way we wished it had been, but the way we are, 'solid with yearning' in the flux and quick of our lives. We are, he warns, 'poor passing facts'. The truth of what happens to us must be recorded before it is gone forever – 'each figure in the photograph given his living name'.

Yet why not say what happened?
Pray for the grace of accuracy
Vermeer gave to the sun's illumination
stealing like a tide across a map
to his girl solid with yearning.
We are poor passing facts,
warned by that to give
each figure in the photograph
his living name.

The effect is, paradoxically, profoundly spiritually sustaining. It gives an incomparable paradigm for the search for authenticity, for the spiritual journey in relationships – based solidly on the reality of subjective experience, the uniqueness of each person's experience, and suffused by feeling. A glimpse of the world as perfect.

Catholic Schools as Communities of Service:
The US experience

Joseph M. O'Keefe, SJ

What can one learn about the mission of Catholic education by examining schools outside of the particularity of one's own context? Why is it productive to delve into schools that have a history, political reality, cultural context and fiscal structure different than one's own? In my experience, opportunities to learn about education in sectors other than my own have proven to be a source of creativity.[1] The sentiment of many people in interreligious work applies here: I need the other not only to know the other; I need the other to know myself.

It is in this spirit that I offer to an Irish audience an overview of Catholic schools in the United States. It is my hope that this volume will be an impetus to further dialogue across the Atlantic, so that the differences between us will illuminate our commonality of purpose. In an actual and virtual world that grows ever smaller and in a Church that is undergoing unprecedented scrutiny and rapid change, Catholic educators across the world need to learn from each other. No matter where on the globe we are located, it is only through a rediscovery of community and service that we will do the work of the gospel. For we live in a market-based world that commodifies education, exalts the autonomous individual and takes as its norm the survival of the fittest. As other contributors to this volume suggest, we need to move beyond our parochialism and our internecine struggles to face the dehumanising forces of the twenty-first century.[2]

I begin my exploration of Catholic schools in the United States through an overview of their history. I then articulate the espoused mission of Catholic education. Next, I depict the circumstances that contemporary

Catholic educators in the United States face. Finally, I offer some thoughts about moving forward on both sides of the Atlantic.

Historical perspectives

The standard history of the Church in the United States describes an immigrant Church fighting for survival in a white Anglo-Saxon Protestant society that, for reasons familiar to an Irish audience, was hostile to Catholicism.[3] For many, the establishment of the US Catholic Church was in the Maryland colony with the arrival of recusant English Catholics in the 1630s. By century's end this community faced discrimination as the Protestant majority grew. In the other colonies, especially those that were founded by English Protestant dissenters, anti-Catholicism was codified in law, before and after independence from the Crown. And long after the end of legal discrimination, prejudice and subtle oppression remained.

At the founding of the republic, Catholics were a tiny marginal group. That changed as immigrants from Europe flooded the United States in the nineteenth and early twentieth centuries. The Irish were the first and the largest in number and influence, scattered across the continent but concentrated in urban centres. Germans, Eastern Europeans and Southern Europeans followed, bringing with their Catholicism a language and culture that threatened the English homogeneity of the young nation. Civic officials in charge of State-sponsored education proposed the 'common school', in which the claim to non-denominationalism cloaked pan-Protestant indoctrination and patriotism was a cover for xenophobia. Predictably, the bishops mandated the parish school as a protective fortress for Catholic children. Their efforts to garner taxpayer money were unsuccessful. As a result, a separate system emerged, financed by Sunday collections but especially by life-long voluntary service in the form of religious communities, the vast majority of whose members were women. Educational institutions, from parochial schools to high schools to colleges and universities, stood next to hospitals and social-service agencies to provide womb-to-tomb service in a parallel Catholic world. For the Irish, faith and culture were to be maintained. Other immigrants tried in addition to preserve their non-English mother tongue. All of them offered to Catholics the opportunities for education and economic security that mainstream institutions would not provide. At the outset of the twenty-first century, the schools had clearly accomplished the latter goal. It is doubtful that they maintained the former, for as Catholics experienced stunning upward mobility, they moved out of their ghettos and into the language, culture and worldview of the mainstream.

In the 1960s came the collapse of the Catholic fortress in the United States. The cultural upheaval that affected everyone did not bypass Catholics, especially regarding sexual norms. Inconceivable a generation earlier, the election of a Catholic to the presidency marked the arrival of Catholics into the political mainstream. Moreover, the Second Vatican Council generated internal changes of polity and belief, encouraging an embrace of the world. Catholics had educational options anywhere, they lived wherever they wanted, they earned as much as their neighbours. Simultaneously, and probably because of a loosening of internal control and unlimited opportunities outside of the Church, novitiates and seminaries witnessed a dramatic decline in numbers. In the mid 1960s, 95 per cent of those working in Catholic schools were members of religious communities; today they number only 5 per cent. The fortress had indeed collapsed and the reason for founding the schools had disappeared.

In the United States, Catholic schools share with their non-Catholic counterparts a tradition of relative autonomy. Just as public schools are run by local governments and chartered by individual states, so too Catholic schools are run by pastors, religious communities and dioceses whose priorities differ widely. As a result, about half of the schools that existed in the early 1960s are still open today. Discounted by many as anachronistic, they struggled to stay open in the midst of skyrocketing personnel costs; sisters worked for nearly nothing, but lay people have to make a decent wage. Many schools discovered a new reason for existing. The Second Vatican Council's call for the renewal of religious communities enlivened many schools. Jesuit schools, for example, echoed the call to social justice that emerged from their post-conciliar general congregations. Many women religious rediscovered the foundress' mission to provide education to the poor, especially girls. And lay people began to take their rightful place in the ministry of education.

In my estimation, the most remarkable story is found in the nation's inner cities. A host of researchers, most notably James Coleman and Andrew Greeley, discovered in their analyses of federal data sets that Catholic schools were remarkably effective for low-income children from ethnic and racial groups that had experienced discrimination.[4] For a host of reasons, but especially because of funding formulae and racial segregation, the public schools were generally atrocious. In many places, only the Catholic school provides the opportunity for a decent education. Among those who have taken advantage of a Catholic education are newer immigrant groups, including Vietnamese, Filipinos, people from the English and French-speaking Caribbean, but especially those from Spanish-speaking backgrounds who will, by nearly all estimates, constitute over half of the

Catholic children in the United States by the mid twenty-first century. Notably, the remarkable measures of academic success were found among African-Americans, the vast majority of whom are Protestant. They migrated from the rural South to urban neighbourhoods that had been abandoned by an earlier generation of European Catholics, whose mobility up was coupled with their movement out to the suburbs. It is imperative to note that these schools are academically successful but financially insolvent; they need to be subsidised by the larger Church community, either through a religious community or, most commonly, through the local diocese. The debate about subsidising these schools brings to light the bedrock question: Why do Catholic schools exist?

The espoused mission of Catholic education: what we say we believe
A detailed analysis of the mission of Catholic education is beyond the scope of this short chapter. Indeed, there are serious differences of opinion, which reflect different visions of the Church itself. Many of the ideological wars in the Church turn schools into battlefields. Whose version of Catholicism gets taught? What are the various priorities that emerge? Who should teach? Who should be allowed to attend? Some people want to rebuild the fortress of former years, motivated by a nostalgia for the 1950s. There would be no room for non-paying African-American Protestants there. As is always the case, nostalgia distorts memory and the past can never be re-created. For some, Catholic schools should cease to exist altogether. But for many, myself included, contemporary Catholic schools in the United States are distinctive and valuable because they espouse their mission of being communities of service.

The Jubilee of the year 2000 provided for many Catholic educators the opportunity to, metaphorically, in the tradition of the Hebrews, 'let the fields lie fallow' while they pondered the individual and institutional priorities.[5] In my pondering, seven features emerge as central. The first is **participation**. The belief in the dignity and inherently social nature of the person, requires individuals and institutions to provide people with what they need to participate fully in civil society, as contributors and as recipients. The United States is a highly bifurcated society, and the division is often the result of educational opportunity. Statistics show clearly that in a post-industrial society, with the decline of manual labour and protective labour unions, education and income are highly correlated. Compounding this correlation is the relative lack of social services that allow people to live in a dignified manner. In a fast-changing world, educated people can negotiate their way through the complex world of work and be relatively assured of a decent home, the wherewithal for a comfortable lifestyle and health care for themselves, their children and their elders. On the other hand, the poorly educated earn a minimum wage, have no job security, paltry health care and they face an ominous old age. Never has it been as important to provide educational opportunity. Catholic schools at their best model the participatory society that is in line with the gospel. Statistics tell us that Catholic schools have higher levels of family participation than other schools, teachers are more satisfied with their ability to make decisions about curriculum, instruction and other school policies, and students feel more cared for than elsewhere.[6]

Hand-in-hand with the teaching about participation is the belief in **the preferential option for the poor**; those who have the greatest need have the greatest claim on our resources. Contrast this with the philosophy that undergirds *laissez-faire* capitalism: belief in the autonomous individual, acceptance of *caveat emptor* as a way to relinquish responsibility for the other, the conviction that competition is the primary motivation of the human heart and the belief that progress is made through the survival of the fittest. The preferential option for the poor should determine budgetary priorities in regard to those within the school and those beyond its doors. This teaching should temper the desire for status and security with a deep empathy for those in need. Wealth and privilege often render the poor invisible. It is the challenge of prophetic leadership to see the needs within and beyond the school and to have the courage to act accordingly. Catholic schools should also raise the consciousness of students to the glaring and widening discrepancies of wealth between developed and developing countries.

Educationalist John Goodlad once called **racism** 'America's congenital disease'. In regard to African-Americans, it is only in the last forty years that legal *apartheid* ceased to exist. Moreover, the history of the United States is strewn with sad episodes of racism: slavery, genocide of Native Americans, xenophobia toward refugees and immigrants, racial profiling by police, residential and job discrimination. Sadly, despite civil rights legislation, racial minority status is still positively correlated with low educational attainment and poverty. Whiteness still has its privileges, be it through inherited wealth or the subtleties of social acceptance. Moreover, backlash is evident in the blatant hatred of white supremacists or the subtle rollback of civil rights. The political right wing often caricatures anti-racism as political correctness, reducing the moral grounding to a passing fad. In fact, racism is a mortal sin, a repudiation of those made in the image and likeness of God. The curriculum of the schools should reflect the Church's teachings about racism for the white majority especially, as well as for members of racial minority groups.

The fourth feature, **multiculturalism**, is related to the previous one. The positive aspect of the teachings about the sin of racism is the beauty of human diversity. Reputable biologists claim that Western categories of race are scientifically untenable – there are more variations within racial groups than between them. The use of the term 'race' to identify a particular group of humans developed during the late-nineteenth-century era of colonialism. Given globalisation of culture and economics, traditional notions of race seem increasingly ludicrous. The Catholic Church is perhaps the most multicultural organisation in the world, and though schools mirror the ethnicities of their location, they should reflect the larger multiculturalism in curriculum, culture and worship. The demographic trends in the Catholic Church are clearly leading away from Europe and North America to other parts of the world. In the years to come it will be the Africans, Asians and Latin Americans who make decisions in Rome. Within the United States, the Catholic Church has a rich multicultural history, at one time from the cultures of Europe and now from Latin America, Asia and Africa.

The fifth feature, **ecumenism**, is particularly important in schools with religious diversity. After the groundbreaking acknowledgement of religious liberty at the Second Vatican Council and its accompanying respect for people of other faiths, hopes for ecumenical vitality were high. While documents such as *Ut unum sint* have given a new rationale for ecumenical activity, others such as *Dominus Iesus* hint at a retraction. Apart from official documents, on a popular level much of the ecumenical fervour of the late 1960s and early 1970s has waned. In the United States, the most sustained institutionalised ecumenical efforts are to be found in the schools. Along with ecumenism among Christians is the increasing presence of non-Christians actually living in local neighbourhoods or taking the attention of Americans from afar in an increasingly small world. Because of demographics in the US, contact with Jews has a long history. Given political realities, dialogue with Muslims has taken on a new urgency. Because of their educational mission, Catholic schools can make a major contribution to interreligious harmony. Finally, large numbers of people are either totally uninterested in questions of faith or professed atheists or believers in God who eschew organised religion. Catholic schools can contribute to society by providing common ground for people of faith across religious traditions.

The sixth feature, **non-violence**, is especially timely. As the only remaining superpower, the United States wields enormous military and economic strength. Yet, as the events of 11 September 2001 so shockingly demonstrated, the nation is vulnerable. The pain of death and destruction gave rise to heroism and compassion and fostered in Americans a newfound sense of solidarity. But these events can also give rise to a new militarism that abandons civil rights and due processes. Moreover, much of the political rhetoric reduces geopolitical complexity to a simple battle between the forces of good and evil. Through indiscriminate bombing of non-combatants or lethal injection on death row, the rhetoric threatens to give licence to vengeance, even at the cost of innocent human life. The Church preaches a gospel of non-violence and a strict moral calculus to justify war, though it has often failed to live up to its own standards. Catholic schools can temper the thirst for violence and allow students to ask the politically unorthodox question, 'Why do so many people in the world hate the United States?'

The last feature, **service**, reflects elements of the previous ones. The call to service is found throughout the Gospels and is evident in the rich spiritual traditions of Catholicism. When the Church is privileged and powerful, leaders face the temptation to be served rather than to serve. The Catholic school, like the Church itself, does not exist for its own sake but as a means to an end, i.e. co-operating with God's grace to make the Reign of God a lived reality. An ethos of service permeates many Catholic schools. Built on the tradition of service given by members of religious communities, lay people today provide generous care to children in schools, often at great personal cost. Sadly, Catholic school teachers on average earn only two-thirds of the salary of their counterparts in public schools and the benefits packages (decent health insurance, retirement pension, etc.) are often worse than the salaries.[7] Parents are heavily involved in these schools, largely because the school cannot exist without their financial donations in the form of tuition payments and benefactions and their contributed services. Scarcity of funds does have a positive side. Students in these schools often exhibit a greater inclination to service than their counterparts elsewhere, in community service activities or engagement in political processes.[8] The latter is especially important in a nation that has a notoriously low level of citizen activism, as witnessed by voter turnout. The schools in the inner city that have managed to survive provide a cornerstone in neighbourhoods that have been abandoned by businesses, Churches and civic associations. Catholic schools are called to the biblical injunction of being a good neighbour, especially in places that are bereft of beauty, safety or hope. Finally, Catholic schools exercise their call to service by providing educational opportunities to children in poverty who would otherwise be relegated to a bleak future. One cannot understand the mission of Catholic schools without examining the other options that would be left if they were no longer to exist; and in the inner cities of the United States most other options are unpromising indeed.

Circumstances that Catholic educators face

Educators in US Catholic schools face daunting challenges created by circumstances beyond their control. These challenges emerge from both the civil and ecclesiastical realms. The decennial census of the United States, last conducted in the year 2000, depicts shifting population patterns in a highly mobile society. Urban centres of the northeast and midwest, which are heavily Catholic, have been steadily losing population to the south and the west, areas that are traditionally Protestant. Whereas dioceses in the urban centres are closing institutions and selling property, those in places like Florida and Nevada have burgeoning churches and schools. Family life has also changed, with less than half of the nation's children living in homes with a mother and father who have been married only once. Increasing financial pressure has made stay-at-home mothers a rarity and schools are called upon to 'raise' children. High levels of geographic mobility create unstable homes and neighbourhoods, resulting in a lack of social cohesion. A new wave of immigrants from non-European cultures has changed the face of many communities, bringing new languages, customs, religions and philosophies to the nation. Finally, because of birthrates and immigration, the United States is becoming a bilingual and bicultural English/Spanish country.

Again and again, social commentators see in demographic trends confirmation of a rootless society.[9] This ambience of *anomie*, combined with highly sophisticated marketing, creates a consumer culture in which human worth is measured by possessions. American children often face a lonely and highly competitive environment. Never has there been as great a need for schools that provide a sense of community and a compelling philosophy of life, that one develops one's talents not primarily for self but for building up the common good. Sadly, politicians have reduced the noble role of the school to numbers on standardised tests. Sweeping federal legislation called the 'No Child Left Behind Act' forces schools to test relentlessly in a misguided attempt to assure accountability. State-mandated curricula threaten to reduce learning to test-preparation. The narrowness of vision ignores the complexity of learning and takes away from teachers the ability to be creative. These tests are called 'high stakes', not only for students (who may not receive a high-school diploma) but also for schools (underperformers lose their funding). Students and schools are thus pitted against each other. Thankfully most Catholic schools are free from such mandated testing, but they will be pressured to prove their effectiveness though similar measures. As voucher plans[10] and other schemes to get some Government funding move forward, Catholic educators should heed a Jewish friend's warning about Government involvement, 'With the shekels come the shackles'.

Indeed, the lack of shekels is a major problem for Catholic educators. Schools are heavily tuition-dependent and thus risk becoming accessible only to the economically élite. Administrators are often overwhelmed by the demands of fundraising. The time they could spend as instructional leader and pastor of the school is spent writing grant proposals or courting benefactors. They are forced to market their product (the school) in a competitive environment. Sadly, some schools have to tailor themselves not so much to the mission but rather to consumer demand. The schools that charge lower tuition cannot provide expensive services required by children with special needs, they have serious capital needs that are unmet, they lag behind other schools in technology infrastructure and they have difficulty in recruiting and retaining underpaid teachers and administrators. Compounding the staffing challenge is the fact that, excepting Catholic clergy, women can choose any career they want, whereas at one time their only options were teaching, nursing and social work.

Catholic educators are also challenged by ecclesial circumstances. Given the US policy of Church-State separation, the Church is reliant on voluntary contributions. Therefore, analysis of financial realities sheds light on deeper issues. Catholic philanthropy was in trouble long before the sweeping scandals of 2002. Since the 1960s the average percentage of income given by Protestant Churches has increased to 4 per cent. During the same period, the percentage of income given by Catholics to the Church has decreased to a current average of 1.1 per cent. Ironically, with greater capacity came lesser commitment. And that commitment has indeed lessened, hastened by shocking stories of sexual predators who were protected by bishops. A Gallup poll in March 2002 found that 30 per cent of the sixty million Catholics in the United States are cutting off donations to the Church. Excluded from these figures are donations given directly to independent Catholic institutions such as universities, hospitals, and the 15 per cent or so of Catholic schools that are separately incorporated from the diocese. Some people continue to give to their local parish church, if they are reassured that the funds are restricted to the local parish, given to causes that the donor espouses. The target of people's anger is the diocese, because the bishop alone has total control of the funds. The degree of anger and boycott differs from diocese to diocese, but the number spreads as the extent of the scandal grows.

Why are lay Catholics voting with their pocketbooks? Because they are no longer passive subjects of episcopal authority; gone are the days of 'pray, pay and obey'. Emerging from the Archdiocese of Boston, epicentre of the crisis, is a politically moderate group of laity called 'Voice of the Faithful', whose motto, echoing the local rallying cry against the Crown at the start of the American Revolution, is 'Donation without Representation'. As bishops have banished them from Church property and forbidden institutions under diocesan control to accept direct donations from them (Voice of the Faithful set up parallel fundraising efforts to underwrite Catholic institutions that serve the poor), the group has grown in number and influence. Mary Jo Bane, Harvard professor and prominent lay Catholic, echoed the sentiments of many in *The Boston Globe*:

> Lay Catholics have no effective bodies through which to exercise responsibility, but we do have one powerful means of influence – our ability to withhold or postpone our financial contributions to the archdiocese. A full public accounting of all archdiocesan funds is the least we can ask as contributors, and would be an important first step in challenging the culture that bred the current tragedy.

The clarion call of the laity in regard to all aspects of Church life is 'transparency and accountability'. As a voice outside of the Church, Jim Wallace, editor of the progressive Christian journal *Sojourners* wrote on their website:

> The real problem here is lack of accountability, and only radical reform that brings new and effective accountability to every aspect of the church's life will suffice as a solution. The bishops should institute far-reaching changes that would bring lay people into virtually all decision-making at the core of the church's life and mission. That means substantial lay involvement in every aspect of the church's business and ministry, including decisions regarding management and administration, finances, grievances, and the crucial decisions about the evaluation and deployment of personnel that are at the heart of this painful situation.

More significantly, standing before the assembly of US bishops gathered in Dallas, Notre Dame Professor Scott Appleby said:

> At the heart of these problems is the alienation of the hierarchy, and to a lesser extent degree many of the clergy, from ordinary lay women and lay men. Some commentators say that the root of this scandal is betrayal of purity and fidelity; others say it is the aloofness of the bishops and lack of accountability and transparency. They are both right: to be faithful to the church envisioned by the council fathers of Vatican II, bishops and priests must trust the laity,

appropriately share authority with them, and open their financial, legal, administrative practices and decisions to full visibility. They must give a compelling account of the faith that is within them and address controversial issues directly, in an open and collaborative spirit.

Sadly, his comments fell upon many deaf ears. During the summer of 2002 the actions of prominent bishops (making priests and religious 'toe the line' through intimidation, silencing people, banning lay people from assembly on Church property, downplaying the spiritual and emotional damage visited upon victims, blaming the media, etc.) indicate that reform will be arduous and slow.

The scandal brings to the fore questions about Catholic education. The scandal is shedding light on problems that have long existed, such as the lack of subsidiarity, mixed messages about shared decision-making and overlooking the unique insights that parents bring to the staff of Catholic schools. Once the ministry of religious communities, the schools are now the ministry of lay people who take on roles of leadership, from day-care centres to universities, from the local parochial school to the entire diocese. Like the bishops, they must exercise transparency and accountability if they are to exercise authority; likewise, bishops must delegate to them authority and power. Second, the scandal makes people wonder if any Catholic institution is a safe place for children or those who are vulnerable and innocent. Schools have instituted new policies against sexual abuse. However, enemies of Catholic schools have an arsenal of weapons in public policy debates about Government support through vouchers and other mechanisms. Third, the moral authority of Church leaders and institutions has been terribly compromised. How much more difficult it is to teach prophetically about the preferential option for the poor, racism, non-violence, consumerism, and so on. The response of people in and out of schools is, predictably, 'Get your own house in order before you preach to us'. Fourth, while the boycott of diocesan fundraising is understandable, the effects will be felt most acutely in those institutions that serve the poor and are reliant on subsidies from central sources. Institutions that serve the wealthy will survive. The essence of power is to be unaffected by external changes beyond one's control. A sad lesson is repeating itself: it is the poor who suffer the consequences of others' sins.

The scandals did not create many of the issues that are surfacing in the US Catholic Church; rather, they shed light on them. For example, unless he is convincing in word and action, the bishop's authority has been empty. People on the left and on the right are consumers of religion; choosing the elements they want, ignoring those they don't. Many people shop for churches and schools, they embrace a Catholic way of life (rituals, traditions, sacraments, culture), but do not feel bound to every codified teaching. Many women feel alienated from the Church; some struggle within the structure (over 85 per cent of teachers in Catholic schools are women), others join women-friendly Protestant Churches and others simply defect in place. Many Catholic immigrants experience the US Church as cold and distant; evangelical Protestants, with small local congregations (often in storefronts) and approachable ministers, have made huge inroads into these populations. Generational differences are stark.[11] For many young people, Catholic identity is focused outside of the institutional Church. How many will continue to perform even rudimentary Catholic activities like marriage in the Church and baptising babies? Pollsters tell us that young people search for God and many seek community in a highly individualistic society. A Catholic way of life is appealing to them, but current leaders have squandered much of their moral authority. Increasingly, the school will be the only Church that children know, and lay leaders will be their *de facto* pastors.

Moving forward

It is often said that a crisis can be seen as a problem or an opportunity. As people of hope, we are bound to consider the latter. I am consoled by the endurance of faith among many people who have been deeply hurt by the current scandals. What we are experiencing is more a crisis of leadership than a crisis of faith. Who can predict the state of Catholic schools in five years, ten years, or mid century? Much will depend on the next pontificate and the quality of those people, men and women, lay and cleric, who will exercise leadership. Much will depend on the socio-political realities within which Catholic schools exist. It is hard to predict the future, but I am certain that the following questions will be raised in the US context.

- Will the Church continue to sponsor schools at all?
- Will Catholic schools be bold and creative, taking advantage of the possibilities that technology and global communication afford?
- Will fiscal realities make Catholic schools accessible only to the economically élite? Specifically, will they be accessible to non-Catholics who have no other education options?
- Will Catholic educators compromise their beliefs for political gain?
- Will they espouse market-based reforms uncritically, leaving those without political power in further impoverished schools, thus perpetuating social inequality?

- Will Catholic educators capitulate to politicians who reduce the richness of learning to quantifiable measures on standardised examinations?
- Will the shame and humiliation currently being visited upon Church leaders make them reluctant to embrace the vocation of the prophet?
- Will Church structures and leaders become intransigent or will they respond favourably to the call for accountability and transparency?
- Will women remain active in the Catholic Church as it is currently structured?
- Will organised religion continue to become a marginal anachronism in the United States and Ireland? In that context, will Catholic educators discover in the call to community and service a distinctive and compelling reason to exist?

Notes

1. I am a founding member of the *International Journal of Education and Religion* at the University of Nijmegen, which is dedicated to fostering dialogue among researchers of religiously affiliated schools across denominational and national boundaries. I have studied Catholic schools and lectured in Canada, Australia, Ireland, Scotland and Chile. My major international effort was with Catholic educators from England and Wales, culminating in the book I co-edited with Terence McLaughlin and Bernadette O'Keeffe, entitled *The Contemporary Catholic School: Context, Identity and Diversity*, published by RoutledgeFalmer Press in 1996. I also participated in a two-year dialogue with Jewish educators in the United States.

2. For an excellent exploration of these issues in the English-speaking world, see Gerald Grace's *Catholic Schools: Missions, Markets and Morality* (London: RoutledgeFalmer, 2002).

3. This standard history takes for granted an Anglo-American perspective. Located in the territories that are now part of the United States were Catholic schools of New France and New Spain. Moreover, the 'immigrant-dominant' history renders invisible some vibrant Catholic communities in Louisiana, expecially among African-Americans. For more information, see the doctoral dissertation written by Sister Addie Walker at Boston College, *Religious Education for the Regeneration of a People: The Religious Education of African-American Catholics in the Nineteenth Century*, 1996.

4. For a detailed analysis of these and other studies of inner-city Catholic schools, consult the following:
   O'Keefe, J.M., Goldschmidt, E., Green, J. & Henderson, S. (2003 – forthcoming), *Sustaining the Legacy: Urban Catholic Elementary Schools in the United States* (Washington: National Catholic Educational Association).
   O'Keefe, J.M. (2001), 'What Research Tells Us About the Contributions of Sectarian Schools in the United States' in *University of Detroit Mercy Law Review* 73 (3) 425-41.

O'Keefe, J.M. (2000), 'Ethnically Diverse Catholic Schools: An Overview of Students, Staffing and Finances' in Youniss, J. & Convey, J. (Eds), *Catholic Schools at the Crossroads: Survival and Transformation* (New York: Teachers College Press), pp. 117-36.

O'Keefe, J.M. (2000), 'The Challenge of Pluralism: Articulating a Rationale for Religiously Diverse Urban Roman Catholic Schools in the United States' in *International Journal of Education and Religion 1* (1) 64-88.

O'Keefe, J.M. (1999), 'Leadership in Urban Catholic Elementary Schools: The Reality and the Challenges' in Hunt, T. & Oldenski, T. (Eds.), *Catholic School Leadership: An Invitation to Lead* (London, New York: RoutledgeFalmer), pp. 225-43.

O'Keefe, J.M. (1997), 'Children and Community Service Learning: Character Education in Action' in *Journal of Education 179* (2) 47-62.

5.   For a summary of the documents related to Jubilee and a sampling of school programs to integrate social teachings into schools, see the book I co-edited with Carol Cimino and Regina Haney entitled *Integrating the Social Teachings of the Church into Catholic Schools: Conversations in Excellence* (Washington: National Catholic Educational Assoaiation, 2001).

6.   For more recent information on teacher satisfaction see the publication by Martha Naomi Alt and Katharin Peter entitled *Private Schools: A Brief Portrait*, published by the National Center for Education Statistics of the United States Department of Education Office of Educational Research and Improvement, 2002.

7.   For a discussion of issues related to teachers in Catholic schools, see the book I co-edited with Carol Cimino and Regina Haney entitled *Catholic Teacher Recruitment and Retention: Conversations in Excellence* (Washington: National Catholic Educational Association, 2002).

8.   See *Private Schools: A Brief Portrait* by Martha Naomi Alt and Katharin Peter, published by the National Center for Education Statistics of the United States Department of Education Office of Educational Research and Improvement, 2002.

9.   See the work of Robert Bellah, a sociologist of religion, who describes the erosion of community in America. See also the recent work of Harvard political scientist Robert Putnam in his book *Bowling Alone*, which substantiates the decline of civic associations in the US.

10. In a landmark decision in June 2002, the United States Supreme Court ruled that giving parents public vouchers to pay their child's tuition at a religiously affiliated school is not unconstitutional. For a full discussion of the benefits and perils of vouchers for Catholic schools, see my chapter entitled 'Catholic Schools and Vouchers: How the Empirical Reality Should Ground the Debate' in *School Choice: The Moral Debate*, Alan Wolfe, Ed. (Princeton University Press, 2003), pp. 195-210).

11. For more information on changes in affiliation patterns among US Catholics, see the work of William D'Antonio et al., *American Catholics: Gender, Generation and Commitment* (New York: Alta Mira Press, 2001).

Partnership:
Towards a richer model of Catholic school as community

Ned Prendergast

The central quest of this book has been for a fresh vision around which Catholic education can be reimagined, a vision that can be stated, embraced and bedded into schools. In that quest a number of central themes have been providing the spine around which the book is unfolding and these themes speak in a special way to the particular topic of this chapter.

The first of these interconnected themes is the spiritual foundation on which Catholic education is based, recognition that 'God is the mystery of man's humanisation' (Baum, 1971:58), pursuit of the meaning and implication for the twenty-first century of Jesus' words 'I came that you might have life, and have it to the full' (John 10:10), and, very importantly, the Catholic school's realisation of how much now depends on the spirituality of the lay teacher.

A second major theme is the primacy and sacramentality of relationships in Catholic schools, recognition that the 'locus of the divine is the interpersonal' (Baum, ibid.) and the belief that 'the person finds true significance only in relationship with others, encompassing both rights and responsibilities, freedom and accountability, self-fulfilment and self-discipline, self-expression and self-denial' (Anglican and Roman Catholic Bishops of New Zealand, 1992).

A third theme relates to the need for a radical re-engagement with the young people in our schools, for staying emotionally close to them as Maureen Gaffney puts it, for re-engaging their religious imaginations as explored by Jacques Janssen.

The upshot and implication of these themes gives rise to the master theme of building community in our schools, ideally faith communities with atmospheres 'enlivened by the gospel spirit of freedom and charity' (*Gravissimum Educationis*, 1965:8 – hereinafter *GE*) to the end that we might state with Bryk et al. (1993:306) that 'For students, the school constitutes a network of caring relations that binds them to the place, its people, and its programs'.

Stating the desire for spirituality, life-giving relationships, engagement and community is one thing; embracing and bedding in these values is quite another. We live in a real world where any school, not to mention schools that call themselves Catholic, may have queried levels of spirituality, good relationship, engagement and community. Why is it that so many students see the work of schooling as 'a monologue followed by a test' (Erickson and Shultz, 1992:481) or as like 'death and taxes, inevitable and unavoidable' (Marx, Grieve and Rossner, 1988:55)? Why is it that 'When those who are managed and controlled, as young people are in schools, begin to speak for themselves, theirs is a discourse against power, a counter discourse' (Lodge and Lynch, 2000:49)? Since when did disaffection become the fertile ground out of which you build a faith community?

How then do you build the values we desire into schools? One answer, one clue, this paper argues, lies in the partnership ideal which is under our very noses, which is the guiding spirit of the Education Act 1998 and now (on paper at least) so much part of the State system with which Irish Catholic education is enmeshed. Partnership, we would argue, is a very Christian ideal, and what we suggest is that if we want to build faith communities in our schools we begin by putting our hearts and souls behind the partnership vision of schooling. Partnership may not bring us all the way to a reimagined Catholic school (much more needs to be said about spirituality, about religion teaching, about pastoral care, about curricula, about liturgical expression, etc.), but it takes us well down the road towards getting relationships right, towards engaging people more deeply and towards building enlivened community, prerequisites surely for the spirituality we desire. Before you build faith community, first you have to build community (Daly, 2002:27). We need, therefore, to run with partnership for all that it is worth. It is time indeed that we reclaimed partnership vision as something deeply Christian, time we recognised the way in which Catholic school vision deepens and gives coherence to partnership, time we harnessed it to create the fertile soil in which faith communities can grow.

Partnership

Partnership is an inspiring and transforming ideal that brings into play a set of fundamental values relating to people and to the culture of their institutions. These values speak to the manner in which people are esteemed, to how they are treated and to how they relate to each other. They speak particularly to the manner in which the institutions where people live or work or learn, should operate.

The partnership ideal proposes three core values. The first of these is a profound respect for persons, expressed as a mutual attitude. The second value proposes a determination on the part of those who manage the contexts of human interaction to be inclusive of all persons in the dynamics of that interaction. The third value heralds the intention to underline the interdependence of people in human flourishing.

After a number of years working with the Partnership Project at the Marino Institute of Education, I came to simplify the concept of partnership for myself by saying that the partnership way is one in which everyone is recognised, everyone is welcomed, everyone is told, everyone is asked, everyone is heard, everyone is included, everyone is involved, and everyone, ultimately, is happy. I also found myself saying that the partnership way leads to community-building because community grows when people share vision and aims, when they feel that they belong, are allowed to contribute, have a say in where things are going, are recognised.

I also came to the conclusion that the only model of partnership that made sense in the school context was a three-way model to include parents, teachers and students. The student part is crucial; we have talked over the heads of young people for far too long and such talk has never been conducive to their engagement. The encounters that take place in schools are most important for the young people whose formative years, affective responses and lifelong learning patterns are at stake in the extent to which partnership values are expressions of the school's nurturing dynamic.

A very Catholic ideal

If you were to ask a teacher in school today where the partnership ideal came from you would probably get a secular answer prompted by the widespread and accurate understanding that the ideal has grown from a more developed critique of society in Ireland, accompanied by an impetus to make society better. Factors contributing to the emerging ideal in education are seen as including: the general growth of participatory democracy in our society; changing paradigms relating to the centrality of the student in learning and to the re-visioning of teaching as the mediation of learning; the increasing politicisation of parents; a concern for quality and effectiveness; an increased focus on social equity and cohesion; a greater understanding of the dynamics of exclusion; and a fresh emphasis on the benefits of inclusivity for the marginalised, the alienated and those with learning difficulties.

What is not always considered, however, is the extent to which partnership has provenance in and resonates with the teaching of Christ, or how expressive it is of the spirit and educational ideals enshrined in the philosophy and values of the Catholic school. The message of Christ, as conveyed in the Gospels, underlines and celebrates the value of persons, calls both in parable and in example for the inclusion of people, even in the most improbable of circumstances, and cries out for the interdependence of persons for love, for all that is lifegiving and human, and ultimately for salvation. The philosophy and value system of Catholic education is based on the gospel of Christ, on the Christian model of honouring the nature, dignity and destiny of persons, on the emphasis on achieving right relationships or justice in communal settings. These values are stated in a fresh way in the documents of the Second Vatican Council and in the documents of the Vatican Congregation for Education, which have developed the teaching of Vatican II.

Decades before the concept of partnership was to gain a footing in secular thinking, the Second Vatican Council was proclaiming that 'it is through the family that [young people] are gradually introduced into a civic partnership with their fellow men' (GE:3) and asking teachers to 'perform their services as partners of the parents' (GE:8). It was the view of the Council that:

> Parents must be acknowledged as the first and foremost educators of their children. Their role as educators is so decisive that scarcely anything can compensate for their failure in it... the family is the first school of those social virtues that every society needs. (GE: 3)

The consequent view of the school was as a 'kind of centre whose operation and progress deserve to engage the joint participation of families, teachers, various kinds of cultural, civic, and religious groups, civil society, and the entire human community' (GE: 5). The Congregation for Catholic Education went on subsequently to assert that 'the educational task of the family and that of the school complement one another in many concrete areas' (*Lay Catholics in Schools: Witnesses to Faith*, 1982:34 – hereinafter WF) and to ask parents 'to commit themselves totally to the cordial and active relationship with the teachers and the school authorities' (ibid.). It also asked 'all who are responsible for education' to 'pool their resources to enable

Catholic schools to provide a service which is truly civic and apostolic' (*The Catholic School*, 1977: intro – hereinafter *CS*). The congregation's most recent document asks explicitly that 'dialogue with the pupil's families… should also be encouraged through the promotion of parents' associations' (*The Catholic School on the Threshold of the Third Millennium*, 1997:20).

Catholic teaching also suggests the desirability of a partnership with students, both for the sake of the students themselves and for the good of society. It asks that young people 'be trained to take an active part in the construction of a community through which the building of society itself is promoted' (*CS*:13). The core motive is 'to develop in them the ability to make correct use of their judgment, will, and affectivity' (*WF*:12) and thereby 'to form strong and responsible individuals' who are 'inner-directed' and 'capable of making free and correct choices' (*CS*:31). The outcome of such a treatment of young people is that co-operation, responsibility and belonging are promoted and that disaffection is countered.

> When students are trusted and given responsibility, when they are invited to contribute their own ideas and efforts for the common good, their gratitude rules out indifference and inertia… They are more willing to cooperate when they feel respected, trusted and loved. (*The Religious Dimension of Education in a Catholic School*, 1988:106)

Catholic inspiration for the value of partnership may be summed up in the following imperatives of Catholic teaching:

- To celebrate the value, dignity and destiny of each person and to express this in extraordinary levels of respect and welcome.
- To recognise the primacy of the spiritual and the moral life in holistic human flourishing and to promote the deep levels of human engagement implied in that.
- To build a community that welcomes everyone as neighbour.
- To proclaim and honour the centrality, ascendancy and sacramentality of relationships in all that we do.
- To maintain at all times a commitment to caring and to service, to social justice and the common good.
- To go the extra mile for lost sheep and to offer 'preferential love' for 'those who are oppressed by poverty' (Catholic Catechism, 2448).
- To share in the Church's salvific mission of redemption and to promote the Kingdom of God.
- To offer a transformational apostolate of hope through leadership that is based on a servant model.

Partnership lies at the heart of the Catholic vision of education and fits into what Hogan (1999:148) calls 'the day to day struggle to exact the values of the Gospel and to embody the Christian vision and vocation in the social context'. It is a vision of how we get relationships right, of how people should be together, of how young people should be treated, a charter of what is human and humane. It is a vision of education in the best sense, a vision that recognises and proclaims that 'transformative education is essentially a spiritual process' (Hope and Timmel, 1984:16).

Embracing and bedding in

If running wholeheartedly with the partnership vision is a major step towards a richer model of Catholic school as community, the next question is: how do you put the partnership vision itself into action? We are back to the search for practical models, for norms organised in such a way that they focus on the nature, dynamics and shape of relationships, of community, of engagement. We are looking for a consistent pattern of assumptions, goals, attitudes, behaviours and strategies relating to school culture, which are transformative and prescriptive, that is, for imitation. We are looking for ways to transform the culture or medium of a school so that it allows a young person to say something to the effect that 'this is my life, this is my school, this is my education, this is what I believe'.

Getting there

It is my belief that the partnership ideal can be worked towards through named strategies and practical measures which relate to how each member of a core partnership is empowered and supported in the roles that are ascribed to them and to how nurturing attention is given to the systemic factors that bind partners together into a community. The following tables suggest, in skeletal and somewhat cryptic form, strategies, measures and outcomes that are proposed as a model that might be helpful as a framework for promoting a triadic partnership in schools between teachers, parents and students.

Strategies to empower

Table 1 offers strategies, measures and outcomes that give pointers to the manner in which partnership members may be empowered in their roles.

TABLE 1: EMPOWERMENT

Strategy	Measure	Outcome
Offer recognition	Role definition	Acknowledgement
Provide rationale	Cogent argument	Conviction
Extend welcome	Sincere outreach	Belonging
Address inner vistas	Personal development	Self-esteem
Promote conversation	Three-way engagement	Contract
Disseminate information	Open communication	Empowerment
Encourage listening	Focused attention	Satisfaction
Deliver challenge	Mobilisation	Responsibility

Strategies to support

Table 2 offers strategies, measures and outcomes that give pointers to the manner in which partners may be supported in their roles.

TABLE 2: SUPPORT

Strategy	Measure	Outcome
Provide resources	Physical, financial personnel, time	Practical partnership
Offer training	Train each partner	Effective partnership
Address needs	Audit, listen, respond	Relevant partnership
Special outreach to the at-risk	Go the extra mile	Life-giving partnership

Systemic strategies

Table 3 offers strategies, measures and outcomes that give pointers to the manner in which nurturing attention may be given to the systemic factors that bind partners together.

TABLE 3: SYSTEMIC STRATEGIES

Strategy	Measure	Outcome
Placing the highest priority on relationships	Pastoral care, pastoral structures	A Christian school, a pastoral school
Promoting high levels of information flow	Multiple vehicles of three-way communication	A school that 'hums' (Bastiani, 2000)
Creating an atmosphere of welcome and invitation	From reception to valediction	An inclusive school
Achieving a shared vision of school	Mission and vision statements	A school with a unifying and coherent vision
Generating community spirit	Community building measures	A school that sees itself as a community
Ensuring effective representation	Parent councils Student councils Effective staff and board meetings with open agendas	A democratic school
Drafting whole-school policies	A range of apt policies	A cohesive school
Broadcasting the positive outcomes of partnership	Celebrating effort, contribution and achievement	A school with high morale
Reaching towards transformational leadership	Leadership roles from many sources	A learning organisation
Waging an attrition on the barriers to partnership	Raising ceilings	An improving school
Pursuing a programme of continuous audit and review	Placed on agendas, on calendars, timetables	An honest school, sincere in its pursuit of partnership

A planning model

Finally, an action-research approach, one useful methodology for putting value into action, might be considered as a way of promoting partnership and the values of respect, inclusion and interdependence that it subsumes. Action research suggests a pattern in which (a) the value of partnership is stated; (b) the denial of partnership values is addressed; (c) an action plan is put into place to promote partnership values; (d) transformations are audited; (e) ongoing challenges are identified; and (f) a new cycle of promoting the value of partnership is instigated. These stages suggest a useful planning model with applicability to the promotion of partnership.

TABLE 4. AN ACTION RESEARCH METHODOLOGY FOR PROMOTING PARTNERSHIP

Element	Strategy	Outcome
The partnership value	Stated	Rationale
Denial of partnership values	Addressed	Concern
An action plan to promote partnership	Implemented	Initiatives
Transformation towards partnership	Audited	Clarification
Ongoing challenges	Identified	New cycle
New cycle to promote partnership	Instigated	Further progress

Conclusion

When partnership is introduced to a school, people are more conscious of their dignity and are raised up, persons are cared for and needs are met, people trust each other, are responsible and accountable to each other, people feel they belong, right relationships are established, institutions become more just, morale is higher, genuine democracy flourishes, richer forms of community ensue.

When partnership vision is infused with Catholic school vision it brings to the ideal an extra depth and coherence. What is now on offer is an educational process that is holistic and inclusive and that holds out a justice framework grounded in 'right' relationships. To all of that it adds, if pursued, a model of vocation, a sustaining spirituality, and models of sanctity. Sacramental and liturgical frameworks, which have not been considered here, add space and occasion in which vision and values are given visible communal expression.

When the partnership values of respect, inclusion and interdependence become active purposes and commitments in education, schools come to be very different and reimagined places. Progress is underway towards that school environment 'enlivened by the spirit of freedom and charity' (*GE*) which can act as a 'leaven in the human community'. Those who promote partnership in schools offer an answer to the question posed by Lane (1991:96):

> ...who will turn our schools into Christian communities that are marked by a sense of caring, sustained by an experience of belonging and missioned by a spirit of justice?

Bibliography

Anglican and Roman Catholic Bishops of New Zealand (1992), *The Purpose of Education – A Christian Perspective*.

Bastiani, J. (2000), 'I know it works!... Actually proving it is the problem!: examining the contribution of parents to pupil progress and school effectiveness' in Wolfendale, S. and Bastiani, J. (eds), *The Contribution of Parents to School Effectiveness* (London: David Fulton Publishers).

Baum, G. (1971), *Man Becoming God in Secular Experience* (New York: Herder and Herder).

Bryk, A. S., Lee, V. E. and Holland, P. B. (1993), *Catholic Schools and the Common Good* (Cambridge MA: Harvard University Press).

Daly, C. B. (2002), 'Values in Education' in Donaldson, A., McKeown, D. & McCann, G. (eds), *Ethos and Education: Contemporary Issues in Catholic Education* (Belfast: Ethos and Education).

Erickson, F. and Shultz. J. (1992), 'Students' experience of the curriculum' in Jackson, P. (ed.), *Handbook of Research on Curriculum* (New York: Macmillan).

Gravissimum Educationis (1965), *The Documents of Vatican II*, (ed.) Walter M. Abbott, pp. 637-51 (New York: Corpus Books).

Hogan, L. (1999), 'Occupying a Precarious Position: Women in Culture and Church in Ireland' in Lane, D. (1999).

Hope, A. and Timmel, S. (1984), *Training for Transformation: A Handbook for Community Workers* (in three books), (London: Intermediate Technology).

Lane, D, (1991), *Catholic Education and the School: Some Theological Reflections* (Dublin: Veritas).

Lane, D. (ed.), (1999), *New Century, New Society: Christian Perspectives* (Dublin: The Columba Press).

Sacred Congregation for Catholic Education (1982), *Lay Catholics in Schools: Witnesses to Faith* (Vatican City: Libreria Editrice Vaticana).

Lodge, A. and Lynch, K. (2000), 'Power: A Central Educational Relationship' in *Irish Educational Studies*, Vol. 19, Spring 2000, pp. 46-7.

Marx, R., Grieve, T. and Rossner, V. (1988), *The Learners of British Columbia* (Victoria: British Columbia Royal Commission on Education).

Sacred Congregation for Catholic Education (1988), *The Religious Dimension of Education in a Catholic School* (Vatican City: Libreria Editrice Vaticana).

Sacred Congregation for Catholic Education (1977), *The Catholic School* (Vatican City: Libreria Editrice Vaticana).

Sacred Congregation for Catholic Education (1998), *The Catholic School on the Threshold of the Third Millennium* (Vatican City: Libreria Editrice Vaticana).

Pastoral Care in Schools:
The role of management, chaplains and teachers

James Norman

Introduction

This chapter will explore the possibility of maintaining a pastoral ethos in Irish Catholic schools at a time when these schools are experiencing both external and internal pressures to align themselves more and more with the needs of the market economy and to cope with the emerging personal needs of their pupils. In order to explore this question I will briefly review some of the recent research on ethos in Catholic schools in Ireland. Arising from this review I will outline some of the pastoral challenges for schools and the role of school principals, chaplains, guidance counsellors, year heads and tutors in maintaining a pastoral ethos in Catholic schools.

Ethos and Irish schools

The ethos of any organisation is that which arises out of the internal relations of those who make up that organisation. School ethos is the atmosphere that emerges from the interaction of a number of aspects of school life, including teaching and learning, management and leadership, the use of images and symbols, rituals and practices as well as goals and expectations. In order for a school to achieve all of its goals it is necessary for it to maintain a balance between the different aspects of school life. Gerald Grace (2002) refers to the Catholic school in terms of its 'mission integrity', that is, the school's ability to maintain an ethos that reflects the goals and charisms of those who founded it.

Research into the ethos of Irish schools indicates that the ethos of many Catholic schools has been undermined by the strength of the pressure to prepare pupils for a terminal exam, not to mention the forces of the market economy to prepare young people to be skilled in such a way as to quicken their entry into commerce and industry. In his research McDonald (1995) found that the operative ethos in the Catholic schools he studied was deeply affected by the expectations of teachers and pupils of the primary purpose of the school being to prepare its pupils for success in exams and readiness for the workplace (Vol. II: 451). In his research into a large Catholic school, O'Keefe (1998) found that the parents and pupils in the school valued preparation for work first and gave their lowest ranking to the pupils' religious development (p. 34). O'Keefe concluded from his research that the Catholic school in his study had an ethos that was quite individualistic and even secular (1998, p. 40).

Scott Boldt's (2000) study into ethos in Irish schools was not particularly concerned with Catholic schools. However, as many of the schools in Ireland are Catholic in one form or another (Feheney, 1998, p. 6), its findings are relevant. Boldt found that pupils in both primary and second-level schools in Ireland perceived their schools to value 'an ethic of hard work' and 'academic achievement' more than anything else. The study also suggests that pupils in general have themselves taken on these values (Boldt, 2000, pp. 36-7). Of particular interest is the fact that most of the teachers in this study said that although they were aware of students' pastoral needs, they felt that they had to give more time to the academic aspect of the pupils' development (p. 41).

It seems from these studies that, arising from external pressures as well as parental expectations, many schools are experiencing a displacement in their mission integrity, resulting in an ethos that is overly academic and gives less time to pupils' pastoral development.

Specific factors working against a pastoral ethos
Streaming
Many schools in Ireland, in order to tailor the academic curriculum to the level of the pupils, have opted to organise pupils into sets of classes according to their intellectual ability (Drudy and Lynch, 1993, p. 245). This form of streaming pupils into ability groups relies heavily on assessments that are primarily concerned with linguistic and numerical intelligence. Consequently, some pupils can find themselves placed in a 'top' or 'bottom stream' class and much of their experience of schooling can be affected by the position they are awarded at entry to their second-level school. Those in favour of this form of streaming will argue that as a system of organising learning it allows the school to focus teaching and resources around the specific needs of the pupils in each ranked class group. However, others will

argue that because of its narrowly defined focus on certain types of ability it can result in pupils in lower streams having a lower self-esteem and ultimately setting their educational goals lower than those in higher streams, resulting in a self-fulfilling prophecy whereby those in the higher streams always seem to do well and those in the lower streams tend not to achieve so well academically. While some schools have tried to alleviate the negative effects of streaming by calling class groups after saints, rivers and national heroes, streaming is hierarchical in nature and it doesn't take a pupil too long to work out where s/he has been placed. This ultimately contributes to an ethos that is competitive and whereby some pupils in top and bottom streams may feel that they are valued more for their academic ability rather than their contribution as a person.

Timetabling

In any school it is the timetable that provides the clearest window into what is valued by teachers and, specifically, management. The school principal and his/her deputy, who in their decisions reflect the values of the school, of parents, teachers, management and ultimately society, normally decides the amount of class time assigned to a particular subject. Most schools will have no problem finding four or five periods per week for academic subjects like Irish, English or Mathematics. However, when it comes to Social, Personal and Health Education (SPHE), Religious Education or Physical Education, these more person-centred subjects tend to have little or in some cases no place on the school timetable. Research carried out by Looney and Morgan (2001) found that the majority of schools give less space on the timetable to the more intra-personal subjects and more time to academic subjects and that boys' single-sex schools in particular give less of a priority to subjects like SPHE, Religious Education and even Physical Education (p. 73ff). Apart from the serious consequences for pupils' emotional and mental health, it is clear that through timetabling schools are contributing to an ethos that seems to place academic achievement over personal development.

Part-time work

Changes in pupils' lifestyles in recent years can also militate against the school having a role in their personal development. In the past, apart from home life, the school was probably the next most important influence on a pupil's development. However, research shows that many young people today spend up to twenty hours or more per week in some form of 'part-time' work (Morgan, 2000, p. 19). The figure is higher in areas of social disadvantage, resulting in a large part of the pupils' development being influenced by their experiences in their workplace. Furthermore, the quality of the pupils' attendance in school is also affected as they are often tired and focused on their concerns outside of school. This culture of part-time work for pupils is presenting a real challenge to the schools' pastoral aims, in that, if the pupils come to school tired from work elsewhere it is extremely difficult for the school to have an impact on their personal development, not to mention that the pupils are also being influenced by the values of their place of work, and this too can undermine the school's role. While these developments in terms of part-time work do present a serious challenge to the schools' ability to meet the pastoral aims of the Education Act (1998) and the curriculum in general, they can be overcome through creative initiatives on the part of the school, by developing links with employers who are interested in the pupils' wider development and building a bridge between the workplace and school curriculum in terms of the pupils' personal development. Some programmes in Transition Year and in the Leaving Certificate Vocational Programme provide a basis for meeting these challenges.

Discipline
The changing culture of the student's home life has resulted to a certain extent in a clash with the culture of the school and this is revealed at times in problems of indiscipline (Martin, 1997). Many schools in recent years have experienced increased non-compliance of pupils in classrooms, violence towards other pupils and teachers, outbursts of misbehaviour and, consequently, increased pressure on teachers and schools generally.

Those schools that react to discipline problems from a purely punitive response are failing to get to the core of the problem and ultimately creating an ethos that is characterised by control rather than care and concern for the individual pupil. Furthermore, the use of programmes such as Discipline For Learning (1996), or DFL, can further undermine the caring ethos of a school as the programme is based on taxonomy of rewards and sanctions that are indifferent to the individual pupil's life context.

For example, today the pupil is doing well; she completes her work in the classroom and receives affirmation and praise from the teacher. If this continues for the rest of the week or the term, she may get a certificate or medal to mark her achievements. The pupil sitting beside her lacks concentration and so causes some disruption to the classroom. She never has her homework completed and can interfere with other pupils, even appear to bully them at times. As the term progresses she gets a number of warnings and sanctions until eventually she has to leave the classroom. Afterwards the teacher reports a great improvement in the class. However, nobody has asked why has this pupil behaved in this way, and the fact that her parents have been fighting a lot and recently separated is not taken into account as a cause for her behaviour and, consequently, she is never helped in school to deal with the emotions and fears that can occur when parents separate.

While some of the methods and skills associated with programmes like DFL can be very helpful when used in conjunction with a wider pastoral approach, these behavioural programmes generally tend to try and focus on changing behaviour rather than addressing the symptoms causing the apparent indiscipline in schools.

Those schools that are dealing successfully with problems of indiscipline are engaging methods that include increased teacher collaboration, parental involvement and, most of all, a pastoral approach to the causes of indiscipline (Martin, 1997).

Pupils' personal difficulties and the pastoral competence of teachers

Research among classroom teachers in second-level schools into the types of pastoral needs that pupils can have has shown that apart from the pupils' general developmental and personal needs, there are a range of specific pastoral needs that spill over into the classroom, mainly from the pupils' home life. When asked to list and rank their pupils' most frequent pastoral needs, classroom teachers reported the following in order of the most frequent to the least frequent:

1. Illness
2. Financial disadvantage
3. Parental separation
4. Chronic low self-esteem
5. Bullying
6. Depression
7. Bereavement
8. Serious aggression in classroom
9. Social exclusion
10. Domestic violence
11. Teenage pregnancy
(Norman, 2003A)

In the same study 64 per cent of the teachers who responded claimed that the above needs can affect their ability to teach on a daily basis, with a further 26 per cent reporting that their pupils' personal needs had an effect on their ability to teach on a weekly basis. These findings clearly indicate the extent to which certain aspects of young people's personal lives can spill over into their school life and their general ability to succeed in their learning. Teachers specifically reported that their pupils' personal needs as listed above affect their participation in school, mainly through absenteeism, lack of concentration, lower attainment levels and disruptive behaviour in the classroom (Norman, 2003A).

While 90 per cent of the teachers who responded to the survey said that they considered pastoral care as part of their duty as a teacher, only 11 per cent of them said that they regularly referred pupils to the school guidance counsellor. This would seem to suggest that the majority of teachers deal with their pupils' personal needs within the classroom. However, 92 per cent of teachers in this study did not consider themselves adequately trained to deal with their pupils' personal difficulties.

Consequently, we can say that teachers are under tremendous pressure in the classroom as they try to deliver the curriculum and provide support for pupils' personal needs at the same time. Considering the extent and type of issues that teachers have reported arising in the classroom and the frequency of effect on their ability to teach, it does seem that there is a need for professionally qualified pastoral carers in schools, who, rather than undermining the pastoral nature of the teacher-pupil relationship, can provide extra support outside the classroom and ultimately enhance the teaching and learning within the classroom.

Pastoral-care roles in the school
The school principal
While the ethos of the school will arise out of the dynamic life and interaction of all those in the school community, there are a number of key figures whose presence and role can influence the ethos of the school considerably.

In terms of developing a pastoral ethos and the actual provision of pastoral care in a school, the school principal is the most important figure. If the school principal is committed to pastoral care, this will be reflected in the space given on the timetable to subjects with a more pastoral bias, such as Social, Personal and Health Education, Religious Education and Physical Education, where teachers through open discussion can learn more about their pupils' needs and the pupils can learn to feel that they are important to the school and develop a sense of well-being and belonging. The principal who is committed to pastoral care will also ensure that there is a post of responsibility for pastoral care within the school and the provision of physical space where pupils and parents can come for support and care.

Fundamentally, the school principal will model best practice in pastoral care through his/her interaction with teachers, parents and pupils. S/he will continuously look for opportunities to praise and celebrate teachers and pupils' achievements alike. If teachers feel appreciated and valued for their contribution, this will have an effect on their ability to care for their pupils. The importance of this type of emotional leadership can never be underestimated as it contributes to the teachers' sense of worth and well-being and helps them to look forward to and enjoy their work.

The chaplain

Research in the Unites States of America has shown that much of the perceived success of Catholic schools there is due to the development of a sense of community, belonging and a common purpose to school life. Through caring for the needs of teachers, parents and pupils, the chaplain as an extension of the school principal, who is often concerned with administration and staff appointments, has been seen to play a key role in the animation of the school ethos (Bryk, Lee and Holland, 1993, pp. 140-41). Research here in Ireland has also revealed the significance of the contribution of the school chaplain to the realisation of a school's pastoral aims. Chaplains in community/comprehensive schools were found to be involved in counselling, supporting other staff with their personal needs, provision of liturgies and meditation, bereavement support, intervening in discipline problems, meeting and visiting parents, and visiting pupils, staff and their families in hospital (Norman, 2002, p. 9). The findings of this study clearly show the extent to which school chaplains are intimately involved in the life of schools (Norman, 2002, p. 14).

The chaplain holds a professional mandate, which is both educational and ecclesial. The educational mandate arises out of the Education Act (1998), which obliges schools to promote the emotional, moral and spiritual development of the pupil (Education Act 9:d). The research mentioned above indicates that the chaplain is a key figure in the realisation of these educational goals. The ecclesial mandate arises from the Gospels, where Jesus says that he has come so that we may have life and have it to the full (John 10:10). While many of the problems presented by a pupil, parent or teacher to a chaplain will be the same as those presented to a counsellor or social worker, the chaplain has a different point of reference in that s/he approaches people and their needs from a faith context. As a minister of the Church the chaplain seeks to realise Christ's mission so that the pupils, teachers and parents will have life to the full.

The chaplain normally will have the time to be available to those with personal difficulties, particularly pupils, and to liaise with other members of staff concerning the pastoral care of the pupil. A crucial role for the chaplain is to judge prudently the level of appropriate disclosure to other staff so as to enhance their understanding of a pupil's behaviour.

The guidance counsellor

The guidance counsellor is also a key figure in the development of a pastoral ethos in a school. In conjunction with the school chaplain and the home-school community liaison, the guidance counsellor can form part of a pastoral-care team in order to provide an integrated support service to students.

The guidance counsellor can make a very clear contribution to a pastoral ethos in the school by being available to offer support and advice to pupils who are at a very important time in their journey to adulthood. Advice given in school may be realised in a place in college, a trade or a position in a company later on, and will have wide-ranging consequences for a pupil's life.

In recognising the totality of the pupils' lives, their gifts and talents, as well as their academic ability, the guidance counsellor will seek to advise them in such a way that they will not only find employment and income but also happiness, fulfilment and contentment, and so the guidance counsellor makes a very important contribution to the pastoral ethos of a school.

The year head

The year head in a school holds a very important responsibility for a year group. Their role will include the overall well-being of a year group as they move up and eventually out of the school. The year head will normally be the point of reference for organisation of activities such as sports, retreats and debates. S/he will also be an important person for referral of pupils who are misbehaving, bullying or bullied, sick, isolated or falling behind in their work, as well as for communication with parents. While many aspects of the day-to-day running of a year group can be dealt with by the head of year, it is important that s/he has an ability to collaborate and refer on to other staff, such as the chaplain or guidance counsellor, when the pupils' needs require it. In other words, the role of year head is not simply managerial but collaborative in nature and so it is vital that the person appointed to this position has an ability to work as part of a team and is able to trust others to play their part in caring for the pupils' needs.

Equally important is the pupils' perception of the year head. As the leader of the year group it is vital that the year head models good communication with pupils and teachers alike, creating an atmosphere in the year group of belonging and purpose. As the pupils journey with their year head through the school they will come to see him/her as someone who cares about them and is not just concerned about grades and exams.

The class tutor

The class tutor is the first point of contact between the pupil and the school, consequently, the pupils' experience of the class tutor is very important. The tutor will meet regularly with the class group and get to know them and their background. As the first point of reference for the pupil in a school, the class tutor is probably one of the most important figures in the development of a pastoral ethos. As many pupils will never have the need to meet personally with the principal, chaplain, guidance counsellor or year head, the class tutor will be the member of staff who will provide them with their lasting memory of school.

The tutor normally liaises with other teachers and parents, not to mention year head, chaplain and guidance counsellor, when a student is experiencing difficulty. It is again very important that tutors see themselves as part of a wider pastoral-care team and are ready to seek help and support for pupils when required.

Conclusions

Irish schools have developed a strong academic ethos in recent years. This ethos has contributed to the personal success of the pupils in their work and careers, not to mention the wider economic success of the country. In exploring this ethos I am not suggesting that we should lose it, becoming less concerned with academic development. Rather, I am suggesting that in order for schools to maintain their 'mission integrity' and to meet the aims of the Education Act, they will have to put as much emphasis into developing the pastoral dimensions of school life.

A pastoral ethos can only be achieved when all of the people involved in a school community share the common purpose of placing the person of the pupil at the centre of their endeavours. All school staff, specifically teachers, play an important role in the development of a pastoral ethos, however, the school principal, chaplain, guidance counsellor, year head and class tutors play a particular role in terms of influencing the ethos of the school.

If a school is serious about caring for its pupils it will have to put in place key personnel such as chaplains and guidance counsellors who have the time to be available to the pupils and accompany them on their journey through school.

As pupils' personal needs continue to evolve and change, there will also have to be ongoing in-service for teachers in aspects of pastoral care so that they can improve their competency in meeting the personal needs of their pupils. Ultimately, if pupils feel cared for and if the right support is available both inside and outside the classroom then teachers will be better able to teach and pupils will be better able to learn.

References

Boldt, S. (2000), 'A Vantage Point of Values – Findings from School Culture and Ethos Questionnaires' in Furlong, C., Monahan, L., *School Culture and Ethos* (Dublin: Marino).

Bryk, A., Holland, P., Lee, V. (1993), *Catholic Schools and the Common Good* (Cambridge Mass: Harvard University Press).

Drudy, S., Lynch, K. (1993), *Schools and Society.*

Education Act (1998), (Dublin: Government of Ireland).

Feheney, M. (1998), *From Ideal to Action: The Inner Life of a Catholic School* (Dublin: Veritas).

Grace, Gerald (2002), *Missions, Markets and Morality* (London: Routledge Farmer).

Looney, A., Morgan, M. (2001), 'An Engendered Curriculum?' in *Irish Educational Studies*, 20, pp. 73-96.

Martin, M. (1997), *Indiscipline in Schools: A Report to the Minister for Education Niamh Bhreathnach* (Dublin: Government of Ireland).

McDonald, M. (1995), *The Ethos of Catholic Voluntary Schools* (unpublished doctoral thesis, UCD)

Monahan, L. (1996), *The Class Tutor: The Why, The What, The How* (Dublin: Irish Association of Pastoral Care in Education).

Monahan, L. (1998a), *The Year Head: A Key Link in the School Community* (Dublin: Irish Association of Pastoral Care in Education).

Monahan, L. (1998b), *The Chaplain: A Faith Presence in the School Community* (Dublin: Columba Press).

Morgan, M. (2000), *School and Part-time Work in Dublin* (Dublin Employment Pact).

Norman, J. (2002), *Pastoral Care in Second-Level Schools: The Chaplain* (Dublin: Centre for Research in Religion and Education (CRRE), Mater Dei Institute).

Norman, J. (2003A), *Pastoral Care in Second-Level Schools: The Teacher* (Dublin: Centre for Research in Religion and Education (CRRE), Mater Dei Institute).

Norman, J. (2003B), *Ethos in Irish Schools* (New York: Peter Lang).

O'Keefe, T. (1998), 'Values in a Christian School' in Feheney, M., *From Ideal to Action* (Dublin: Veritas).

Smyth, A. (1996), *Discipline for Learning* (Langford).

The School and the Parish:
Changing patterns of involvement

Anne Codd

Introduction

The participants in this workshop (sixty in all between the two sessions) brought a wide variety of experience, interest and expertise to the exercise. Dioceses, parishes and schools were all represented. There were diocesan advisers, priests, parish pastoral council members, parish sisters, parish programme coordinators, principals, teachers, catechists and chaplains, as well as people involved in the production and publication of catechetical materials.

My own background in school, in parish and in training of pastoral ministers, as well as the many conversations I have had with people in the field, helped me to offer:

- familiarity with the present reality of school and parish;
- a reading of its genesis;
- a theoretical basis from which to critique practice and inform vision;
- some examples of good practice.

Focus of the workshop

We agreed to concentrate on school–parish links as they relate to faith development.

Assumptions
- We were all seeking change for the better in school–parish co-operation.

- Such change generally involves a shift of focus.
- As participants were not present as teams, the most useful aspect of the workshop might be its method, as one by which dialogue might proceed in their local contexts.

Aim
That everyone would leave the workshop with enhanced conviction that:

- The school–faith community link is not just important, it is essential. 'The coalition is imperative' (Thomas Groome).
- The present, in all situations, is the product of the past. Understanding this is liberating. It is also challenging, since the future will be the product of our present choices, decisions and actions.
- In so far as this field is problematic, the school is part of the problem and must be part of the solution.
- The future is ours to make, and people in school, parish and diocesan roles are testing creative ways forward.

The reality

The following points guided the workshop. Obviously, we could not go through them in any depth and still allow for the kind of participation that people would expect. Given the cross-section of people attending, I believe we could have had a very fruitful dialogue had time allowed.

The school as an institution in society

The Catholic secondary school has moved with time, and in particular with the introduction of the Education Act, into the mainstream of education provision in the Republic of Ireland. The inclusion of most voluntary schools in State provision of second-level education since 1966 formalised this development. The school is, therefore, very fully engaged in its tasks as an institution in society. Its function as such, against a background of the instrumentalism of *Investment in Education*,[1] puts constraints on its role as an agent of faith-formation, in terms of its student intake, educational priorities, use of resources, and so on.

Joseph O'Keeffe's presentation at the conference highlighted, by contrast with the American context, the fact that, by and large, our students come to the Catholic school by default.

Peter McVerry draws our attention, in prophetic manner, to the influence of technical, rational pragmatic purposes in the schools, and to the consequences of this influence in our society. In this context the introduction in recent times of personal development programmes such as CSPE, SPHE, RSE can, in some cases, be thought to replace Religious Education in school planning.

The findings of educational research on the role of the Catholic school in perpetuating social inequality in Ireland must not be ignored.[2] In Ireland the schools, including Catholic schools, have reflected rather than changed society.

Present-day challenges and questions to Catholic philosophy and ethos
While the stated philosophy of the Catholic school, for example, in Schedule 1 of its Articles of Management, still upholds the founding principles of the school in terms of formation of young Catholics for life in Church and world, the ethos of the school in its present-day existence is greatly challenged by the changes that have taken place in Ireland as elsewhere in the last four decades. Joseph O'Keeffe suggested a way to gauge this reality: compare and contrast the mission statement and the budget.

The economic, cultural and religious transformations in our society since the 1960s have been well documented.[3] While the population still registers as 95 per cent Catholic,[4] falling numbers of committed (actively involved) Catholics among the families, the students and the staff of the schools make for a scenario that is radically different from the time when all or most of the student population and their families took part in Church life regularly, and the staff comprised religious, priests and 'practising' Catholic lay people.

Add to this the more recent phenomena of students, families, and ultimately teachers of races, cultures and faith traditions other than Catholic/Christian, and the task becomes complicated indeed. The struggle to redefine Catholic and Christian identity in the pluralist, and in a real sense secularised,[5] context of today is ongoing. Thomas Groome emphasised the call to schools to model the Christian ethic of dialogue and mutual respect.

Fundamental questions need to be asked, therefore, and are being asked in this new scenario: What is the role of religious faith in a pluralist society? How are we to understand the Christian Church in a multifaith context? What is the mission of the Church in the world as we know it now? Can Christian, Catholic belief and practice play a meaningful role in our lives, in community and society today? On what basis are young people to be introduced to the teaching and practice of the Catholic faith tradition? Should the Catholic school give priority to particular categories of applicants?

Changes in Religious Education
The introduction of RE as a subject for examination is now a *fait accompli*. The implications of this development for the handing on of faith have yet to unfold. It is arguable that the new situation has the possibility, not only of

helping young people to become well-informed, but also of bringing the task of faith development into focus, and of opening up the role, in this task, of the wider faith community.

While the distinction between Religious Education and faith formation has validity, it is not absolute. Rather, the methodologies used in RE feature many aspects of faith formation. An example of the interplay of life in faith community and pedagogy of the classroom is the discussion that is envisaged in the curriculum for the Junior Certificate on the students' experience of worship in their tradition and their local assemblies.

Local faith community
The parish as local faith community reflects the social change that has already been referred to above. How it has responded varies from place to place. It is true to say, on the overall, that there has been little coherent, constructive action for renewal in pastoral practice in Ireland, not least because there has been no strategic planning at national or, in most cases, diocesan level, though there are hopeful developments in some places.

The inclusion of young people in the life of the parish is limited. Where there is some form of liturgical action (e.g. music) or where young people have parish-based social outlet or social action, they still have a sense of belonging.[6]

Falling numbers of priests, and increasing demands in terms of administration, compound the stresses of day-to-day life, where the ministry of the parish is still largely the work of the priest. Hence, the work of the school, and in particular the secondary school, in handing on the faith comes up for consideration only occasionally within the ministry of many parishes. Rarely is time invested in understanding the processes in which the school is engaged, the approaches that good catechesis must involve today, the need for serious parish involvement, the importance of liturgical adaptation to communities of young people and their teachers, etc.

It is not surprising, therefore, that the experience documented in at least one significant piece of research on faith development in a network of Catholic voluntary secondary schools, is of great disappointment with the scale and quality of co-operation forthcoming from the parishes.[7]

Questions must be asked of school personnel. What understanding of Church are they, at least implicitly, presenting in their catechesis and exemplifying in their way of working? Is it a welcoming, inclusive and caring Church? What is expressed in their expectations of the parish or parishes? Do they run with the institutional hierarchical aspect alone, or recognise the faith community in a much wider sense?

Chaplaincy

One of the immediate problems regarding chaplaincy is that, very often, appointments of local priests to this role are made without consultation with school principal or anyone else, without negotiation with RE or other staff, without regard for the aptitude of the person in question, and without job specification. Moreover, the role of part-time priest-chaplains is often limited to the liturgical one. As will be pointed out later, this is not an adequate reflection of the totality of faith formation.

The importance of training for chaplaincy is at present being recognised, and training programmes have become much more accessible in recent times (for example, Mater Dei and its outreach centres).

The case for paid full-time chaplains in voluntary secondary schools is progressing. In the event of such appointments being possible, the potential for serious engagement between the school and the wider faith community will be greatly enlarged. Changing patterns of involvement will not, however, come about automatically. They will require conviction and vision, which will be discussed below.

Diocesan context

In the research it was found that where diocesan personnel and resource centres were accessible they made a valuable contribution to the work of the school in catechesis and Religious Education. The possibilities for creative development at diocesan level feature in two examples of good practice below.

Historical background to the present situation of the Catholic school in Ireland

'*The remembering of the genesis can release repressed dialogue. The seeing of interest unmasks ideology.*' (Thomas Groome)[8]

The Catholic Church in modern Irish society

The Catholic school in Ireland emerged within a period of consolidation, here, of the Catholic Church, namely the nineteenth century and twentieth century to 1960. Historian J.J. Lee, among others, highlights the role of the Church in preserving the status quo of Irish society of that time, especially after the famine.[9] Sociologist Michel Peillon attributes the pervasiveness of the Catholic ethos in Irish society then to the presence of two distinctive forces – the hierarchy in Tridentine mode, and the religious orders, present in great numbers within health, education and social-care services.[10]

In penal and post-penal Ireland, education played a major role in the emergence of a national and Catholic identity. Anne Looney suggested that our education, like our Catholicism, was, especially in the Republic, to some degree an expression of defiance and territoriality.

Role of the school
While the Church maintained a dominant role in the ordering of life in society locally and nationally, the work of the school in teaching the faith was corroborated implicitly in family and community/parish life. Now, however, the assumption of almost total responsibility by the school for the task of catechesis is arguably a great systemic weakness of Irish Catholicism.

Role of the parish
The role of the parish, as local faith community that includes the family, in introducing young members systematically to its beliefs and practice, has not been developed in Ireland, and the consequences have become increasingly more evident. It is recognised, for example, that Confirmation at the end of primary school marks for many also the end of engagement with Church for a long time if not for all of life.

Present-day situation
In global terms, the near identification of a society with the Catholic tradition is of necessity a passing phenomenon. What is surprising is that in Ireland this phase lasted so long, a fact accounted for by economic and social factors, which reinforced our insularity. All has changed now, but our view of Church and the call to Christian community living within society is only gradually evolving. It has been said that Vatican II was called to answer questions, which, in Ireland, had not even been asked.[11]

Foundational principles
While they may be considered theoretical, basic axioms are necessary in order to critique practice and inform vision. They can give us the courage to 'question the seemingly unquestionable' (Sr Joan Chittister). Such principles include:

•   The parish, as local faith community, is central to the invitation to faith.

•   Growth in faith is a lifelong process.

•   The parish, while headed up by the clergy, is not to be identified solely with the priests.

- Faith development requires a community context wider than that of the school.

- The school, from this perspective, is an agency within the faith community.

- The school is well placed to call the parish to its mission.

The parish (as Church here and now) and the invitation to faith

Vatican II invited us to understand the Church as the sign and sacrament of God's self-giving to humanity, to see the Church as serving the coming of the kingdom, rather than solely as a means to individual salvation.[12] Like the People of God in the Jewish scriptures, the Church exists within the world for the sake of all people. By its life of 'faith, liturgy and love',[13] it is to witness to the presence of God in the world.

On this view, membership of Church becomes a matter of invitation and response. Catechesis becomes not just teaching but also witness, and the offer to share life based on faith in Jesus Christ. Clearly it is by experiencing the life of the community and being guided in interpreting their experience, that young people can grow in understanding the Christian vocation, and make commitment to live it. The focus of our faith is not just Jesus of Nazareth, but Jesus Christ, risen and witnessed to by the community.

The presentation of catechesis as 'shared Christian praxis'[14] assumes this faith-community context and at the same time points up the potential of the school-based dimension of the process, as the privileged place of experiencing community, as well as of teaching and reflection.

Growth in faith is a life-long process

When we recognise faith as an interpretation of experience in the light of our tradition it is clear that this task cannot be accomplished on a once-for-all basis during school years.

Faith is real in so far as it is lived out historically and socially as well as personally. Therefore, the unfolding circumstances of our lives call for ongoing reflection in the light of our beliefs, and our faith must be continually enlarged as we move through each phase of our life.

Finally, even during school-going years, the decision to live by faith needs to be symbolised by choices made in 'free' time. Parish-based faith development complementing work done in school offers this opportunity.

The parish, community of faithful

While in principle it is understood that the parish is the community of Christians in time and place, in practice many still express their expectations of the parish in terms of what the priest ought and ought not do. This is hardly surprising in the light of how little change has actually taken place in parish structures. Through its programme of action, the parish community needs to become much more visible, socially as well as liturgically. This and more is what parish development is about.

By giving expression to parish as community, in language and in practice, the school itself can foster new awareness. The example that will be discussed later of one school in inviting parishioners to share their stories of belonging in parish will demonstrate this.

There is, nevertheless, no doubt that priests play a key role in how a parish is organised and how all in the community, including the school community, experience Church.

The process of faith development

According to sound catechetical principles, new members must grow into the life of the community through becoming versed in the apostolic teaching, sharing the fellowship, participating in the prayer and worship, and contributing to the life of Christian service.[15] The confines of the school, even as Christian community, are such that these functions cannot be fulfilled in isolation from the wider parish and Church.

In practice, the students in a secondary school may live in many different parishes. Moreover, it is highly likely that they will not live within their home parishes after school, as they move on to further education, training or employment. What is, nevertheless, important is that they experience fellowship, prayer and service in heterogeneous faith communities, and have opportunity to reflect on their significance.

In the research,[16] students said that they knew they could return to their parish when the need arose, for example, when they would need marriage papers. It is clearly necessary to broaden the young people's sense of what a parish is, what it could be, and what they can contribute to its development.

The school, agency within faith community

The work of education in faith, which is accepted by the Catholic school, originates in the mission of the Church. The school should, therefore, be critically conscious of any assumption of a self-appointed task. In a canonical sense, the local church is primarily the diocesan Church, and it is within the diocese that the school's mission of faith development finds reference.

The school cannot function in isolation. In practice, no school even tries. More importantly, the impact of the school within the wider ecology of the community of parish, parishes and diocese, is unavoidable.

Despite the challenges that have been enumerated, and the problems that have been reported, it is very important that catechists, principals and all others within the school resist the trap of laying blame uncritically on priests, parishes or dioceses. The school, as every other part of the whole organism, is part of the problem and part of the solution.

The school – well placed to call the parish and the diocese to their mission
If the foundational principles are accepted, the school will expect the diocese and the parishes not just to support it, but to recognise it as working on behalf of Church, and in particular on behalf of the local church. Language, attitudes and practice in schools that suggest that they carry primary responsibility for the faith formation of young people need to be reviewed critically. The role, and understanding of role, of diocesan advisers and diocesan resource centres is critically important in this regard.

Given the present real situation, what is probably required, first of all, is a sustained dialogue between the school and local church. This is a process that may be shared at diocesan level with schools in the State sector. Nationally, managerial and other associations need to continue in conversation with, or where necessary open new conversations with, influential groups – the Bishops' Conference, Commissions, NCPI, pastoral development offices in dioceses, and so on.

Current initiatives
Four avenues to creative action are exemplified in practice. Each could be said to 'redefine success'. (Thomas Groome)

School
Teachers in some schools, in co-operation with principals and colleagues, take account of the parishes from which their students come, and invite from each parish the priest and/or some parishioners to come together for an exchange of stories, on an arranged day and time, with their student-parishioners.

A former parish priest of one of these parishes remembers with joy how a woman of the parish shared with a class group her family's experience in a time of bereavement, and the support and services that were available to her in her parish. Her sense of being cared for, and her ongoing sense of belonging, made a lot of sense to the students.

This activity requires some imagination, good organisation, the co-operation of colleagues, and good communication, so that all concerned are clear on what is being asked for. The possible outcomes are surely worth the effort.

The same PP recounted having two parishioner-students spend a day in the parish. He himself was the one to introduce them to what was happening at the Day Centre, and other aspects of life as they happened. This experience made a significant difference to how these young people perceived what local church community is about, Monday to Friday.

Once again, what is needed as well as a co-operative PP, or delegate of his, is some vision on the part of the school, and the commitment to allow time for such an exercise. Also assumed, of course, is a local church context in which there is, in fact, some activity in the name of the parish in addition to Sunday liturgy and the personal ministry of the priest.

In other contexts (the ones I have encountered personally happen to be rural), students from Transition Year are invited to commit themselves on a rotation basis (and with all necessary parental approval) to share in clubs run within the parish for young people, notably those with mild mental or physical handicap. They are greatly challenged by this experience, and can reflect on it in their RE class group.

The potential for faith formation of this kind of exercise is huge. The methodology of reflection on action is, especially for young people, very effective.

Parish
Young people are often willing to get involved in action-projects in response to local or global needs. Parish-based initiatives offer points of meeting and co-operation between parish and school. Obvious examples are social events for the senior citizens of the community. It is important that reflection on these experiences takes place, so that students may make connections between their experiences and the gospel message.

Many priests look to second-level schools for potential readers and other ministers for parish liturgies, and are sometimes dismayed at the response. But it has to be recognised that they are not approaching the students in their own idiom, but rather that of Church.

By contrast, when an occasion arises that is important for the young people, and for which they themselves make plans, their interest and engagement is transformed. When a priest of the parish is willing, in preparing to preside at their liturgy, to enter into the significance of the event, the meaning with which it is invested and the ritual expressions that grip the imagination of the young people, then the parish is experienced as a place of welcome, respect and life. Examples abound: rituals that mark important transitions, for example, the beginning and ending of the school year, funeral and memorial services, and graduations.

Another example of parish initiative involves the first-year students who go out of their locality to post-primary school. Clubs that are founded in the parish, through which they can stay in touch with their peers there, are greatly appreciated.

Diocesan Advisers

What follows is a creative and practical example of school–parish link-up: first-year students from a number of schools in a region have been invited to take part in conversations with the Parish Development and Renewal (PDR) groups of their parishes, who of course had also agreed to the idea. Orientation for each group was organised, so as to develop mutual understanding. Over three nights, conversations took place within the parishes.

What this exercise highlights is that today, while it may be difficult for adults and young people to find common ground on which to exchange views and reflections, it can still happen with the help of some structure and planning.

What such an initiative requires is co-operation between teachers and the programme co-ordinator, willingness on the part of the students (and their parents), the PDR groups and the priests to get involved, and innovative thinking and a lot of organisation on the part of the co-ordinator, perhaps the DA or other persons with his/her support.

Diocese

In some dioceses assemblies of young people have taken place, in parallel with other diocesan developments. Such initiatives ideally include school personnel, and provide material for discussion and reflection in the classroom.

The merit of such diocesan initiatives, especially when young people themselves request them, is that they recognise the youth as members of the diocesan community. Hopefully the participants are also empowered to take initiative at local level, both in school and parish, with the authority and some resources of the diocese behind them.

Summary

Throughout my research in preparation for the workshop, the topic evoked interest and varied responses. Nobody, across the broad spectrum of those with whom I discussed it, dismissed it as unimportant. At the same time, many seemed to consider development in school–parish co-operation an impossible dream.

However, we are not talking here about a *dimension* of the school's life and mission. We are talking, metaphorically, about the ground on which the school stands. The reality is that the school cannot be true to itself if, like an anchorless vessel, it invites young people to participate in the Christian, Catholic tradition without reference to its wider church community context.

There is need for a fair appraisal of the current situation and recognition of its history, for a return to first principles in order to review practice and form vision, for sincere dialogue between school and wider faith community at all levels, for creative action and for patience.

The expectation of full commitment by all students to active Christian community in the school is as unreal as the expectation of full participation by all the baptised in the parish. The ecclesiology promoted by Vatican II accommodates this reality. What is called for, in both school and parish, is a strong witness by those who profess the Christian faith, so that the Church is truly there as 'sign and sacrament' of God's loving presence, of the saving work of Jesus and of the power of the Holy Spirit. Those who attend a Catholic school are entitled to be invited to belong in such a Christian community, and they may also legitimately expect the formation and group support that will help them to respond.

The practical implications of what has just been said include policy decisions on the allocation of time and resources to Religious Education and faith formation, on whether attendance at liturgy will be optional or not, on how prayer is included in the regular schedule in the school, and on inter-religious conversations. Moreover, it becomes abundantly clear that relationship with a wider faith community is essential to the processes of invitation to and formation in the Christian faith.

The examples of practice that have surfaced in the course of my conversations around the country are, most likely, replicated many times over, and I am sure that there are other fine stories to be told. They are, in themselves, relatively simple and manageable programmes of action. Nevertheless, I would argue that they demonstrate, in however seminal a way, understanding, imagination and commitment. Most especially, they stand up to critique in terms of the understanding of the role of the school that they express, and the long-term goals that they are serving.

Review

The main outcome of this workshop, in my view, was the agreement of the participants that the essential relatedness of the parish as faith community and the school as an agency within that community needs to be revisited. I can only hope that the event, and the conference as a whole, offered something to further the very important task of renewing and strengthening the collaboration of the school and the parish in the mission of Religious Education and formation in faith.

Notes

1. Department of Education, 1966.
2. Ref, for example, the work of CORI Education Office.
3. See, for example, the helpful outline in Oliver Brennan, *Cultures Apart? The Catholic Church and Contemporary Irish Youth*, Chapters II and III (Dublin: Veritas, 2001).
4. Greeley and Ward, *Doctrine and Life* (December 2000).
5. The concept of secularisation is a contested one. Cf. Greeley and Ward in *Doctrine and Life* (December 2000). The term is used here to signify the changes outlined above in religious attitudes, belief and practice.
6. *Beyond Nostalgia*, David Tuohy SJ, Mary Maume and Roger Maxwell. This research report to the Northern Province of the Presentation Sisters is available from Presentation Ministries Office, Portarlington, Co. Laois. The researchers surveyed and analysed the experience of catechists, principals and chaplains in seventeen secondary schools, in six dioceses.
7. *Beyond Nostalgia*.
8. 'Shared Christian praxis: a possible theory/method of religious education' in Astley, Jeff and Francis, Leslie, *Critical Perspectives on Christian Education* (Leominster: Gracewing 1994), p. 227.
9. Lee, J.J., *The Modernisation of Irish Society 1848–1918* (Dublin: Gill and Macmillan, 1989).
10. Peillon, Michel, *Contemporary Irish Society: An Introduction* (Dublin: Gill and Macmillan, 1982).
11. Freyne, Seán, Introduction to *Church and Change: The Irish Experience*, Hans Kung (Dublin: Gill and Macmillan, 1986).
12. *Gaudium et spes*, 1.
13. *Ad gentes*, 14.
14. Groome, Thomas, *Christian Religious Education, Sharing our Story and Vision* (New York: Harper and Row, 1980).
15. Bouley, Alan (ed.), *Catholic Rites Today, abridged texts for students* (Collegeville, Minnesota: The Liturgical Press, 1992), pp. 68-9.
16. *Beyond Nostalgia*.

Engaging with Ethnic Minorities

P.J. Boyle

Introduction

Current demographic changes and recent Government policy towards non-nationals (including refugees and asylum-seekers) have culminated in many social debates around the concept of interculturalism in Ireland. One of the greatest challenges facing schools and the education system in Ireland is their ability to cater appropriately for the existing and newly arrived people of different ethnicity. In practice, engaging with ethnic minorities in the context of Irish education will involve a whole organisation evaluation of cultural competencies. Perhaps more importantly it will involve an examination of attitudes and the acquisition of knowledge by individuals and organisations at all levels within education towards these new service users, i.e. non-national pupils and their families, and the consequences by which they found themselves here.

This chapter explores some of the influencing factors concerning current demographic changes and looks briefly at some of the 'push and pull' factors that have resulted in people of other cultures coming to live in Ireland. Furthermore, this chapter will examine current theories in relation to interculturalism and cultural competency and suggest some useful methods in helping to engage people of ethnic minority and schools in embracing cultural diversity.

Multiculturalism in Ireland

Despite popular belief that multiculturalism in Ireland is a relatively new phenomenon, Ireland has always had some degree of heterogeneity when it comes to social demographics (Cullen, 2000). For centuries the Irish travelling community has experienced difficulties around the acknowledgement of their ethnic identity by the majority community of 'settled' Irish. There is also an established Jewish history in Ireland over many years tracing back as far as the eleventh century. In more recent times other communities have sought refuge in Ireland during times of conflict. Such groups have included Hungarian refugees in the 1950s, Chilean and Vietnamese refugees in the 1970s, Iranians in the 1980s, and in the 1990s people from the Balkan wars, including Bosnians and people from Kosovo. However, it is perhaps the recent and continuing increase in the numbers of asylum-seekers and refugees to Ireland from more non-traditional destinations that has brought the concepts of *multiculturalism* and *interculturalism* to the fore. Since the mid 1990s the numbers of asylum applications in Ireland has increased from just over 400 in 1992 to over 10,000 in 2001, with the majority of new arrivals coming from the West African continent and Eastern Europe.

The arrival of families from these countries (the majority of which are considered 'developing world' destinations) has resulted in calls for examination and evaluation of services in relation to current needs, focusing particularly on equality and cultural appropriateness. In particular, education and health-sector staff are faced with the daily realities of having to meet the needs of people from these communities, a percentage of whom have experienced traumatic events as a consequence of fleeing persecution. It is unavoidable that some school staff throughout Ireland will encounter experiences of having to deal with multi-ethnic pupils, whether Travellers, asylum-seekers or immigrants. Of particular concern is the profile of young asylum-seekers. For the year 1999 and the first six months of the year 2000 the age profile of young asylum applicants aged eighteen years and under was put at 18 per cent. Within this group 37 per cent were aged under four years, 39 per cent aged between four years and twelve years, and 24 per cent were aged between twelve and eighteen years old. As the dispersal policy in place for asylum-seekers continues to be implemented, the question remains as to how prepared schools and staff are to deal with encountering pupils and families from other cultures.

Factors influencing current demographic changes in Ireland
Irish missionaries and overseas development work
Ireland has a long history of contributing towards the development of communities abroad. The Irish Church, in particular through religious orders and communities founded in Ireland, for example, the Irish Christian Brothers, Presentation Sisters, the Irish Sisters of Mercy and Irish Sisters of

Charity, have contributed enormously to the development of essential services (education, health and social services) in many countries of the developing world, particularly in the African continent. Consequently, for the indigenous people living within these communities who have used and benefited from such services, it would appear that Ireland would be an attractive and safe destination should they require refuge and security in times of conflict or persecution.

Similarly, Ireland's involvement over many decades in international humanitarian efforts (for example, bilateral Government-aid agreements, peacekeeping missions, and NGO emergency relief efforts) has contributed to its popular international profile as a country of generosity and concern. The appointment of former Irish President Mrs Mary Robinson as United Nations High Commissioner for Human Rights may also have added to this notion of Ireland as an attractive destination for asylum-seekers and migrants.

Ireland's economic success and labour shortage

It would be wrong to associate exclusively the recent emergence of Ireland's multicultural make-up with the arrival of asylum-seekers/refugees or people from developing countries alone. Of particular significance in recent years is the performance of Ireland on the international economic stage. Having experienced an economic 'boom' in the late 1990s, which contributed to the phenomena of the 'Celtic Tiger', Ireland has become a popular destination for people from other industrialised nations. Apart from returning Irish emigrants, migrants from other EU members States and non-EU States continue to arrive as part of work visa/permit schemes (Watt, 2001). In addition, the employment shortage experienced by both the private and public sectors in Ireland has resulted in a significant number of people from many countries being recruited to work in these sectors. An example of this in the public sector has been the phenomena of healthcare staff and nursing shortages. Large recruiting drives have been undertaken by Irish hospitals and health boards in countries such as the Philippines, India and Nigeria. It would appear as a normal part of human development and the migratory process that in the future these newly arrived workers will begin to unite with family members here or start families of their own, thus contributing to the cultural diversity of Ireland. One of the first places in which this will manifest itself will be in the schools of Ireland, when children from these families present for formal education.

Irish peace agreement

The significance of our own domestic political history as represented for decades on the international platform may also be significant in the context of recent inward migration. Since the acceptance of the Good Friday Agreement in 1997 on the whole island of Ireland, and the perceived notion of stability and peace by people in other countries, there are those who may now find Ireland a more attractive destination than in times past. There is anecdotal evidence to show that there are increasing numbers of people from other countries coming to live and establishing communities in Northern Ireland and in the border counties of the Republic.

Whatever the reasons for people choosing Ireland as a destination to live in, the fact remains that Ireland is now a country of inward migration for peoples of many different cultures and ethnicities. This provides opportunities and challenges to all who are entrusted with the responsibility of providing services to society as a whole. Such challenges will include the evaluation of our own definitions of pluralism and cultural diversity. It would seem obvious that schools as centres of learning are one of the most appropriate places to commence this process.

Interculturalism in schools

The Christian conscience to which the Catholic School subscribes remains constantly challenged by the gospel to respond to situations that history places before us. Roe points to the fact that 'the theme of asylum and refuge is woven into the whole tapestry of God's relationship with human creation and that the drama of the gospel story is that the very survival of the Saviour depended on the hospitality of a foreign people towards the fleeing asylum-seekers, Mary, Joseph and the infant Jesus' (Roe, 2000).

In addressing the issue of interculturalism in Irish schools (in the context of the demographic changes outlined above), there is a need to revisit our understanding of the aims of Catholic education as expressed through documents like *The Catholic School* (1997) and recent Government legislation on education in Ireland, such as the Education Act (1998) and Education and Welfare Act (2000).

The Vatican Document *The Catholic School* (1997) states that Catholic schools exist for the Church, for the common good of all society, and for the poor and the marginalised. The arrival of children and families from other cultures to Ireland provides Irish Catholic schools with an opportunity to fulfil in a new way these aims of Catholic education as outlined above. For example, the implementation of a specific programme of induction and support for non-national students. Such a programme may involve a number of staff and student-body members, including pastoral-care, home-liaison and teaching staff, offering not only educational or academic support but social, pastoral and cultural support. Such an initiative would help to contribute to an ethos of interculturalism and inclusiveness in the school environment. However, the development of such initiatives is clearly dependent on resources and funding, which can be often difficult to access (Tuffy, 2002). One group who are in particular need of such support are separated children or unaccompanied minors. These are children under eighteen years old who arrive in Ireland alone. These children may be fleeing persecution and have come to Ireland to seek refuge. A percentage of them may have experienced traumatic events personally or witnessed such events in their families, among close friends or neighbours. Consequently, their opportunity to gain access to school and education and all that goes with school life (making friendships, finding support) may provide a sense of normality to their situation as separated-children asylum-seekers.

Regarding the obligations of the Education Act (1998) for schools to promote the overall development of the pupil, a recent research study noted that the needs of non-Catholic asylum-seekers in denominational schools raise particular questions. Some parents of asylum-seeking children who responded to the survey expressed concerns about religious 'assimilationism' in Irish schools (Fanning et al, 2001). That is, due to the integrated nature of the curriculum in Catholic schools, it can be difficult for the children of non-Catholic parents to avoid taking on aspects of Catholicism. Both the Children's Rights Alliance and the Constitution Review Group have described this situation as being in breach of Article 14 of the Constitution regarding the rights to freedom of thought, conscience and expression. It is clear that there is a challenge here for Catholic schools to embrace pupils of other religions and maybe even to develop collaborative links with members of other Churches to meet the obligations of the Education Act (1998) regarding pupils' spiritual and cultural development.

It is clear that the education system has a key role to play in supporting individual students and in transmitting civic and moral values to all students. These values must include a respect for diversity and a commitment to equality. The introduction of legislation, i.e. Equality Employment Act 1998 and Equal Status Act 2000, in this regard should go some way towards the establishment of a society that places serious emphasis on respect for diversity and equality.

From multiculturalism to interculturalism

If we are to address the issue of interculturalism in schools we must be clear not only in our understandings of the philosophy of education and the ethos and function of schools but also in our definition of interculturalism.

The word *multiculturalism* is mentioned frequently in discussions and debates about cultural diversity. However, the word multiculturalism in itself is minimalist in its explanation of different cultures. As a definition, the word multiculturalism only acknowledges the existence of many cultures. Consequently, in discussing issues in relation to cultural diversity, the concept of interculturalism is more appropriate and in recent times has replaced the concept of multiculturalism in cultural-diversity discourse.

The National Consultative Committee on Racism and Interculturalism defines *interculturalism* as follows: 'Interculturalism suggests the acceptance not only of the principles of equality of rights, values and abilities but also the development of policies to promote interaction, collaboration and exchange with people of different cultures, ethnicity or religion...' (NCCRI, 2001). Such a definition clearly explains and points to the challenge for those concerned with and entrusted with the development of society. Therefore, in the context of current demographic changes Irish schools, including school management, staff and student bodies, have a moral and legal obligation to contribute positively towards the development of interculturalism within the life of the school.

The first and most important step in the process of developing an intercultural approach is the acknowledgement and acceptance of cultural diversity. Diversity involves many different aspects of people's living and doing. It encompasses issues related to class, age, gender, ability, ethnicity, religion, sexual orientation, politics and socio-economic status. These differences exist within all communities globally and, consequently, may be bound by similarities such as language, geography or history. Therefore, while communities may differ in some aspects, they also share common ones. By each community recognising what they have in common (the commonalities) and also by learning about each other's differences (diversities) there exists an opportunity for interaction between communities. It is this interaction when engaged in with respect and understanding that gives rise to interculturalism. There can be no better place for such an opportunity to exist than in the school environment, where pupils and staff come together in an atmosphere of mutual learning. Should this dynamic be facilitated and allowed to develop within the school, both students and staff alike may benefit positively from this cross-cultural experience. The following section will outline some ways of developing and contributing towards interculturalism and engaging with ethnic minorities in the school environment.

Characteristics of an intercultural school

Immigrants bring with them a richness and vibrancy. Ireland can benefit tremendously from the increase in cultural diversity that people of different ethnicity bring with them. However, Toner highlights the fact that this benefit can only be experienced if Ireland and its institutions promote the maximum degree of integration that is favourable to promoting the dignity and self-identity of immigrants and native Irish alike (Toner, 1998).

From a practical standpoint the school is an ideal place to pioneer the new methods and programmes to address interculturalism. Schools can provide a safe and secure environment where learning and negotiation can take place. The emerging dynamic among pupils, staff and the wider community will be multifaceted, involving changes in values and attitudes, not to mention the development of skills and knowledge.

Curriculum
The curriculum as defined by the National Council for Curriculum Assessment encompasses the content, structures and processes of teaching and learning which the school provides in accordance with its educational objectives and values. The curriculum includes specific elements such as concepts, skills, areas of knowledge, and attitudes that children learn at school as part of their personal and social development. However, it is not just these specific elements alone that constitute the curriculum. There are also implicit elements present. These elements are those factors that contribute towards the establishment of the school ethos and the general environment of the school. Such elements are lived out in the daily life of the school, between students, staff and the wider community. In considering this understanding of curriculum we can see that as a concept curriculum is something that reflects the real experiences of those in the school. Consequently, as Irish schools begin to experience the reality of cultural diversity within the communities to which they serve, perhaps there is need to re-evaluate and adapt elements of the curriculum in schools.

In order for cultural diversity to be respected and for interculturalism to emanate from the school, the taught curriculum must contain components that deal with intercultural issues such as language and communication, and world religions/cultures. In addition to these subject areas students and staff should be provided with the opportunity to explore in more detail and in an experiential way development issues that influence cultural diversity, such as migration, debt, social justice and discrimination. Currently there exists the opportunity to make the curriculum 'real' for both pupils and staff by engaging in collaboration and partnership with ethnic-minority community solidarity groups or field trips to ethnic-minority community development projects. A number of these newly established groups provide very informative intercultural education sessions at the invitation of schools.

However, caution must be paid in relation to issuing invitations to such groups, particularly if there are perceived or noticeable negative attitudes by students or staff towards people of ethnic minority. Prior to such invitations, preparatory work on tackling racism and/or discrimination should be undertaken.

In some schools there are arrangements between the school and religious order whereby students from transition year may experience working overseas in a project run by the same religious order. The availability of a bursary and the running of a competition may give some student(s) the opportunity to discover at first hand an intercultural experience by travelling and helping in a development project, for example, building of a school or community housing. A similar type project could be undertaken in the context of working with the travelling community, or the establishment of a partnership between schools in designated areas of disadvantage with schools in more affluent areas. Clearly this type of informal curriculum contributes to the social and moral development of the students and will contribute to a society where efforts are concentrated on equality and justice.

Fundamentally, the curriculum provides many opportunities to promote an intercultural world-view among the teachers, parents and pupils. It would be incorrect to associate interculturalism solely with issues such as overseas development, migration and poverty. Each pupil and staff member brings to the school some element of their own cultural identity, whether it is from urban, rural, socio-economic, or gender differences and commonalities. It is here, through the informal and formal social interaction of those present in the school, that the 'real' intercultural dynamic occurs. Similarly, the curriculum as we know it does provide for an intercultural world view in subject areas such as religion, geography, economics and even school tours. However, in the context of the recent demographic changes in Ireland there exists the possibility for all members of the school community to engage in experiential learning at local level by learning from each other in a personal and respectful way through the sharing of knowledge and experiences, and in doing so promote understanding.

Symbols and images
In the day-to-day functioning of the school, what must first be evident to all is the acknowledgement of cultural differences. One effective way of addressing this is by paying attention to the symbolism and imagery that is visible in the school. For example, if all of the posters, photos, advertisements on display in corridors, classrooms or libraries exclusively depict *'white Irish people and Irish scenes'*, what message does this send to

pupils and families of other ethnicity who attend the school? Similarly, if signs denoting *welcome* or *directions* are only written in Irish and English, what message of welcome does this send to newly arrived pupils of other cultures who do not speak English as a first language? We have noted previously that when we speak of diversity it encompasses many factors, such as gender and ability. Therefore, in addressing issues of minority in the school environment, schools must be conscious of the way in which they can contribute in an unconscious way to excluding individual pupils. For example, schools with an established tradition of success in a particular sport and who display outward signs of rewards to pupils involved may be at risk of excluding pupils who do not ordinarily conform to the 'traditional' sport but may have won awards for some other activity. While these examples focus on external or superficial aspects of the school environment, visible symbols and imagery are important factors in contributing to inclusiveness. Symbols are more than just mere decorations: they help the pupils to construct meaning about themselves, their community, and society in general. A school's choice of symbols and images can contribute to an intercultural experience of education.

Practical ways to engage in interculturalism for staff and pupils in schools

A whole-school approach is essential for the development of any type of programme in addressing interculturalism. Therefore, it is imperative that management, staff, pupils, parents and the wider community be involved in the drafting of strategic planning on this issue. Three basic elements will underpin the development of any such plan. These are the *examination of attitudes, the acquisition of knowledge,* and *the learning or further development of skills* in the area of intercultural communication and cultural diversity. Fundamental to the development of such an initiative is the establishment and employment of a monitoring tool built into the original plan. Likewise, an essential component of any project is a commitment to funding. It is necessary to undertake an evaluation of the proposed financial cost and other costs, including time and commitment by the people involved. Appropriate funding will enable some of the more important aims of the initiative to be undertaken, for example, *acquiring resources* and *teaching materials, implementing support structures for staff,* such as training, or the employment of support teachers or teaching assistants. Information concerning the availability of the entitlements for individual schools in relation to non-national pupils and teaching/support staff ratios and resources is available from the Department of Education.

Support team
A number of recommendations have been put forward by the Department of Education in addressing the issue of working with pupils of ethnic minority in schools. These include *the setting up of support teams.* Such a team may be comprised of multidisciplinary staff members, such as home-school liaison, chaplaincy/pastoral care, support teachers and/or year heads. The development of such a team of committed and experienced staff can be useful not only in supporting ethnic-minority students and teachers, but it can also be a useful resource in awareness-raising and educating other staff and pupils about relevant issues, i.e. asylum procedures, acculturation process, intercultural issues and anti-discrimination education. Similarly, the use of 'key workers' within the team who may work on an individual basis with a pupil, perhaps with an 'unaccompanied minor', may prove beneficial in liaising with social care or healthcare personnel should related problems manifest in the school environment.

Buddy system
The creation of a 'buddy' system has also been recommended. Such a system would enable the development of a cross-cultural dynamic from the outset between the non-national pupils and their peers in the school. An essential part of developing this type of project would be the training and preparation of pupils who are motivated to work within the programme. The involvement of members from ethnic community development groups in partnership with school staff and other interested parties, for example, local youth initiatives, may prove beneficial in the development of peer-led integration programmes. Pupils and staff may implement a number of positive cross-cultural learning experiences through the media of arts, sports, music or outdoor activities. Examples of a 'buddy' system could be modelled on other established 'buddy-type' programmes', such as the Gluais or Meitheal programmes. Providing pupils with the opportunity to evaluate the programme in a safe and structured setting would also be an essential element of the programme. Likewise, the leadership within the programme should ideally come from the pupils themselves, with support and facilitation being offered by relevant school staff members, i.e. some member of the 'support team'.

Very often in the absence of any formal programme to address interculturalism by the school authority, pupils have already begun to engage in positive cross-cultural social interactions, for example, sharing ideas and information on popular culture issues such as music, fashion and the use of language, etc. When provided with the opportunity, the student body of the school itself may suggest a number of creative and resourceful methods of engaging with their own peers who come from diverse cultural backgrounds.

An example of ideas and activities that may be put to use in the classroom or as a part of other initiatives addressing interculturalism in the school environment is outlined below. (Further examples and information on implementing similar activities may be found in training packs or teaching aids used in other subject areas, such as Development Education and SPHE, and may possibly be adapted for use accordingly.)

Generating discussion by using film

This may involve showing a brief film-clip that depicts some type of intercultural issue. A clip from a relevant mainstream movie (age appropriate) or from a specific educational video pack may be used. The clip can be used to develop a guided and facilitated discussion around cross-cultural discrimination, racism, human rights or injustice. The film-clip may also be used in preparation for a formulated debate by two teams or individuals on a related topic. If there is a group, they may become involved by voting or by participating in the debate. The use of film often maintains pupils' motivation and can be a beneficial learning tool. The use of a prepared questionnaire on the film-clip may also be a useful tool for stimulating discussion, as pupils are asked to complete it while watching the clip or immediately afterwards. There are a number of suitable resources for this type of activity available from the library of the National Council for Development Education (NCDE, 1999).

Intercultural zone

The idea of an intercultural zone can prove particularly useful as it involves participation and sharing of information. The 'zone' should be established in a prominent area of a classroom, library or school. Responsibility for the area may be given to a member of the 'buddy team', who can generate ideas by consulting his/her fellow pupils on what the 'zone' should contain. One idea may be a competition for pupils to design the layout or display area (stand, wall, floor space, etc.) once it has been agreed what the area is to exhibit or function as. Staff and pupils may then pick a theme that they wish to address on a rotational basis, for example, food, dress/costume, artefacts (lamps, crockery, tools, artwork, etc.). Items may be gathered by pupils or staff from holidays, student exchanges or collectors. Alternatively, pupils may be encouraged to enquire about artefacts used worldwide for various tasks, for example, collecting water. They may then be asked to draw or design their own model based on their inspiration from examining these topics in another culture. The availability of a globe or world map in the area to pinpoint and mark where the artefacts come from or where people may be from (including places in Ireland!) will prove informative and interactive. The availability of a large world map can also be useful in the creation of 'personal family histories'. Pupils may be encouraged (with sensitivity) to trace family members' whereabouts or origins. This can be expanded to include that person's reasons for travelling, emigrating, etc. The pupils can then mark on the world map an area of interest and personal experience for them. Should there be enough space for a large area and depending on resources the intercultural zone may also be used for performances from pupils or invited guests. If music is used as a medium for teaching about cultural diversity, the 'zone' could be used as the venue to perform a song or piece of music composed by pupils. In the intercultural zone pupils should be encouraged to question issues and discover the cultural significance of what may be on display, and relate it to their own cultural experiences. The development of rules and regulations that govern the area and what takes place there may be drafted by pupils and staff. The most important rule is that all people are treated equally and respectfully within the intercultural zone and that this is mirrored throughout the school environment.

Bibliography

Cullen, Paul (2000), *Refugees and Asylum Seekers in Ireland* (Cork: Cork University Press).

Department of Education and Science (2001), *Information Booklet for Schools on Asylum Seekers* (Dublin: Government Stationery Office).

Dolan, Rose (2001), Student Leadership Programmes, an unpublished Masters thesis (National University of Ireland, Maynooth).

Fanning, Bryan, Veale, Angela, O'Connor, Dawn (2001), *Beyond The Pale: Asylum Seeking Children and Social Exclusion in Ireland* (Dublin: Irish Refugee Council).

Farrell, F., Watt, P. (eds), (2001), *Responding to Racism in Ireland* (Dublin: Veritas).

Guidelines on Anti-Racism and Intercultural Training 2001 (Dublin: NCCRI).

MacLachlan, Malcolm, O'Connell, Michael (ed.), (2000), *Cultivating Pluralism: Psychological, Social and Cultural Perspectives on a Changing Ireland* (Dublin: Oak Tree Press).

Making the Links, Breaking Barriers: Annual Report 2001 (Dublin: Vincentian Refugee Centre).

Raising Awareness of Diversity and Racism, An Activity Pack for Schools and Youth Workers (Dublin: NCCRI, 2002).

Refugee Information Service, *Progress Report 1999-2000* (Dublin: RIS).

Roe, Paddy (2000), 'Asylum Seekers and Refugees in Ireland Today' in *Intercom*, October 2000 (Dublin: Veritas), pp. 8-9.

Shade, Barbara, Kelly, Cynthia, Oberg, Mary (1997), *Creating Culturally Responsive Classrooms* (Washington DC: American Psychological Association).

Smith, Suzanne (1999), *Tools For Change* (Dublin: National Committee for Development Education).

Toner, Bill (1998), 'Wanted: An Immigration Policy' in *Working Notes*, December 1998, Issue 33 (Dublin: Jesuit Centre for Faith and Justice).

Tuffy, Gemma (2002), 'Embracing Interculturalism' in *ASTIR* (Dublin: ASTI), pp. 19-20.

Watt, Phillip (2001), 'The Challenge to Build an Anti-Racist and Intercultural Society in Ireland' in *Focus*, Issue 64 (Dublin: Comhlámh), pp. 34-5.

REALISING THE PURPOSE

Improving Our Aim:
Catholic school ethos today

Joseph McCann, CM

Targets

Once upon a time, not so very long ago, a stranger arrived in a small town
in the American west. One thing caught his eye. Everywhere he went, he
noticed paper targets, concentric circles with small black spots in the middle,
attached to buildings, fences, poles, all over town, and the bullet hole was, in
every case, exactly in the bull's eye. The stranger enquired who the brilliant
marksman might be. The inhabitants told him that it was Bill, the village
idiot. The stranger went in search of Bill, and asked him the secret of his
marksmanship. 'Aw shucks,' drawled Bill, 'Aisy. Ah just shoots first and draws
the target afterwards.'

Sometimes our school mission statements, school ethos declarations and
other documents are products of the village idiot. Like him, we shoot first
and draw targets later. In other words, it looks as if we continue to operate
regardless of mission, and justify our actions. Nowhere is this more true
than in the case of Catholic ethos.

We are not entirely to blame. Schools are going concerns, armies on the
move, and they each have their momentum, their tradition, their tried and
true habits of action deeply embedded in their operations. And it is difficult
to examine a commitment that is old, strong and taken-for-granted. It is like
operating on oneself to find how one's heart ticks or pulling up a cabbage to
see how it grows. Ethos, some allege, is something organic. It is in the
atmosphere. It has to be cherished by individual staff members, responded
to by individual students, and valued by individual parents for it to be strong
and vibrant. Management decision cannot impose it.

There is an element of truth in this. Culture has to be taken for granted or it is not cultural. The unquestioned elements of attitude are at the deepest level of commitment. A good example of this in Ireland is our national compulsion to attend funerals, something that is quite unusual in modern Western society. Yet Irish people never question it. It is valued unequivocally, and when it is questioned it will have changed.

Nevertheless, culture can be created, norms initiated and ethos encouraged. It is possible through the conscious and deliberate decision of authority to do so, and history provides many examples of nations, institutions, colleges and companies that have done so. In fact, all Catholic schools were themselves deliberately established, and their original ethos was very far from a casual emergence. So, while management decision, in the absence of staff co-operation, can do very little to create or sustain ethos, without energetic, focused and wide-ranging engagement by leadership, ethos cannot be initiated nor continued.

Schools are organisations, not spontaneous gatherings, nor natural social groupings. Schools are intentional societies, created for specific goals, formed by particular groups, and directed with distinctive spirits. Management has a decisive influence on operations and spirit, because it is management.

Catholic educational ethos is no longer an unquestioned element of school culture. It is severely contested. Therefore, attention must be paid to it by those in management to see what it is and how it can be supported, and what changes need to be implemented to ensure its continuance. A target must be drawn before we aim.

Religion and school

Religion should make a difference to the way schools are run. Religious people establish schools to make a difference for religions. There are obvious differences between religions as far as education is concerned, differences that raise questions for Catholic schools.

In particular, the different educational approaches of the major religious traditions to secular learning are very striking. Hindus stress 'unfolding the individual's personality' as the core of formation in its faith, and regard secular education as entirely a separate concern, irrelevant to religion. Jews regard religious formation as understanding sacred scripture and its consequences for daily life. For them, knowledge of other subjects is extraneous or ancillary to religious knowledge. Classic Islamic education, by contrast, valued and therefore preserved secular knowledge and pursued the disciplines of human reason, but in the end, historically and practically, maintained that ultimate truth and knowledge of God is principally obtained through revelation. Eastern Orthodox Christian education is traditionally very spiritual, and focused entirely on religion; and so secular education is, for the Christian school, separate and subordinate. Protestant Christian education, on the other hand, stimulated secular learning as a sphere of activity both for receiving the Word of God by reading the Bible and for carrying out the will of God in the duties of one's state in life.

For Catholics, the exercise of human reason and scholarship is neither irrelevant for, nor contradictory to, the revelation of God. Catholic schooling absorbs secular education. Catholic schools accord 'parity of esteem' to the subjects of the general curriculum, which accounts for the strong streak of rationalism observable in typical Catholic education. The Catholic attitude to education recognises a parallel between the book of the Word and the book of the world in the quest for truth.

No less than adherents of other faiths, of course, Catholics believe that religion is the centre of human life and that God is the ultimate reality. All life, being and activity come from God and return to God. The universe is created by God and depends totally on God's will for its life and development. Nothing has value independent of God. Everything has value in so far as it shows forth the glory, the being, the goodness, the truth and the beauty of God. God is not totally separated from the created world in the Catholic view. God is the highest reality, but not the only reality.

The hand of the Creator can be discerned in a close study of creation. Furthermore, God the Father has sent the Son and the Spirit into the world to bring all people and things back together again to the Father. The doctrine of the Trinity ensures both God's presence and God's transcendence, God's sovereignty and God's dynamic providence. God is, in Donal Dorr's memorable phrase, 'God beyond us, God among us, God within us'.

Catholics recognise that this is the educational environment for every student and teacher. No knowledge is irrelevant to the search for truth. But Catholic educational theology believes that everyone and everything is separated from God by sin. Catholics are particularly conscious of failure and very aware of evil, but still hope in the coming reunification of the human race under God. Though the vision of community among all humanity may seem 'an impossible dream', it is possible in the reconciliation of Jesus Christ. The mission of the Catholic school is to convince people of this hope. The school does this by discerning the sign of the Spirit, the mystery of the Son and the face of the Creator in the revelation of Word and sacrament, and in creation, especially its aspects of integrity, goodness, truth and beauty.

This outlook on secular learning is one common to all Christian Churches, but there are other characteristics special to the Catholic approach to education, particularly as they manifest themselves in practice. These qualities distinguish the ethos of the Catholic school from other kinds of school. They have been identified as an appreciation for tradition, an emphasis on the symbolic, an insistence on worship, and a respect for community. The hard question arises: how do they differ from the qualities shown in the schools of other Christian denominations? Indeed (with the exception of worship) from the qualities exhibited in well-organised secular schools? Can the Catholic qualities of school ethos be distinguished in practice from those shown by any optimistic, genial, amiable, approachable, open, sensitive, sunny, happy, contented, energetic and concerned sets of students and teachers whom we may encounter in any school staffroom, corridor and class?

Odious comparisons

All comparisons are odious. Yet comparison and contrast remains one of the surest ways of clarifying our ideas and cataloguing our discoveries. That is why we continually ask our examination candidates to 'compare and contrast'. To 'comparison and contrast', therefore, we now turn. But we shall try to avoid making the comparisons odious, by being true to the mission and vision, not just of the Catholic school, but of other schools as well. In particular, we shall avoid pejorative labels that do less than justice to the ideals of committed educators.

The first attempt at comparison is between Christian schools and non-religious schools. We will take five kinds of school and compare them on a number of dimensions. The five kinds of school are: the Elite School, the Selective School, the Secular School, the Humanist School and the Christian School. The Comparative Dimensions are the Reference for the School, the Relationships in the School, the Purpose of the School and the Result of the School.

The Reference Dimension designates the part of the public that the school serves and to whom it looks for guidance and direction, and which it regards as a criterion for assessing its progress or lack of progress. The word 'Reference' stands for the Reference Group, which is the primary source of the school's own self-identity. It could involve a civic reference (as in the Secular School) or a religious reference (as in the 'Bible' or Christian School).

The Relationship Dimension seeks to describe the kind of atmosphere obtaining inside the school. This is notoriously difficult to put into words, yet often very clear to the observer. This dimension involves both the social and official realms; it tries to capture the quality of personal interactions, the root of personal attitudes, and the foundation for communal decision-making. Relationships can range from the co-operative to the competitive, from the idiosyncratic to the communal, and so on.

The Purpose Dimension articulates the goal of the school. This is inferred from action and choice, and not explicitly derived from formal documents and mission statements. Accordingly, some schools may well protest that the Purpose described here is not true to their vision. But these labels are comparisons suggested only for the purpose of argument and for the clarification of minds. If these suggestions lead to clearer school aims and objectives, they will have achieved their aim. For it is by this Dimension particularly that schools come to terms with installing and maintaining their Ethos. The proposed Purposes extend from Tradition, to Investment, to Redemption.

Finally, the Result Dimension captures the output or product of the school in terms of the education of students. Again, some schools may well dispute the representation provided here of their own educated student. There are two responses to that objection: one robust and the other diplomatic. The robust answer is the well-known phrase: 'If the cap fits...'. The picture of the educated student leaving one's school may not be one espoused by the staff and management of the school, but it may be recognisable by the general public (or even by alumni).

The diplomatic answer is that the school labels are generic. An individual school will not fit easily under any of them. In a manner similar to Max Weber's 'ideal types', these kinds of school will not be found in a pure form anywhere. Reality is always mixed. Accordingly, the Result, the Educated Student peculiar to each type of school, does not exist in real life. All that could be said is that the different characterisations of the educated student represent tendencies that schools would do well to consider.

FIGURE 1: COMPARISONS BETWEEN DIFFERENT KINDS OF SCHOOL

	Elite School School	Selective School	Secular School	Humanist School	Christian School
Reference	Class	Industry	Society	Humanity	Church
Relations	Sponsored	Competitive	Egalitarian	Individualist	Communal
Purpose	Tradition	Investment	Politics	Maturity	Redemption
Product	Culture	Success	Citizen	Person	Disciple

With all of this in mind, we turn to the comparison itself (Figure 1). Each of the School Types will be discussed in turn under the Dimensions for comparison.

The Elite School is intended to serve a particular Class of pupil and parent, for instance, upper middle class or high society, and this is its Reference group. Entrance is dependent on membership in an identifiable social group. The Relationship characteristic of this kind of school is a Sponsoring one, whereby suitable students are afforded access to the school, and retained by it, because of criteria other than scholastic or competitive ones. One gets into the school because of membership of a social class, and remains on, not because of success in examinations, or academic progress, or competitive edge, but simply because one is who one is. The student is 'sponsored'. The judgement is made that he or she is 'one of us'. The Purpose of the School is the handing on of Tradition. The past plays an important part in the policy of the school; the way things have always been done influences what is done now. One notices, in many such cases, alumni who are very active, and who exercise a conservative influence on the evolution and development of the school. Though obvious illustrations of the Elite School involve privileged and preferred social classes, there is no reason why other social groups might not provide other examples. The Product of the education given in the school is Culture: that is, a student familiar with and at home in the Ethos that that society can offer. Elite Schools call forth phrases like the 'old boy network', 'alma mater' and the 'old school tie'.

It has to be understood that there is nothing wrong with an Elite School. It is a very successful institution. In fact, when beginning to establish an educational tradition, the Elite School is the way to start. When education of any type is rare and unvalued, schools have to be very careful about taking only 'suitable' pupils, because the new venture cannot survive dissenting voices or counter cultures. In a way, the Elite School might manage to inculcate the public that it serves with its own Ethos in a kind of reverse reaction. The pupils are already attuned to the school values before even they enter its portals.

The Selective School takes as its Reference the world of work or Industry. Its internal Relationships are Competitive. Education for the Selective School has the Purpose of Investment. The promising pupil is encouraged to improve his or her knowledge and skill, because it increases his or her utility to professional or commercial life. Its typical Result is a student who is a Success in terms of work and employment.

How does the Selective School differ from the Elite School? The Reference is the key to this kind of school. Whatever leads to success and achievement in the world of work is what is valued in the school. These qualities can change, and in the contemporary world can change rapidly. The past has no purchase here. Otherwise, the two kinds of school can be, and often are, confused.

The Secular School corresponds to the publicly founded and funded non-denominational system intended by the State to educate all the children of the country. Its Reference Group is Society as a whole as it is represented inside the boundaries of the State. Its dominant Relationship, in Western democracies at least, is Egalitarian. Its Purpose is Political; it answers to the needs of the State as expressed by the legislature, especially as expressed in its social agenda. Its Result is the Citizen, the student ready to take his or her place in adult life as an interested and capable member of society. Obviously, in other regimes than the Western democratic one with which we are best acquainted, other Relationships and Results might apply, though the Political Purpose remains.

The Humanist School has a quite different emphasis. Its focus is the pupil as an individual. Its Reference is Humanity as such, not confined by national boundaries. Its quality of Relationship is Individual. Its educational Purpose is Maturity, as the pupil is encouraged to develop in his or her own terms to the limits of potential. The hoped-for Result is the Person, fully human and fully alive. The Irish National School 'child-centred curriculum' acquires its philosophical and educational foundation here, but its political economic driving force is the Secular School described previously. Whether or not it is a Christian School as well, in any meaningful sense, remains to be seen.

Finally, the Christian School can be compared to other kinds of school. The Christian Referent Group is the Church – not a social class, nor the world of work, nor the national society, nor humanity as a whole. It looks to the people of God, local and universal, of this age and of all the ages, committed and non-committed. Its Relationships are based on Community, not a gathering of the like-minded, but a unity of differences, young and old, committed and lukewarm, saints and sinners, with very different visions of what it is to be a Christian. Its Educational Purpose is Redemption, which acknowledges sin and failure in every human being, the evil in fallen creation, and yet the graced-filled potential for good as well. Its Result is the Disciple, a follower of Jesus, still a sinner, but filled with hope.

If these characterisations make any kind of sense to the reader, it is because the various Dimensions ring true to the atmosphere and practice found to some extent in many particular schools. They are explored here in order to clear minds and sort ideas, not to identify and describe individual schools. It is not possible to use these types to do that, because real schools exist in a mixed state. Nevertheless, sharpening one's vision is crucial as we separate one idea from another. Hopefully, this explanation helps to avoid some confusion.

Kinds of Christian religious schools

Christianity displays an array of different approaches to schooling. Even inside the education offices of various Christian Churches, different assumptions are made and different approaches constructed to the common task of education.

There are a number of possible ways of categorising approaches to Christian education. The best known is drawn from the Protestant theologian Richard Niebuhr. Niebuhr suggested over seventy years ago that there are five possible relationships between Christianity and Culture: Christ Against Culture, Christ Transforming Culture, Christ in Paradox with Culture, Christ above Culture, and Christ with Culture. Each category expresses a particular point in the relationship between Christ and Culture. These categories of Richard Niebuhr can also be employed to articulate the gamut of vision, mission and perspective available to Christian educators and schools of any denomination.

The Hartford Congregational Religious Presence Research also provides a particularly interesting categorisation. McKinney and his team at the Hartford Seminary investigated parishes and communities of all the Christian denominations (and Jewish congregations) in Hartford, Connecticut. They were interested in Religious Presence, that is, the way in which religion is present to a society. The team noticed four principal mission orientations: the Activist, the Sanctuary, the Evangelist and the Civic Orientation. The Activist parish or religious group emphasises justice issues and engagement in social and political action. The Sanctuary group focuses on worship, tradition and its doctrines in the company of committed believers. The Evangelist parish or group stresses witness and faith-sharing with others, and the Civic congregation is supportive of the social status quo, celebrating the local community. The Hartford researchers suggested that these four orientations represent different types of Religious Presence. These orientations can be linked to the four aspects of the pastoral mission of the Christian Church: *Diakonia, Leitourgia, Kerygma* and *Koinonia*, that is, Ministry, Liturgy, Announcing and Community. It is now possible to develop and elaborate a grid to outline five different kinds of Christian-school ethos.

FIGURE 2: THE DIFFERENT KINDS OF CHRISTIAN-SCHOOL ETHOS
Developed from Neibuhr and the Hartford Religious Presence Research.

RELATIONSHIP WITH CULTURE

	Against Culture	Paradox of Culture	Above Culture	Transforming Culture	With Culture
Typical Action	Ignoring Culture	Confronting Culture	Relating to Culture	Humanity Culture	Assimilating Culture
Christian Mission	–	*Kerygma* announcing	*Leitourgia* – liturgy	*Diakonia* – ministry	*Koinonia* – community
Religious Presence	Sectarian	Evangelical	Sanctuary	Social	Civic
Kind of School	Fundamentalist School	Proclaiming School	Worshipping School	Serving School	Celebrating School

The first of Neibuhr's positions, with its pastoral and educational applications, may be briefly discussed. It is the stance of Christ Against Culture, a sectarian response of defensive isolation, and is easily identified in a 'Fundamentalist School'. Mainstream Christians would be uneasy with this ethos, because it seems to fly in the face of what they would understand as any variety of Christian mission to the world. It is important to describe it, though, because some liberal educators today would identify it with a genuine Christian educational ethos.

The second position is that of Christ in Paradox to Culture, a confrontation of culture connected to the theology and mission of proclaiming the Word of God to the world. A school based on this theology and attitude to culture will be very clear about the distinctiveness of its witness and insistent on the religious contribution to every aspect of its education. Students and staff will be in no doubt of the challenge to their ideas and assumptions by gospel values. This type of school clearly corresponds to the Evangelical Religious Presence described by the Hartford team in a number of congregations in that city and reflects the *Kerygma*, one of the perennial aspects of the universal Christian mission. We call it a Proclaiming School.

The third position is Christ Above Culture. This is the classic Catholic educational theology or philosophy: grace does not deny nature, but builds on nature. Nevertheless, reality does not exhaust human potential for, at the heart of human nature, or beyond the natural world, there is another sphere – the supernatural – that equally has to be acknowledged and honoured. The parallel with the Sanctuary religious presence observed by the Hartford research is clear. The typical Catholic school, with its liturgies and ceremonies, its images and pictures, its feasts and festivals, belongs here. This is the Worshipping School, and parallels *Leitourgia*, the work of the Christian assembly to adore God in prayer, thanksgiving and penitence.

The fourth position is that of Christ Transforming Culture. This is, according to Brian Kelty, contemporary Catholic educational philosophy. He detects it in the Second Vatican Council's move towards the signs of the times and the needs of the world. In this view, culture has to be changed and transformed by the Christian gospel. The Church in its mission must engage with the contemporary culture, and the educational mission of the Christian School is not immune from this challenge. Hence, we can place in this category the Christian School that emphasises social activism and service of the poor – the Serving School – discerning here another aspect of the perennial Christian mission – *Diakonia* or ministry.

Finally, the fifth position – Christ and Culture- is seen in Christian communities that exist in reasonable harmony with the surrounding society. Culture and world are not perceived as hostile to Christianity. Indeed, Christianity reinforces and bolsters the status quo. Such a Christian congregation, in the Hartford research, was designated as Civic, indicating its happy relationship with public authorities, with the general population, and with its social environment. Christian Schools that play a part in the country's general educational provision will probably be coloured with not a little 'civic' gloss. Such a school is characterised here as a Celebrating School, assimilating the culture, creating a supportive community for students and staff, but one that generally conforms to the prevailing norms and conventions of its society. This is not to say that the Church, congregation or school that finds itself in this position is acting against gospel values. One of the aspects of the mission of all Christians is the creation of community – *Koinonia* – and that must inevitably at times involve compromise and the creating of common ground with the surrounding culture, especially at times and in places where culture seems to be particularly amenable to Christian values.

Catholic-school religious ethos

A conceptual framework is useful for locations, connections and omissions. It is useful for locations, that is, to show where an idea pops up, what is its origin, how it develops, what it can lead to. It is of assistance, too, for connections, in order to demonstrate the relationship of ideas to one another, where they differ, and where they are similar, what is their range, how they compare and contrast. Finally, it is invaluable for omissions, to see if there are any ideas left out, or ignored, or obscured. A conceptual framework points towards new ideas as well as measuring the territory covered by old ones.

This article offers a conceptual framework of School Religious Ethos. In effect, it suggests a target, an area at which a school administrator can aim one's efforts. The conceptual framework tries to be faithful to the theological mission of education, to the educational realities of school practice, and to the variety of religious educational mission.

Furthermore, it demonstrates how the social environment of an educational institution or the theological stance of an educator can, and perhaps ought, to result in contrasting practices. Teachers and educational administrators, religious professionals and ministers, parents and politicians can use this framework to make sense of their observations.

If it does nothing else, this conceptual framework, or target for the educator's aim, can clarify an argument between David Tuohy, Teresa McCormack and Peter Archer in recent issues of *Studies*. Tuohy advocates the 'evangelical' model of Catholic education in contradistinction to Archer and McCormack's alleged espousal of the 'social' or counter-cultural model. He also reads Irish Catholic education history as involving an educational emphasis on the 'individual'. Many traditional Catholic catechists and teachers, however, would adhere to the 'sanctuary' or worshipping school model, with class Masses and retreats and prayers and devotions. Others principals and teachers, however, maintain that their aim is to develop a school community, inclusive and supportive of all the individual students, clearly in terms of the religious conceptual framework offered here, a 'civic and celebrating' aim.

The conceptual framework or ethos target outlined here does not resolve the educational or historical arguments about the Irish Catholic-school system. It does, however, suggest that there are four legitimate types of Christian educational mission. Accordingly, there are four typical Christian ethoi in our schools. It would be true to say that the 'worshipping school' would have been typical of the Catholic school in the past, that the 'serving or celebrating school' would be the typical Catholic school in the present. Whether or not we need a return to more worship, or an injection of proclamation, is a matter of aim and eye.

The Culture and Ethos Process:
Releasing the future of the Catholic school

Noel Canavan

Introduction

The purpose of this paper is to show that the culture and ethos process is useful to Catholic schools that want to review and renew their mission; useful to those schools that want to release the potential of their community. The project's aim was to produce a specific process, tools and a theoretical model that could be used to describe the culture and ethos of any school. Given that the process was not specifically designed for Catholic schools, we will examine the various aspects of the process, and the tools and theoretical model that were developed as part of it in order to draw attention to those aspects that are crucial for Catholics to focus on in the light of some of the main concepts and thinking on Catholic education. But before we do so we will look at what renowned Catholic educators have to say about the benefit of looking at a school's culture and ethos in terms of enabling a school to live out its Catholic mission.

The culture and ethos that a Catholic school has is important with regard to that school fulfilling its purpose and vision. If the culture and ethos values are not in keeping with the aims of Catholic schooling and with the aims and processes of a Catholic philosophy of education, then the school will not be able to create the kind of community that is necessary to educate persons and to nurture their growth and development. So, having a handle, as it were, on culture and ethos allows one to lead effectively. If we do not know where we come from and where we are, it is difficult to plan for the future.

The need for a culture and ethos review

In order to release the future of the Catholic school it is necessary to know what the school culture and ethos is. Being aware of the value set that drives the school culture will enable the school to check the integrity of its value set against the charism or founding values and, in a Catholic school, against the objective understanding of what it means to be a Catholic school. As Barry Dwyer says:

> Exploring the aspects of a school's culture gives [school] communities a chance to reflect more deeply on the nature of the school and to identify aspects that are consistent with or antagonistic to the gospel vision. Such a cultural review would go well beyond the more superficial approaches to school evaluation which often focus on meeting formal requirements, organisational efficiency, and public relations.[1]

Thomas Groome also states:

> Every school should look regularly at its whole environment and review its many aspects for integrity with the values the school intends to teach.[2]

Marino School culture and ethos process

I am proposing that the culture and ethos process developed by the culture and ethos project at Marino will enable schools to describe their present culture and the values that drive it and that this process will be an important way for Catholic schools to reculture their schools and live their mission with integrity as proposed by Groome and Dwyer. The process will enable them to state their culture and ethos explicitly and to identify if changes need to be made when they compare what is with what is desirable. Let us now describe the Marino Culture and Ethos Process in general.

The School Culture and Ethos Process was developed for Marino Institute of Education at the Centre for Education Services in the Institute. The process is a result of research carried out in both primary and secondary schools, both Catholic and Protestant, north and south of the border, in Ireland. A conference on School Culture and Ethos was also held at City West Hotel in the year 2000. As a result of this conference and the research, a culture and ethos process was developed which enables schools to describe their culture and ethos in a systematic way and also to make changes to that culture and ethos if it is deemed necessary.

As well as containing all the tools and materials necessary to carry out a review of a school's culture and ethos, the pack also contains a dynamic model of how culture and ethos works in a school. This model facilitates the identification of appropriate intervention strategies. In order to support and encourage schools to engage in this process the Centre for Education Services at Marino Institute of Education also trains members of school staffs to be able to facilitate the culture and ethos process in their own school. In short, the School Culture and Ethos Project has provided a process, tools, materials, a model and training which will enable schools to describe their culture and ethos and to initiate change if necessary. The whole process was also designed to lock into the Department of Education and Science school planning initiatives at both primary and secondary level by providing a description of ethos necessary for a school plan.

The Culture and Ethos Process (CEP) in question is available in a resource pack – 'School Culture and Ethos: Releasing the Potential'[3] – so a general overview of the process will be given here (see fig. 3.1). (The numbering of figures here corresponds to that used in the resource pack.) The key stages and elements of the process are as follows: data collection, dialogue 1, dialogue 2, and policy formulation and implementation.

Data collection
Specialised questionnaires are used to gather accurate data about all aspects of school life in terms of values and culture. The resulting data is then organised and synthesised into a coherent statement of what the culture and ethos of the school is at the time of the investigation. The questionnaires also provide some data on what the culture and ethos of the school was in the past and what values the participants would like to see being expressed in the culture in the future. All of this information is presented to the teachers, parents and students who participated in the study and to a wider audience of parents and students in the school if this is deemed appropriate. It is highly recommended to do this.

Dialogue 1 (see fig 2.3.3)
At the next stage a dialogue (Dialogue 1) is entered into between the facilitators of the process and the participants to make sure that the detailed statement of what the present culture and ethos is deemed to be is correct and free of major bias. Any agreed corrections to the statement are noted and all of the findings go into a written report. The clarifications and additions arrived at through the dialogue process are placed in appendices. The report is then made public.

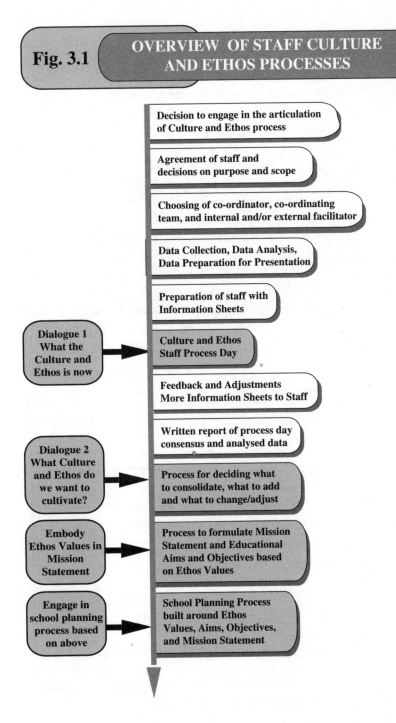

Fig. 3.1 OVERVIEW OF STAFF CULTURE AND ETHOS PROCESSES

Decision to engage in the articulation of Culture and Ethos process

Agreement of staff and decisions on purpose and scope

Choosing of co-ordinator, co-ordinating team, and internal and/or external facilitator

Data Collection, Data Analysis, Data Preparation for Presentation

Preparation of staff with Information Sheets

Dialogue 1
What the Culture and Ethos is now → Culture and Ethos Staff Process Day

Feedback and Adjustments More Information Sheets to Staff

Written report of process day consensus and analysed data

Dialogue 2
What Culture and Ethos do we want to cultivate? → Process for deciding what to consolidate, what to add and what to change/adjust

Embody Ethos Values in Mission Statement → Process to formulate Mission Statement and Educational Aims and Objectives based on Ethos Values

Engage in school planning process based on above → School Planning Process built around Ethos Values, Aims, Objectives, and Mission Statement

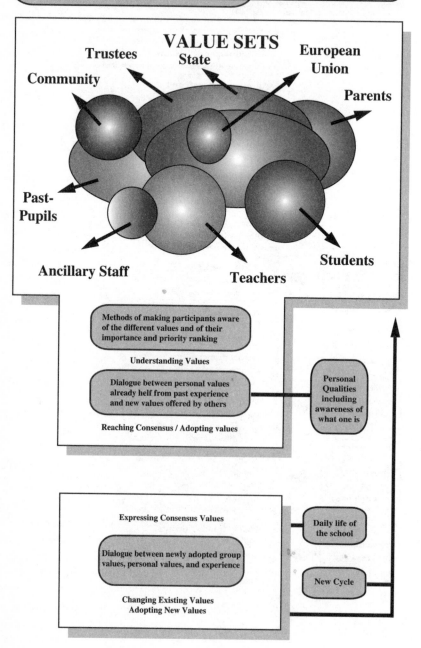

Fig. 2.3.3   **THE DIALOGUE PROCESS**

VALUE SETS

Trustees State European Union

Community

Parents

Past-Pupils

Students

Ancillary Staff   Teachers

Methods of making participants aware of the different values and of their importance and priority ranking

Understanding Values

Dialogue between personal values already helf from past experience and new values offered by others

Reaching Consensus / Adopting values

Personal Qualities including awareness of what one is

Expressing Consensus Values

Dialogue between newly adopted group values, personal values, and experience

Changing Existing Values Adopting New Values

Daily life of the school

New Cycle

Dialogue 2

When the school community have been given sufficient time to read, absorb and discuss the content of the report, a second dialogue process (Dialogue 2) is entered into to allow the community to consider those elements of the culture and ethos that are toxic, those that are acceptable, and those that are desirable but missing. It is at this point that an explicit annunciation of the values that Catholic Education aspires to should be placed before the partners who are engaged in the dialogue process. It is in this way that the school is recultured and the value set that underpins that culture is formally identified and accepted as part of the overall set that will be put into practice. In a Catholic school this value set should be in keeping with a Catholic world view and value set.

As the culture and ethos of a school is dynamic and changing, the official formally stated and agreed ethos and culture will soon come into conflict with new value sets, which will enter into competition with the official set. This is why constant review is always necessary if there is to be a real congruence between the officially stated culture and ethos and the one in operation on a day-to-day basis.

Policies and implementation

When all the partners have agreed as to what constitutes the value set that will underpin the work of the school, these values have to be translated into policies, structures and procedures. Leadership is always important, but very much so at this stage of the process.

The culture and ethos process and Catholic educational philosophy

We will now examine various aspects of the process to see if the process itself is in keeping with Catholic values and educational philosophy. This is important because participation in the process itself becomes part of the reculturing of the school and it is therefore vital that the kind of participation enabled is in keeping with the Catholic philosophy of education that one wants to see being lived out in the school. The parts and aspects of the process, especially the theoretical model, that are the most important for Catholic educators to focus on in their attempt to renew and reculture their schools, will also be highlighted.

One of the main concepts in a Catholic philosophy of education is the building up of a Christian community and respect for the individual. The structure of the culture and ethos process helps to build community and to encourage the development of personhood in individuals. Community formation is facilitated because data is collected from parents, students and teachers, and these three groups are involved at the various dialogue stages and participate in creating a vision that they will share with other members of the community. Individual personhood is developed by facilitating and encouraging individuals at the dialogue stages to become aware of their personal values and to choose new ones in freedom, if necessary. It would be important for Catholic leaders to ensure that all these processes are carried out within an atmosphere of Christian spirituality and prayer so that both the individual and the community come progressively to centre on the person of Jesus Christ.

The dialogue processes are the core of the whole culture and ethos process. It is here that values meet: charism values, organisational values and personal values. People become aware of the whole set of different values. Discussion takes place. If this process is handled properly it allows for individuals to choose values, it respects people's dignity, allows for inclusion, sharing, co-operation, tolerance, understanding, and a search for meaning. It mirrors what one expects teachers to do in the classroom, where educational dialogue takes place.

Many of the personal qualities required for the development of the person can be cultivated in these dialogue sessions: critical thinking, active participation, development of self, self-revelation, honesty, respect for others, justice and compassion. Committee work can be seen as service, freeing people from personal inadequacy and self-absorption. The spiritual aspects of Catholicism should also be cultivated and prayer encouraged.

Thus the dialogue processes can release the potential and the creative imagination of the group, individuals can grow, and the whole process, if handled correctly and carried out in a manner that is in keeping with a Catholic philosophy of education, will mirror the kind of community and relationships that one would like to see being lived out on a daily basis in the school.

This approach to the dialogue stages would prepare the way for deeper staff development, which in turn would enrich the next dialogue process, as the more developed the participants on a personal level the richer the dialogue processes will be. We need good facilitators and leaders for this to happen.

The atmosphere created should enable participants to set themselves free from the brokenness that hinders them from being what God intended them to be. There ought to be a sense of hope. We live in a redeemed world. Failings and limitations can be overcome and our school communities can be renewed. The use of creative imagination should be encouraged for visioning and participants should be encouraged to engage in reflective practice.

Now that we have looked at the structure of the overall process and have shown how it is in keeping with a Catholic philosophy of education, we will examine the theoretical model of culture and ethos to see what parts of it Catholic leaders should pay most attention to if they are to gather the relevant data necessary to review their culture and ethos and to understand how culture and ethos works. This will enable them to make appropriate interventions to reculture their Catholic schools if and when necessary.

The theoretical model (Fig 2.3)

The theoretical model of how culture and ethos works in a school setting underpins the design of the data-gathering tools – the questionnaires. As most of the questions gather data about different aspects of the theoretical model we will only examine various aspects of the model and not the questionnaires. All aspects of the culture and ethos of a school are of interest to the school community. However, there are some parts that are more important than others and especially for the school that wants to provide a Catholic education. Let us now examine the parts of the model that would be of crucial importance for Catholic educators to explore and emphasise. How each part relates to Catholic principles of education will be outlined and comment will be made based on the insights gained while researching and carrying out the school culture and ethos processes in different types of schools.

Founding purpose and charism

The founding purpose of a religious order and its charism is based on the gospel message. It usually emphasises an aspect of that message. This part of the model would be of immense importance to a Catholic school. The founding purpose and charism of a school is the equivalent of corporate culture in the business world. For business, getting the corporate and organisational cultures to harmonise is usually a challenge. It is the same for all schools and particularly for schools that require a specific culture and ethos to be lived out in their school. How does one get both to agree?

This is where the whole culture and ethos process has meaning. By establishing what the culture and ethos of a school is and by engaging in dialogue processes as outlined above, any dissonance between what Catholic culture and ethos requires and what pertains in the school can be addressed. This can be done in a manner that builds Christian community and liberates members of that community to choose to work out of a set of Christian values.

In reality, there is a big problem in this area in schools. Teachers, students and parents are not actively aware of the educational philosophy of Catholic

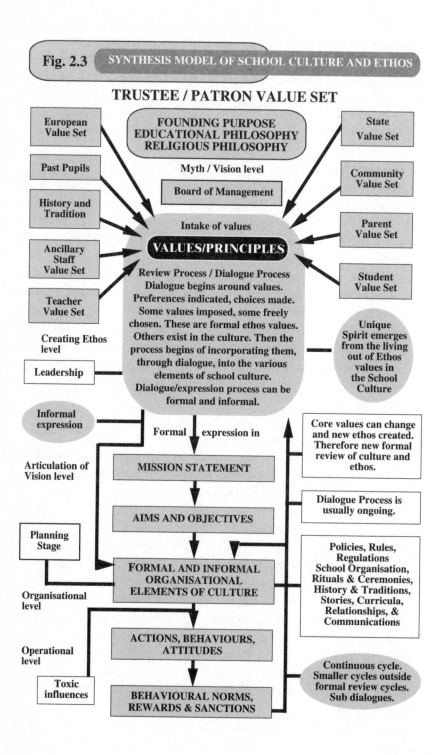

Fig. 2.3 SYNTHESIS MODEL OF SCHOOL CULTURE AND ETHOS

TRUSTEE / PATRON VALUE SET

European Value Set

FOUNDING PURPOSE EDUCATIONAL PHILOSOPHY RELIGIOUS PHILOSOPHY

State Value Set

Past Pupils

Myth / Vision level

Community Value Set

Board of Management

History and Tradition

Intake of values

Parent Value Set

Ancillary Staff Value Set

VALUES/PRINCIPLES

Student Value Set

Teacher Value Set

Review Process / Dialogue Process
Dialogue begins around values.
Preferences indicated, choices made.
Some values imposed, some freely
chosen. These are formal ethos values.
Others exist in the culture. Then the
process begins of incorporating them,
through dialogue, into the various
elements of school culture.
Dialogue/expression process can be
formal and informal.

Creating Ethos level

Leadership

Unique Spirit emerges from the living out of Ethos values in the School Culture

Informal expression

Formal expression in

Core values can change and new ethos created. Therefore new formal review of culture and ethos.

Articulation of Vision level

MISSION STATEMENT

Dialogue Process is usually ongoing.

Planning Stage

AIMS AND OBJECTIVES

Policies, Rules, Regulations
School Organisation, Rituals & Ceremonies, History & Traditions, Stories, Curricula, Relationships, & Communications

FORMAL AND INFORMAL ORGANISATIONAL ELEMENTS OF CULTURE

Organisational level

Operational level

ACTIONS, BEHAVIOURS, ATTITUDES

Toxic influences

Continuous cycle. Smaller cycles outside formal review cycles. Sub dialogues.

BEHAVIOURAL NORMS, REWARDS & SANCTIONS

schools. How can these values be brought into the discussion during the dialogue stage of the process if they are not known to the school community! A series of induction days and a programme of preparation in Christian spirituality and the principles of Catholic education would be necessary in order to benefit from the dialogue stages.

Relationship with Catholic communities/parish/Vatican

One of the distinguishing characteristics of a Catholic school is that it is part of a larger and wider community: the parish community, the national Church and the worldwide Church. These are aspects that a Catholic school would value and use to the full. It is important that aspects of the school culture in relation to outside communities are examined in great detail. How does the school community view its relationship with these other communities?

This aspect is neglected in some schools or is not very developed. Some schools have programmes to send students to Africa or India to do social work and to become aware of the poverty and deprivation in the world community. Some schools do not seem to have a policy of integrating themselves into the local community and the parish community. This integration happens more naturally with primary schools. There is an opportunity here to promote one of the most important aspects of Catholic education – the evangelisation of the wider society.

Relationship with the secular culture

The European community and the Department of Education and Science, through directives and laws and the examination system, have a huge influence on the culture and values of a school. At times this can go against the idea of the Catholic school being counter-cultural and changing society. These influences, especially the points system, make it difficult for schools to focus on personhood and creating a school community that supports the development of personhood as defined by Emmanuel Mounier,[4] the French personalist philosopher.

In schools one gets the impression that the influence is just accepted as a given, with no chance of changing it. Perhaps it is not seen as a problem. A group of parents that we encountered thought that personal values such as relationships, maturity and purposeful learning were achieved through engagement in State examinations. The primary values contributed were in the area of the academic, which gave a sense of structure and discipline to students.

From this it is perhaps the case that most parents see the State examination system as being positive rather than negative, and this is why it has not changed. This poses problems for Catholic educators who want to ensure that the curriculum and examination system reflect Catholic Christian values. It needs to be investigated and incorporated into the discussion on curriculum. This may not be a problem for teachers either, as a large percentage tend to be very practical in nature and may see the points system as a practical solution to a difficult problem.

Relationship with parents and students

The data generated by the questionnaires will be useful in revealing whether the ethos and culture of the school supports the Catholic view of community, inclusiveness and the concept that parents are the primary educators of their children. Structures would need to be put in place to enable real participation by parents and students in school life. This is happening in some schools at present.

However, schools would be weak in this area and it is also part of the wider problem that they have in relating with the wider society. It is less of a problem for primary schools. Teachers at second level have great fears of interference from parents in what they consider their professional domain. The culture around the real participation of parents in the life of the school is going to be difficult to change.

Leadership

This aspect is of major importance to Catholic schools. In Irish education there is at present a lack of training in leadership, and especially in Catholic leadership. Apart from the usual tasks of leadership, a Catholic school leader would need to be able to build up a faith community and to draw people to a vision of education based on Christian values. According to Ken Blanchard,[5] the best style of leadership would be that of a servant leader. Servant leaders are concerned with spiritual significance. Spiritual significance is about who you are in relationship with God. Effective leadership comes from the inside. Jesus wants us to change, to become new people by surrendering to the transforming power of God's unconditional love. The aim of servant leaders is the best interest of those they serve.

The leadership aspect of the culture and ethos process is really important. A school needs a good leader in order to prepare for and carry through on all the work of the dialogue stages. A Catholic leader has even more to do. The leader is the person who communicates the corporate value set and vision to the staff and enables them to grow through an example of Christian service. In reality, this is not happening in many schools. We need training for aspiring, newly appointed and practising principals. If the leadership is weak in a school, the dialogue stages of the process will not work well and could cause more problems than are solved. In this situation a school might be better served in sorting out the leadership issues before engaging in the process of review and renewal.

Formal organisational elements of culture: Signs and symbols/rituals and ceremonies/history and tradition
The signs and symbols, rituals and ceremonies in a school reflect and express the underlying values of the school and, therefore, great care should be taken with regard to these areas. Cultivating an interest in the history and traditions of the school can be vital in passing on values that are core for the community. The data-gathering questionnaires will provide a large amount of information and an examination of the data will suggest ways to proceed in furthering the principles of Catholic education.

These areas contribute to many of the key concepts of a Catholic education being put into practice. They can help in creating the right atmosphere, in building a Christian faith community, in fostering a shared vision, in facilitating positive relationships among the community, and offer unique opportunities to express respect and gratitude to specific people. Leaders need to understand these areas and to use them.

From our research experience the difference between schools is immense in relation to these aspects. Signs and symbols are the worst. Staffs cannot agree on what values the signs and symbols represent. There is a wide variety of interpretation. This would suggest that it is not sufficient to place symbols on corridors and not explain what they mean. In some schools the rituals, like Mass and carol services, seem to have a non-religious meaning. They are simply regarded as community-bonding activities. There is a huge problem in Catholic schools in terms of practising Christian inspired values without wanting to mention Christ explicitly.

Relationships/Communication
How persons relate in a school is central to the whole idea of the development of individual personhood and community formation. This would be one of the brightest areas on the model if areas vital to releasing the potential of the members of the school community were to be lit up. A community is a collection of persons who relate. Community also involves the idea of developing faith, belonging, acceptance and trust. How relationships are in the community is therefore vital. We transcend our limitations and brokenness if we are supported by a loving community. Jean Vannier's ideas on community would be ideal for Catholic schools. The questionnaires generate large amounts of data on the state of the relationships in the school and this information is vital to enable changes to be made if all is not well.

Some schools do not have great communication systems and the relationships between members of the community are not always great. Some Catholic schools do not seem to settle disputes in a Christian way. A Christian community involves the concepts of belonging, connectedness and interdependence. It also involves friendship, co-operation and partnership. If disputes are left unattended and not addressed, this destroys the fabric of the community. We are all called to holiness and love. Tolerance of mistakes and weaknesses is not part of the culture of some schools. Principals are afraid of staff, staff are afraid of each other, and the students and parents are at times afraid of both. This is not a right basis for Christian community formation.

Overall, I feel that the whole area of the development of personhood and community is neglected and also that of a faith community with each person being encouraged to develop a loving relationship with Jesus and with each other. Teachers are not willing to mirror major Christian concepts in their classrooms and in their relationships in school.

Rules and regulations/rewards and sanctions

All schools need rules and regulations. In terms of the culture and ethos process the data produced in regard to these areas is of major interest to Catholic educators. The rules and regulations should serve to promote and develop the Christian community and the person within it. There are always toxic elements in any culture and these have to be dealt with in accordance with gospel values. This also brings up issues around discipline.

According to Groome, the whole area of discipline is important in regard to the moral climate of a school. He says:

> I suspect, however, that the touchstone of the moral culture of a school is how it administers discipline. This measures the school's integrity and effectiveness in forming students in a host of the great virtues, including justice and non-violence, respect and responsibility, mercy and compassion.[6]

The area of discipline surfaces so often in all work in schools that we gave it its own category in the analysis of the questionnaires. Staffs are obsessed with it. It is central to the Catholic school but unfortunately has been reduced to control. So, while great strides have been made in other aspects of relationships, these can be undone by staffs who falter at this hurdle – afraid to devise a system based on Christian values. If justice, compassion and forgiveness are central to Catholic thought, then the school must pay great attention to the area of discipline, rewards and sanctions, rules and regulations. The actions, behaviours and attitudes of members of the school community are central to the attempt to foster Catholic-school values. In practice, these areas are not reflected upon with enough creative imagination.

Curriculum

In terms of the normal culture and ethos process, the values that underpin the curriculum seem to concentrate on achievement and the requirements of the examination system. The evangelisation of the curriculum is central to Catholic education. As Barry Dwyer says, a Catholic curriculum helps students to find meaning and to make sense of the world. It should help develop the spirit, the will, as well as the mind and body. Students must be taught that success does not necessarily mean worldly success. Members of the school community should realise that there is a Christian response to life's questions and to the nature of reality.

In reality, schools compartmentalise the curriculum, and this would be opposed to a Catholic world view because there is a loss of unity, simplicity, and a holistic approach to life. Service to others is not encouraged in a lot of schools and neither is a spiritual and prayer life outside the religion class. For example, how many school guidance counsellors ask their students to pray about their career choice?

Conclusion

According to Barry Dwyer the task of the Catholic School is to pass on beliefs, values and behaviours that humanise us and enable our spirit. A Catholic school with an evangelised curriculum centred on the person of Jesus Christ should enable members of that community, including parents, students and teachers, to search for personal meaning and self-knowledge; to develop their faith in order to make a personal response to Jesus' invitation to love; to want to engage in prophetic action, to give witness to the kingdom; to develop critical thinking, independence of thought, and the ability to challenge value systems not in keeping with the Christian message.

Catholics believe that society can be regenerated, that the world can be renewed. We are a people of hope. As a result of the Resurrection our status as human beings is raised. We value social justice, freedom, and caring for the poor and the oppressed. Let us embrace these values and make our schools places that transform the person and eventually society.

Notes

1. Barry Dwyer, *Catholic Schools: Creating a New Culture* (Newtown NSW: E.J. Dwyer (Australia) Pty Ltd, 1993), p .28.
2. Thomas Groome, *Educating for Life* (Allen, Texas: Thomas Moore, 1998), p. 207.
3. Noel Canavan and Luke Monahan, *School Culture and Ethos: Releasing the Potential* (Dublin: Marino Institute of Education, 2000).
4. Emmanuel Mounier, *Personalism* (London: Routledge and Keegan Paul Ltd, 1952). Translated by Philip Maret.
5. Ken Blanchard, *Leadership by the Book* (London: HarperCollins Publishing, 1999).
6. Thomas Groome, *Educating for Life*, p. 207.

Bibliography

Blanchard, Ken; Hughes, Bill; Hodges, Phil, *Leadership by the Book* (London: HarperCollins, 1999).

Vannier, Jean, *Community and Growth* (London: Darton, Longman and Todd, 1979).

Dwyer, Barry, *Catholic Schools: Creating a New Culture* (Newtown NSW: E.J. Dwyer (Australia) Pty Ltd, 1993).

Mounier, Emmanuel, *Personalism,* Translated by Philip Maret (London: Routledge and Keegan Paul Ltd, 1952).

Groome, Thomas, *Educating for Life* (Allen, Texas: Thomas Moore, 1998).

Canavan, Noel and Monahan, Luke, *School Culture and Ethos: Releasing the Potential* (Dublin: Marino Institute of Education, 2000).

Furlong, C. and Monahan, L. (2000), *School Culture and Ethos: Cracking the Code* (Dublin: Marino Institute of Education).

Mapping the Search for Identity:
Accessing the core characteristics of the Christian Brother network of schools

Seamus O'Brien and Tommy Coyle

Mapping the search for identity is a particularly apt description of the processes utilised by this research project over the past three years. The cartographers who produced the recent Discovery series of ordnance survey maps surveyed a landscape that had in many respects been transformed since it was last mapped twenty years previously. The new motorways, bypasses, apartment blocks and housing estates are the most obvious evidence of this transformation. If we roll back the carpet on the educational landscape and specifically the Christian Brother educational landscape, an even more significant transformation is revealed. Less than twenty years ago all the schools had Christian Brother principals, several brothers taught in each school and there were no boards of management. The typical Christian Brother campus comprised a primary school, a monastery and a post-primary school. The monastery was the locus of identity formulation, and a succinct formulation of the identity of the school then was a school administered by a Christian Brother and in which a number of brothers taught.

When we survey the Christian Brother educational landscape today we can almost say that the past is a different country. Boards of management/governors now administer all the schools; there is just one remaining Christian Brother principal at post-primary level and a handful at primary level in the 122 schools that now comprise the network. Many of the monasteries have closed and those that remain are no longer an integral part of the Christian Brother campus. However, despite this transformation, significant elements of continuity can be discerned. Almost 90 per cent of the lay principals at primary level were either appointed from their own staffs or were promoted from other Christian Brother schools. The corresponding figure at post-primary level is almost 75 per cent. There is only one female principal at post-primary level and a handful at primary level. Also, a significant proportion of the teachers in the schools were either educated by or taught with Christian Brothers.

Despite these elements of continuity the fundamental question of definition remained – how to define the identity of the schools network in the post Christian Brother era. It was in this context that the trustees, in consultation with the education offices of both Irish provinces of the Christian Brothers, commissioned the Centre for Education Services in Marino to carry out a quantitative and qualitative survey of the schools network in September 1999.

Objectives:
•   To sensitise the stakeholders to the issues and possibilities in the schools network.
•   To map and articulate the core values of Christian Brother education.
•   To enable the school communities to access a precise understanding of the Christian Brother educational identity – its foundational values, beliefs and structures.
•   To articulate key principals around which the Christian Brother school can plan for the future.

Methodology
A consultative ethos underpinned the methodological approach at all three stages – research, implementation and planning phases. This was and remains a defining element of the research methodology. It is based on the following principles:

•   Change and planning for moving forward emerges from within; it cannot be imposed from outside.
•   Accepted organisational development strategies suggest that significant and productive change only occurs through maximum participation of members and shared responsibility for that change.

The consultative-collaborative model designed for this project evolved since the first statement of the philosophy of Christian Brother education was issued in 1986. This statement, now referred to as Schedule 2, was formulated following consultations conducted within the religious orders, which probably accounts for its general theological tone. Each congregation adapted it to suit its own particular requirements. As boards of management/governors were established and increasing numbers of lay principals were appointed it became obvious that more extensive consultations with the lay partners would be necessary. These consultations coincided with a significant re-evaluation of the core values of a Christian Brother school as the sesquicentennial commemorations of the founder's death took place in 1994. His subsequent beatification by Pope John Paul II in Rome in 1996 augmented the search for a new Ricean ideology or identity for the network of schools. A conference organised by St Helen's province in 1994 focused on education and social justice; this represented the first step in the evolution from the traditional perception of a Christian Brother school, which was stereotypically functional, effective, conservative and defined by the presence of a Christian Brother principal, as well as by its extracurricular sporting activities. This ethos was essentially pragmatic, reflecting the philosophy espoused in the Christian Brother motto – *facere et docere*. This sufficed in the more stable pre-Vatican II era, when the articulation of a vision and a belief system was not deemed necessary but was challenged by the rapid societal changes that occurred in Ireland in the post-councilor era. A creative tension emerged between this purely pragmatic approach and the more idealistic pastoral identity associated with the emerging Ricean ethos. The search for identity was now increasingly focused on the ideals espoused by Edmund Rice.

The colloquium organised by St Mary's province in 1997, following the beatification ceremonies, furthered this search for a new radical identity for the schools network, which would be distinctive on the educational landscape of third millennium Ireland. Significantly, the emphasis was now on the vision and values of the Christian Brother school. We were essentially witnessing the transformation from a Christian Brother ethos to a Ricean ideology. This transformation of identity impacted on the schools as new iconographical representations of the founder were placed in the schools and new social-action initiatives such as the Edmund Rice Awards and the Third World Immersion programmes in India and Zambia were instituted.

The Education Act of 1998 enshrined in legislation the schools' right to articulate and live out of what was called 'the characteristic spirit of the school'. This is the context from which the decision to commission this research emerged; it was essentially an evolution from the prescriptive tone of Schedule 2 through the increasingly consultative approaches of the conference and colloquium models to what is now an essentially community context, as each school is facilitated in reflecting on the organisational identity as well as being enabled to articulate its own particular identity.

The process and the product

Three distinctive phases emerged during the current three-year duration of this project. The research phase encompassed the first year of the project. All the partners were invited to complete the survey questionnaires, which were designed in consultation with the ESRI. The main objective of the survey questionnaire was to enable the stakeholders to identify and prioritise the core values of an ideal Christian Brother school and then compare this to the reality in their own school. The principles underpinning this approach were based on the belief that the first step in the perpetuation of values is their identification and that these values are identified subsequent to the articulation of vision. The identification and prioritisation of the value set gave a valuable snapshot of the core characteristics of a Christian Brother school on the cusp of the new millennium. They are indicative of a network in transition, as the more pastoral approach of the nineties took precedence over the comparatively narrow functional approach of the previous era. Elements of continuity are also evident as three of the stakeholders prioritised effective discipline as the core value of a Christian Brother school. A strong sense of organisational identity at principal and board of management level also emerged from this survey. This is evident from the order of priority they apportioned to the core values of Catholic ethos and the Edmund Rice charism. This differentiation in levels of engagement with and ownership of the Christian Brother identity was a significant finding of the second part of the survey questionnaire. The level of ownership of the Christian Brother identity of the schools was in direct proportion to the level of engagement the various stakeholders felt they had with the organisational structures at trustee and education office levels. Consequently, the principals and the board members had a very high level of ownership of the identity, whereas teachers were least engaged with this concept. This reflects the fact that the principals meet regularly as a group, are conversant with trustee thinking and are actively engaged in defining the identity of their schools. The absence of a strong sense of identity with the network at teacher level reflects the dearth of developmental work processed with these vital stakeholders and suggests the need for regional or provincial gatherings of teachers if a sense of ownership of the philosophy of the network is desired at this level.

The qualitative research was conducted with a representative sample of twenty-three school communities from all over the country. Three guiding principles were utilised to sensitise the stakeholders to the issues and possibilities around the concept of identity:

- Founding intention of their school and the network of schools.
- Inherited legacy over two centuries.
- Lifeline of the school.

Linear and conceptual models were also used to enable the partners to access the particular identity of their school and to reflect on the organisational culture as it evolved over time. A particularly effective model utilised during the action-research phase was called the 'life line' of the school. This methodology portrayed identity as an evolving, dynamic organic concept and utilised the school communities' lived experiences in the network as the basis for discovering the various layers of identity in the selected schools in the lifetime of the current stakeholders. This methodology was successful as it enabled school staffs to name the core values of their schools as these were espoused by principals in particular. The researcher's role in this process was that of catalyst, listener and formulator of the emerging core values. This mapping exercise entailed sketching the context of Christian Brother education, as it was currently perceived by the partners, and the context for its potential development.

The eight core values identified by the two methodologies formed the basis for the final report on the research findings, *Towards an Identity and a Contribution*. Summary and pamphlet versions of the main findings were also produced and these formed the basis for the implementation phase, which is currently underway throughout the network. The need to set down clearly defined future directions for Christian Brother education became obvious during the implementation phase. The approach during the planning phase was also premised on the belief that any plan for moving forward would emerge from within the network and could not be imposed from the outside. There was also a need, however, to set down clearly defined future directions around which the Christian Brother school communities could build their school plan. The **Four Pillars** – Forming a Faith Community, Creating a Caring School, Seeking Excellence and Fostering Leadership – are a synthesis of the core values identified by the partners. They also challenge today's school communities to vision the distinctive layer they will add to the evolving palimpsest that is Christian Brother education in Ireland.

Bibliography

Grace, Gerald, *Catholic Schools, Mission, Markets and Morality* (London, 2002).

Judge, Harry, *Faith Based Schools and the State* (Oxford, 2001).

Canavan, N., Monahan., L, *School Culture and Ethos: Releasing the Potential* (Dublin: Marino, 2000).

O'Brien, S., Coyle, T., *Towards an Identity and a Contribution, The Christian Brother Network of Schools* (Dublin: Marino, 2001).

Hogan, P. and Williams, K. (eds), *The Future of Religion in Irish Education* (Dublin, 1997).

Cassidy E. G. (ed.), *Faith and Culture in the Irish Context* (Dublin, 1996).

Blake, D., *A Man for Our Time* (Dublin, 1994).

Monahan, L., 'Charting the way forward for Catholic Schools in Ireland', a paper presented to the AMCSS Killarney, 1999.

Groome, T., *Educating for Life* (London, 1998).

Vatican Documents: *The Catholic School* (1997); *Lay Catholics in Schools: Witness to Faith* (1982); *The Religious Dimension of Education in a Catholic School* (1998); *The Catholic School on the Threshold of the Third Millennium* (1998).

Trusteeship:
A Model in Progress

Marie Celine Clegg, IBVM

The title of this workshop was carefully negotiated with the conference organisers to ensure that those choosing to attend would understand that they were not about to be presented with a finished product or template but, rather, with a model in progress. CORI Education Commission initiated a study on three models of trusteeship in the mid to late nineties. There were two collaborative models: congregations of similar charism coming together nationally or schools of all congregations in a particular region forming a single trust. The third model – all the schools of one congregation being placed under a single trust – was the one chosen by Loreto (Institute of the Blessed Virgin Mary – IBVM) and a decision was taken by the Irish Province of Loreto in 1997 'to make the path by walking it'.

There are seventeen secondary schools, two grammar schools, eight primary schools and four community schools in Ireland for which Loreto has trustee responsibility. Traditionally, the function of trusteeship was exercised by the provincial superior and her council, and support structures began to be put in place in the mid eighties when the Loreto Education Network of Schools was formed, giving more formal recognition to the link that always existed between Loreto Schools in Ireland from their foundation. The first Steering Committee of the network was set up in the eighties and in 1991 the Loreto Education Office was established. These groups took on responsibility for certain aspects of the Loreto enterprise of education, while the provincial and her council continued to be responsible for the legal and financial obligations associated with ownership. CORI makes a clear distinction between two important types of responsibility that trustees have in relation to any school with which they are associated:

- Those that relate to ensuring that the school, in its ethos and otherwise, is consistent with the founding intention (i.e. the trust).
- Those that derive from the legal and financial liabilities associated with ownership.
  (CORI, 1996)

In 1997, following consultation at Loreto Province level, a decision was taken by the provincial and her council to delegate the exercise of trusteeship to a group of Loreto Sisters and this marked the first phase of development of the Loreto Trust Board. In 2000, four non-Loreto people were appointed to the board. Meetings are held approximately four times per year to plan and co-ordinate the work, which is mainly carried out by the board's officers and agencies. The brief of the Trust Board is twofold:

- To take responsibility for the function of trusteeship at present.
- To vision for the future appropriate exercise of trusteeship.

A two-day facilitated meeting held in 2000 enabled Trust Board members to be involved in a reflective discernment exercise on their *modus operandi*, which began with the formulation of a Mission Statement:

> Holding in trust and finding a gift for our time in Mary Ward's distinctive vision, we undertake trusteeship of the Loreto enterprise of education, including the properties designated for that purpose.

Working out of IBVM core values and facilitating their contemporary expression within the Loreto schools, we exercise the function of trusteeship through:

- ongoing dialogue with the wider Loreto community;
- two-way communication with the schools;
- support of the Loreto Network of Schools;
- leadership development.

It is clearly our responsibility to establish a real connection between the essence of the Mission Statement and the tasks to be done if our schools are to receive the support that they deserve into the future. 'Heart and soul' ideals must indeed be closely linked with effective strategies if they are not to sound hollow to those who work at individual school level. The 'wheel' diagram is a useful instrument in attempting to describe the 'vehicle', which will enable the ideals in the Mission Statement to be realised. So we on the

Loreto Trust Board continue to ask: what are the human, organisational, physical and financial resources that we need to put in place and/or develop?

Currently, the Loreto Network Steering Committee, representative of trustees, teachers, principals and parents from both primary and post-primary level, play an active part in the leadership/management functions vis-à-vis the service of the Loreto Education Office, while also influencing, monitoring and responding to educational developments and issues at national level. Their role includes initiating various projects that are designed to facilitate schools in reflecting the Loreto Philosophy of Education at local and/or network level. Other officers involved in acting on behalf of the Trust Board are the education development officer, an office administrator, the executive secretary of the Trust Board and a schools' properties officer.

Education Development Officer
- Support of the Loreto network as 'executive arm' of the Steering Committee.
- Developmental work with key school personnel.
- Visits, on request, to school Boards of Management, staff groups, parent groups, etc.
- Advisory role re. recruitment procedures.
- Specific tasks delegated by the Trust Board.
- Liaison with other relevant bodies.

Office Administrator
- Secretarial services.
- Routine telephone communication with schools and others.
- Production of Newsletter / Directories, etc.
- Organisation of meetings / conferences.
- Accounts for the office.
- Receive funding for courses from DES.

Executive Secretary of Trust Board
- Oversees the ongoing development of the Trust Board.
- Co-ordinates the work of the various sub-groups of the Trust Board.
- Manages the finances of Trust Board, administers loans to schools, grants for ministries, etc.

Schools' Properties Officer
- Delivery and updating of Schedule One.
- Approval for capital alteration.

- Receives annual budgets and audited accounts.
- Receives licence fees on behalf of Trust Board.
- Ensures that proper insurance is in place.

An organisational consultant is currently engaged to facilitate the process of clarifying the roles and responsibilities of each of the officers while also establishing lines of communication and accountability. Organisational resources are also becoming formalised through the work of a legal sub-committee. This group is pursuing the possibility of the Trust Board becoming a Company limited by guarantee and not having a share capital. It has been confirmed that transfer of ownership is not a prerequisite for the proper functioning of the Trust Board as a Company. A draft Memorandum and Articles of Association prepared by a legal consultant are currently under consideration. We are aware of ongoing research on the part of CORI in relation to the variety of ways in which a Civil Trust Body might receive approval from a canonical point of view in the long term. The concept of 'juridic person' is central to this discussion since a 'juridic person' would hold the property – movable and immovable, intellectual and spiritual – of a religious institute, thus ensuring that, since the religious institute has a mission to become involved in Catholic education, every effort is made to create some kind of succession.

Physical and financial resources are essential in the exercise of trusteeship. Loreto has considered a purpose-built Education Development Centre but has had to reconsider the extent of such a project because of costs involved. In the context of financial resource provision, an initial donation from the Province is invested to give some annual income and this is augmented by income from school licence fees.

To facilitate the visioning for the future aspect of the work of the Trust Board, a number of Trust Board sub-groups have been put in place:

- IBVM Vision and Ethos
- support structures
- Legal Instrument
- Primary Schools
- Community Schools

Significant documents have been prepared and these include:

- Handbook for Boards of Management of Loreto Post-Primary Schools.

- Manual for Boards of Management of Loreto Primary Schools.
- Annual school update pro-forma.
- Educational Philosophy for Post-Primary Schools – Schedule Two.
- Educational Philosophy for Primary Schools.
- Operational Guidelines for interim Trust Board.
- Process used in the appointment of Principals.
- Process used in the nomination and appointment of Board of Management members in schools.

At this point in time, the Trust Board is very conscious of its responsibility in relation to supporting an already existing vibrant network of schools. Planning for leadership succession is perceived as extremely important. While it is difficult to plan for an unknown future, the desire to give contemporary expression to Loreto's core values remains very much alive at individual school community level. Management, teachers and ancillary staff, parents and students alike are encouraged to define what their schools' values are against the background of the Loreto Philosophy of Education. Their insights as Loreto educators will inform and inspire the work of upholding and developing Loreto's characteristic spirit in the years ahead.

Reflection questions at workshop

Q.1   What do you consider to be the essential characteristics of trusteeship into the future if it is to have 'a positive and distinctive influence on the educational experiences of young Irish people and on society as a whole'? (The Trusteeship of Catholic Voluntary Schools, CORI, 1996)

Responses from the workshop groups

- Trusteeship that provides 'renewed heart and soul' in the vision for schools into the future. This is considered to depend very largely on the commitment of lay people, teachers in particular, to the underpinning vision and philosophy articulated by trustees.
- Trusteeship that recognises the importance of vision becoming translated into a culture that extends to the classroom and the whole learning environment of the student. This ideal has implications for relationships, structures and systems, with particular reference to the leadership role of the Board of Management in the individual school.

Q.2   What factors are likely to have the greatest impact on the successful development, or otherwise, of new models of trusteeship?

Responses from workshop groups

- The clarity and dynamism of the religious congregations as they face their own situations, involve lay people, make the hard decisions facing them with wisdom, discernment and detachment, not allowing issues of control or status to cloud central issues.

- The recognition of diversity of schools in the Education Act 1998 raises the question of State funding towards the cost of trusteeship. It seems necessary for denominational schools to have a 'united front' in order to enter into such negotiations. A certain 'corporate recognition' of denominational education is necessary.

- Lay teachers who attended the workshop spoke passionately about their sense of 'vocation', making an appeal to religious congregations that lay teachers be offered the chance to 'walk the journey with us'. One person spoke of the need for religious to tear down the limitations that they put on 'vocation'. Teacher involvement at Loreto Network Steering Committee level was considered a very worthwhile way of enabling teachers to exercise a leadership influence in the context of the Loreto network of schools.

Bibliography

Conference of Religious of Ireland, *The Trusteeship of Catholic Voluntary Schools. A Handbook for the Leaders of Religious Congregations* (Dublin, 1996).

The Religious Educator:
Keeper of the Flame

Fiona Gallagher

In considering the religious educator as 'The Keeper of the Flame', it becomes apparent that the religious flame that burns in schools must be 'kept' by all members of the school community. Teachers, administrators, students, parents and non-teaching staff are all keepers of the faith. We are all guardians of the flame. But what a task!

The recurring theme in many of the Vatican Council documents on Catholic education is the emphasis on the community of faith and the need for mutual dialogue and collaboration. We are all part of this educative community of faith which is responsible for religious education. (*The Catholic School on the Threshold of the Third Millennium*, 1998, Article 18.) An educative community of faith is a body of persons finding in Christ the meaning of their own lives and the purpose of their shared educational project (Donaldson *et al.*, 2002, 27). Being a member of the educative community of faith involves commitment, not just to teaching subject and skills, but to awakening wonder – a wonder that can find its proper object in Christ, who is 'the radiant light of God's glory and the perfect copy of its nature, sustaining the universe by his powerful command' (Letter to the Hebrews 1:3). On a practical level, how can a school create and achieve an educative community of faith?

Creating and achieving an educative community of faith

An educative community of faith must first of all examine its ethos. Brick (1999) believes that a school is as good as its ethos. He maintains that individual schools revitalise themselves and heighten their effectiveness when they regularly revisit their underlying ethos (Brick, 1999, 88).

An ethos cannot exist on its own. For an ethos to permeate the entire life of a school, it must engage in deep soul-searching and self-effacing. In so doing, it is necessary to examine how this ethos permeates and infiltrates the entire life of the school. In particular, this article will examine how ethos permeates and infiltrates the educative community of faith.

First of all, to be an educative community of faith we need to ask soul-searching questions:

- What is distinctive about our school?
- Are we a school of the gospel, which has its roots in justice and respect for one another?
- Does the school ethos cultivate concern for the weak and underprivileged or is it more likely to cultivate a spirit of survival of the strongest?
- Do students learn to respect one another because the school ethos is one that cultivates respect for pupils generally?
- Is there a culture that supports personal growth?
- Does the entire educative community of faith regularly ask: 'Why are we doing things the way we are?'
- What support structures are put in place to assist new teachers to integrate well and quickly into their new workplace?
- Is the school environment one that encourages and promotes creative expression by decorating the school walls with students' work, e.g. paintings, etc.

This is not an exhaustive list of questions. These questions, like all the questions in this article, are simply there to act as a catalyst or vehicle to begin exploring what it means to be a keeper or guardian of the flame. We cannot as a faith community become complacent and hope that 'what we are doing is fine'. We need to be constantly clarifying and defining our vision of education if we are an educative community of faith.

In an attempt to explore how a school can undertake this task and develop its role as 'Keeper of the Flame', this article will examine this issue under two headings. Firstly, the writer will examine how a school can become a 'school of the gospel', with particular reference to the work of Sullivan (2000). Secondly, the writer will outline the means by which a school can *audit* the status of its religious education and religious ethos, using a *blueprint* as refined by the *An Tobar – Resourcing Religious Education* project.

A school of the gospel

The distinctiveness of a school or a 'school of the gospel' is characterised by the distinct and unique qualities that underpin its entire school curriculum. At its foundations, a school of the gospel is grounded in love, justice, solidarity and respect, and above all else is centred in Christ. However, we cannot be called a school of the gospel without living out its demands and responsibilities.

The document on *The Catholic School*, says: 'Often what is perhaps fundamentally lacking amongst those who work in a school is a clear realisation of the identity of the school and the courage to follow all the consequences of its uniqueness'. Sullivan (2000) provides some very interesting and thought-provoking insights into what it means to be a school of the gospel.

The evangelisation process of a school, which is, as Sullivan observes, part of the mission of the Church, must be shared by all members of the school. In so doing, 'a school, as part of its mission of the Church, should always allow its policies, its priorities and purposes, to be illuminated, inspired, guided and challenged by the teaching of the gospel' (Sullivan, 2000, 109). This sharing and work must be spiritually fortified and sustained on a regular basis. With this fortified and united approach, the school of the gospel should be evident in all aspects of the school, i.e. the budget, timetable, resourcing, curriculum, pastoral care, and its internal and external relationships. This approach has also been advocated by Gerard Rummery (JRE, 50(2), 2002, 64). Specifically, Rummery highlights the fact that a good school is where good relationships are valued. The school is a place that is experienced as a place where the gospel of Jesus Christ is taught, celebrated and above all lived out in the lives of those who make up the community (Rummery, 2002, 65).

However, Sullivan is anxious to point out that the leaders and power-brokers in this evangelical approach must undertake their role with a degree of humility and openness to criticism. He reminds us that 'the power of the gospel will affect and upset humankind's criteria of judgement' (Sullivan, 2000, 110). This effect will extend to all members of the school community. With specific reference to teachers, the power of the gospel needs to be taught in the classroom and beyond. In their classroom work, teachers need to be prudent, imaginative and sensitive. Furthermore, Sullivan outlines that teachers are only listened to if they 'walk their talk' – they must live their words. Sullivan is not a unique advocate of this view of teachers. Rummery observes that today people listen more willingly to witnesses than to teachers, and if they listen to teachers, it is because they are witnesses *(Evangelisation in the Modern World,* 1974, 41).

Before a school can embark on a comprehensive adoption of Sullivan's ideas it firstly needs to examine the status of Religious Education in its own school. In short, it needs to undertake some form of audit to ascertain its priorities in relation to Religious Education. The following section looks at a Religious Education Audit as refined by the *An Tobar* team over the past few years.

An Tobar – Religious Education Audit
Looks are not always deceiving – they often reflect our priorities!
It can be very difficult to assess the degree to which an ethos permeates the life of a school. Yet in our pluralist and increasingly secular society the necessity for examining and understanding the degree to which ethos permeates the life of a school becomes ever more significant. *An Tobar* has attempted to respond to this necessity. Following consultations with schools and teachers of Religious Education who are at the 'chalk face', *An Tobar* has sought to develop a 'user-friendly' and contemporary *blueprint* by which schools can 'audit' their Religious Education programme.

This audit in Religious Education will be explored under a number of headings. Each section will begin with a number of questions for reflection, and one or two of these questions will be explored further. There are five central themes to examine:

1.   **Policy issues**
2.   **The physical environment of the school**
3.   **School and faith formation**
4.   **Practice in respect of faith formation**
5.   **The partnership between the family and the school**

1. POLICY ISSUES
In deciding on policy issues, it is recommended that a school should consider the following questions:

- **Is there an induction programme for newly qualified teachers of Religious Education?**
- **When you make your budget, what gets first priority?**
- **Is the allocation of teaching staff consistent with school policy in respect of faith formation?**
- **Is policy in respect of Religious Education regularly reviewed and evaluated by the Religion department?**

Let me begin with the new graduate of Religious Education in our schools. Very few of our schools have deliberate and structured supports in place to ease the transition from teacher-training college to full-time employment in a school. As an educative community of faith we must never forget that we began somewhere some time.

The induction of newly qualified teachers of Religious Education
The newly qualified teacher of Religious Education is a key player in helping schools fulfil their religious mission. However, the new graduate must be given the necessary professional supports to achieve this. The demands of a quality induction-programme system must be recognised, planned for and resourced (Carr, 1996, 17-24). Coolahan (1990) advocates that the enthusiasm, energy and positive attitudes of the newly qualified teacher 'are not blighted by a too abrupt and isolated exposure to full teaching responsibilities and difficulties' (Coolahan, 1990, 12).

Induction in a supportive learning environment
The author's experience with newly qualified teachers of Religion referred to the importance of implementing an induction programme in a supportive learning environment. This learning needs to be focused with care on teaching, its methodologies and applications (Gallagher, 1999, 124). Induction programmes will only succeed where school communities provide stimulating, creative and supportive learning environments. Schools must, therefore, become learning organisations where good practice can be observed and emulated (Carr, 1990, 23).

A school staff should actively seek to cultivate an environment that encourages learning. The need to implement induction programmes with care and professionalism was aptly pointed out by one newly qualified teacher of Religious Education:

> We need to induct our new teachers into a system with considerable care and professionalism. This will allow us to enjoy our initial years and harness the enthusiasm and eagerness we all have for the betterment of our schools and pupils.
>
> (Gallagher, 1999, 124)

It is imperative that schools harness the enthusiasm and eagerness of our newly qualified teachers of Religion in developing a positive learning environment. The teacher of Religion has a distinct contribution to make to the school community and the wider community in terms of creativity, enthusiasm, ideas and energy for projects. The presence of a young teacher on a staff enhances and invigorates the staff and can be a rewarding experience for the established members of the staff. From the information provided by teachers of Religious Education over the years, there are a number of characteristics one can associate with a positive learning environment:

- Frequent communication among staff and management.
- Sharing of resources.
- Discussion of classroom methodologies.
- Open and frequent analysis of effective and ineffective teaching methods among experienced teachers.

Underlying the rationale for induction is a concern for the personal growth, professional development and retention of newly qualified teachers of Religious Education during the first years of teaching. They are acquiring and refining new skills and building on what has been learned during pre-service. The induction phase provides many opportunities to continue learning, as well as the opportunity to develop a deeper understanding of the internal organisation of schools.

The specialised needs of Religious Education

As mentioned earlier, looks are not always deceiving – they often reflect our priorities! Our actions speak louder than words. The funding of resources may be a barometer of the priority 'in action'. The religious identity of schools is not something that happens by accident. It is an identity that is achieved by careful planning and the allocation of appropriate resources. In short, is the level of resourcing for Religious Education on par with that of other subjects?

The issue of accommodation is frequently raised by teachers of Religious Education, i.e. the use of a Religion room or an oratory to facilitate different types of learning experiences. Teachers of Religious Education feel that if Religious Education is a priority in a school, then it is imperative that the necessary accommodation is given. A Religion room in a school not only gives the subject a very visible status but it is also a very real and tangible symbol of the ethos of the school 'in action'. In a very practical way it also allows the RE department to 'house' all the resources, hence contributing to a collaborative approach to Religious Education. Students are very quick to perceive and detect what is given priority in a school and, consequently, will soon decide the more important areas of the curriculum within the school.

2. THE PHYSICAL ENVIRONMENT OF THE SCHOOL

The physical and aesthetic environment of a school is possibly the most tangible evidence of its religious ethos and identity.

- **What visible signs and symbols are displayed in the school?**
- **Can the Mission and Vision Statement be clearly seen and does it reflect the true nature of the school?**
- **Is there a calendar of significant liturgical celebrations planned for the school year? And is this circulated to staff, pupils and parents?**

The visible evidence of Religious Education

The physical expression

The physical expression of the distinctiveness of a school and the importance given to Religious Education is nowhere more evident and obvious than in its visibility within the school walls. Precisely, what gives a school of the gospel its distinct flavour is the quality of its 'religious' physical environment. Pious aspirations and sentiments which are articulated in ethos documents and mission statements but do not find expression in practice are simply, in the words of Terence McLaughlin, 'edu-babble' (Groome, 1996, 138). The visibility of RE in the school displays to what extent 'lip-service' is being given to Religious Education.

There was a time when the visible nature of the school was never an issue. Many of the leadership personnel were religious sisters, brothers and priests. They were, and still are where present, the living symbol or 'vivid image' of religious faith (Grace, 2002, 140). New lay leadership now has a prime responsibility and duty to guard and enhance the mission integrity of the school. It would be naïve of me to ignore the competing needs that exist within a school, but if we are to call ourselves schools with a gospel-based mission, then we have to be truthful to ourselves and our students. Should the only visible signs in a school be about promoting the academic excellence of students; equipping students to take their place in a technologically advanced and rapidly changing society? Or should the visible signs be about promoting the spiritual dimension of education? If a school is committed to being a school of the gospel, then this commitment should be clearly visible throughout the school, for example, RE displays, an oratory, RE classroom.

Lay witness

No other subject on the curriculum, it could be argued, has the same degree of visibility in a school. Religious Education permeates and pervades the entire school community. It is important that lay teachers who work in a school participate actively in the liturgical and sacramental life of the school. Students who witness and experience the concrete involvement of lay adults in the liturgical and sacramental life of the school will share more readily in the life of the school. We must begin to promote lay spirituality in our schools.

The 'visibility' of Religious Education depends on a number of factors, but the religious development of students can be supported in a number of practical ways in a whole-school context, such as:

- The school ethos, which is the responsibility of the whole staff, can cultivate a sense of community among teachers and students, respect for one another, and foster values such as care for the weak and underprivileged.
- The contribution made by pastoral-care programme and team within a school.
- Chaplaincy service.
- Outreach programmes, for example, the Developing World Immersion programme; the Edmund Rice Awards.
- An oratory or a Religion room.
- Religious Education noticeboard.

3. SCHOOL AND FAITH FORMATION
Faith formation is about the development of an educative community of faith which expresses its beliefs.

- **Are there opportunities for staff to avail of personal self-development courses; to go on retreat?**
- **In what ways do you provide your teachers of Religious Education with the encouragement that will nourish their sense of vocation?**
- **Does prayer have a clear place in the school day?**
- **What visible supports do you provide for teachers of Religious Education in your school?**
- **The introduction of the RE examination – are the necessary support structures in place so as to facilitate the introduction of the subject at Junior Certificate level?**
- **Is the whole school aware of its introduction and its consequences?**
- **What can be done to enhance collaboration among teachers in your school?**

Professional and personal development of all staff

The existence of a Religious Education programme alongside the rest of the curriculum or a privileged space for worship does not make a school a Catholic school. Effective Religious Education does not just happen spontaneously or accidentally. The very nature of the Religious Education class requires teachers of Religious Education to keep 'upgrading' and enhancing their teaching skills and resources. In short, there is the need by management to give the necessary financial assistance to provide the necessary professional development. This is especially true for the untrained teacher of Religious Education or the non-RE teacher.

However, it could be argued that every teacher teaching in a school is contributing to the religious ethos of the school. And the role of the non-RE teacher is equally as important. Every subject on the school curriculum is value-laden. Consequently, there should be provision made by management for all staff members to avail of 'formation experiences' that nurture their spiritual needs so that their own world of meaning is brought into a life-giving encounter with the tradition (Sharkey, 2002, 40). Effective leadership is about reading the needs of staff and responding to them appropriately. Sharkey puts forward a three-level approach to the formation of staff in a school. His *Staff Formation Profile* articulates quite clearly what supports should be put in place for the whole school and delivered in an ongoing way by the school.

(a) All staff

The first level is basic, general and compulsory and is designed for every teacher who accepts a teaching position in a school.

- Everyone employed in a school has embraced a commitment to support the ethos of the school.
- Ongoing professional development in the religious domain is both legitimate and essential for all staff in the school.

(b) Extension experiences

This level is voluntary and is responding to the needs of teachers as they arise in their professional career.

- Whilst every member of staff needs to have a base level of professional formation in the religious domain, a range of extension formation experiences also needs to be provided for staff to access, for example, retreats, courses etc.
- These experiences are taken up by staff according to their particular roles and circumstances.

(c) Roles of leadership and specialisation
The third level is for staff with designated responsibilities in the religious domain in the school.

- A number of staff shoulder particular responsibilties in the religious domain, for example, school leaders, RE co-ordinators, liturgy co-ordinators, outreach, etc.
- Special training and resourcing is necessary for these staff.

Sharkey is aware that the Religious Education co-ordinator requires ongoing professional development in order to:

- support and guide the teachers within the RE department;
- provide a Religious Education programme that is of a high quality.

It is evident from the stages of staff formation as outlined by Sharkey that each member of staff has an invaluable role in the mission of the school of the gospel and to keeping the flame burning. However, this is not something that will happen automatically or on an *ad hoc* basis. A deliberate and structured staff formation programme that builds upon individuals, to form a coherent whole, would have to be created, taking into consideration teacher needs and school resources.

Prayer having a clear place in the school day
Sullivan suggests that within the life of the school community, one might consider the priority given to and the creative energy and resources devoted to the fostering of personal prayer and public worship, drawing upon the richness of the liturgical tradition and its diverse forms of spirituality (Sullivan, 2000, 83).

There are various forms of prayer that can take place during the school day, as the Religious Education Junior Certificate syllabus shows. Section E5 on Prayer, for example, studies different types of prayer – meditation, contemplation, petition, praise and thanksgiving, penitence. These do not necessarily have to be the sole responsibility of the teacher of Religious Education.

Tuohy (2000), in his book *Youth 2K*, a study of the religious values and attitudes of young people, found his interviewees recalling the school senior retreat as being an element of school life that had an impact on them. The prayer life stimulated on the retreat was nourished and affirmed (Tuohy, 2000, 78). Interviewees found the 'sacred space' experience, organised and created by RE teachers, in particular, extremely rewarding (Tuohy, 2000, 78).

If we belong to a school of the gospel it is important that we encourage and nurture the spiritual appetite of adolescents for personal relationship with God.

Enhancing collaboration among teachers in your school

It is becoming ever more apparent from talking to teachers of Religious Education that there is a need for teacher reflection and team teaching, especially at senior cycle level. This not only enhances their teaching but also reduces the risk of teacher burnout and fatigue. While there are no statistics or figures to prove this, it is becoming increasingly obvious that our teachers of Religious Education are moving into other areas of the curriculum, for example, school chaplaincy, guidance counselling, transition-year programme, etc. If we are to keep our teachers of Religious Education, we need to provide support structures in specific areas. Let me begin by looking briefly at critical reflection and its value.

The importance of critical reflection

Vonk (1994) maintains that analysing and reflecting on experiences, both positive and negative, can help in building up a 'practical knowledge base' and a 'flexible repertoire' (Vonk, 1994, 14). Critical reflection is a vital component of teaching. Without critical reflection on what we are doing, our teaching will have limited opportunities for improvement. In relatively few professions are people appointed to a position to face the challenges of their job with minimal support and subsequent training. Teachers of Religious Education need a way of recording evaluative information that is both constructive and manageable. In acknowledgement of the lack of training/professional development most schools now build staff development days into their academic calendar. These days can serve as opportunities for the whole school to reflect on the religious nature of their school and to see where its strengths and weaknesses are.

The value of team teaching

The An Tobar team have often noted that where there is a collaborative and united approach to Religious Education the RE department are at their most innovative and creative. Murgatroyd and Morgan (1989) maintain that teamwork should be encouraged for the following reasons:

- Teams provide an environment in which learning can be articulated, tested, refined and examined against the needs of the organisation and within the context of the learning of others.
- Teams are self-managing.

- Teams can examine cross-functional issues more effectively than individuals acting on their own initiative. (Murgatroyd and Morgan, 1989, 241-258)

Religious Education departments should have regular departmental team meetings. These meetings are opportunities for the team to organise and prepare school liturgies, to discuss teaching methodologies and to share resources. From the author's experience of working with RE departments, the value of team teaching allows individual teachers to speak openly to their colleagues in the RE department, thus giving them a sense of empowerment. Empowering the teacher energises the teacher. It will reinforce experimentation and creativity in teachers' work and participation. It will enhance and develop teachers' professionalism, making them happier and more effective teachers. Senge (1992) makes a good argument for teamwork when he states that 'the IQ of the team can potentially be much greater than the IQ of the individuals' (Senge, 1992, 239; see thesis, p.135). The teacher of Religious Education no longer feels isolated but rather is involved in a collaborative process or activity with other teachers of Religious Education.

There has to be a whole-school approach to Religious Education that is both sympathetic and understanding to the needs of teachers of Religious Education. It is through team planning, lesson debriefing and continual discussion that teachers of Religious Education are enabled to develop new insights and skills.

4. PRACTICE IN RESPECT OF FAITH FORMATION
The rhetoric and the reality!

- **Does Religious Education and faith formation policy influence the construction of the timetable?**
- **What opportunities are available to teachers of Religious Education to undertake in-service and professional training?**
- **How visible is RE in the school?**

The school timetable
The timetabling of Religious Education is possibly one of the most contentious and divisive issues for teachers of Religious Education. For the majority of teachers the position of RE on the timetable is a yardstick as to the real importance of Religious Education in the school. The school timetable is as much an expression of school culture and ethos as it is of school resources. It is not a question of packing everything in but of

establishing priorities (Looney, 1998, 91). From the author's experience, teachers of Religious Education single out certain timetabling issues, such as:

- Timetabling Religion as a pre-lunch class, which is seen by some teachers as diminishing its importance on the school day's calendar.
- Timetabling two class periods of Religious Education one after the other requires careful planning with the Religion department. Otherwise, inaccurate timetabling of double-class periods can cause stress and anxiety.
- Balancing the Religion teacher's timetable evenly between the subject of Religion and the teacher's elective subject has been perceived by many as giving them a sense of empowerment and justification.
- Using Religion class periods to teach other subjects undermines the Religion teacher and the value of Religion classes.
- Using Religious Education to 'fill up' a teacher's timetable.

In focusing on school timetables and class periods it is important to remember that our Religious Education also extends beyond the walls of the classroom.

5. THE PARTNERSHIP BETWEEN THE FAMILY AND THE SCHOOL

- **Are parents encouraged by management to meet teachers of Religious Education at parent-teacher meetings?**
- **Is parental involvement in Religious Education encouraged and actively sought?**

There can be no doubt that the attitudes of parents are among the most important factors in the formation of religious attitudes (Argyle, 1958). Flynn (1975) in his study of sixth-form students in twenty-one boys' high schools in Australia found that schools were most successful in achieving their religious goals when the school and the home 'mutually reinforce each other' (Flynn, 1975, 179).

However, from the author's experience this is something that needs addressing and developing. It is felt by most teachers of Religious Education that at the time of parent-teacher meetings, parents are reluctant to queue to meet the teacher of Religious Education. Teachers of Religious Education are left sitting at their desks with no parent in front of them.

There must be communal responsibility for the religious identity and ethos of the school. Furthermore, school management should actively encourage parental involvement in Religious Education. In so doing, schools will hopefully avoid the scenario where Religious Education becomes a showpiece or a public relations exercise at key times or moments in the school calendar.

Conclusion

This article is about the educative community of faith as keepers of the flame, with specific reference to the role of the teacher of Religious Education. The keeper of the flame is not the sole responsibility of a Religion department, but rather the responsibility of everyone in the educative community of faith, a community of believers. There is a very real and urgent need for us all, as members of the educative community of faith, to be keepers or guardians of the flame in a very practical sense. No one person is responsible for the religious ethos of a school; we are all keepers of the flame and we all have a significant light to bring to bear on our schools. Sometimes that light needs unveiling to reveal the inner spirituality that is within each of us. One brief flash of light may illuminate a huge darkness.

Cardinal Cathal Daly believes an educative community is one with a shared vision of the aims of education and of the aims of the school in particular; with a common commitment to the tradition and spirit and educational project of the school (Donaldson et al., 2002, 27). This is a challenge that all of us must take ownership of if we are to be a genuine educative community of faith.

There is no denying that our teachers of Religious Education play a huge role in creating the religious ethos and identity of our schools by their lay witness to gospel values and by their commitment to their students and enthusiasm for their subject. Because no one makes the journey of faith alone, I believe that our teachers of Religion have a unique opportunity to contribute to the building of the community of the school through their willingness to be witnesses to their faith.

Teachers of Religious Education often comment that school management perceive them as 'the conscience of the school'. Furthermore, teachers of Religious Education often note that they feel solely responsible for creating the religious ethos of the school. Obviously, this should not be the case. As this article outlines, the development of an educative community of faith is the responsibility of the entire school community. A considerable task! In addressing this task, this article has focused on the Religious audit.

The Religious Education audit is a response to a need to address the nature of Religious Education in our schools. It has come at an opportune time, when schools are considering the Religious Education examination at junior-cycle level and when schools are defining what it means to be a Catholic school. The Religious Education audit asks 'easier said than done' questions. It demands that schools raise their heads above the parapet and face the reality of what is happening in terms of Religious Education.

Obviously, an audit of this nature needs a time-frame and requires the support of the whole school community. Certainly, the full implementation and development of the audit should be set within a five-year plan. This plan will need to be regularly reviewed. Not everything in the audit can be achieved immediately but it raises questions as to the priorities of the school.

In seeking to provide developmental ideas for Religious Education in Irish Catholic schools, this article has spent little time lauding the continuous and creative developments that have been taking place over the past number of years. It has to be acknowledged that there are schools that have marvellous support structures in place and the necessary personnel to carry out a very effective Religious Education programme. It is interesting to note that these schools often boast many specific characteristics mentioned in this article, for example:

- A nominated co-ordinator of Religious Education
- Regular departmental meetings
- A Religious Education room
- An oratory
- A team of qualified catechists
- Team teaching or modular teaching at senior-cycle level
- The support of management
- Religious Education as a priority in the school
- Adequate class periods
- Teamwork and collaboration

This essay has not attempted to address all areas of the educative community of faith, for example, the relationship of the parish. Nor has it addressed the Religious Education examination, but has instead provided a flavour of what it means to be a keeper of the flame in the communal or communitarian sense. It must be acknowledged that there are a number of areas that should be included in this audit, for example, the relationship between the parish and school, the input of students in Religious Education and ethos, and the Religious Education examination.

Furthermore, although this article strongly encourages the role of the entire school community in the development of an educative community of faith, the Religion department has a major responsibility as the driving engine behind this development. The Religion department is the most visible religious identity presence of a Catholic school. The Religion department needs to nurture the passion for an educative community of faith. In a way, the Religion department is a keeper of the 'keepers of the flame'.

Finally, it must be said that in the process of 'keeping the flame', the keepers will be energised. In striving for an educative community of faith, all those keepers of the flame should experience an ignition of pride and fulfilment in their own professional lives. In short, the keepers of the flame will be warmed by its strength.

Bibliography

Assocation of Secondary Teachers, Ireland (ASTI), *Issues in Education – Changing Education, Changing Society* (Dublin: ASTI House, 1998).

Conroy, James, *Catholic Education Inside-Out/Outside-In* (Dublin: Veritas, 1999).

Coolahan, J., 'Teacher Education in the Nineties: Towards a New Coherence', *ATEE*, Volume One, 1990.

Donaldson, A.; McKeown, D.; McCann, G., *Ethos and Education: Contemporary Issues in Education,* (Ethos and Education, 2002).

Gallagher, F., Towards the Creation of an Induction Programme for Newly Qualified Teachers of Religion in the Diocese of Meath (Unpublished Thesis, 1999).

Groome, T.H. (1996), 'What Makes a School?' in McLaughlin T., O'Keefe, J. and O'Keeffe, B., (eds), *The Contemporary Catholic School: Context, Identity and Diversity* (London: Falmer).

Francis, J. Leslie; Kay, K. William; Campbell, S. William, *Research in Religious Education* (Leominster/Malon, Gracewing: Smyth and Helwys, 1996).

Senge, P. M., *The Fifth Discipline: The Art and Practice of the Learning Organisation* (C. Century Business, 1992).

Sullivan, John, *Catholic Schools in Contention* (Dublin:Veritas, 2000).

Tuohy, D. and Cairns, P., *Youth 2K – Threat or Promise to a Religious Culture* (Dublin: Marino Institute of Education, 2000).

Vatican Congregation for Catholic Education, *The Catholic School on the Threshold of the Third Millennium* (1997).

Vonk, J.H.C., *Handbook of Teacher Education in Europe,*

Carr, J., 'Teacher Induction and the Teacher Unions' in *Teacher Induction* by Swan and Leydon (1996), pp.17-24.

Murgatroyd, S., 'Kaizen: School-Wide Quality Improvement' in *School Organisation,* Vol 9, No 2 (1989), pp.241-58.

Rummery, Gerard, 'Catholic Teachers for the New Millennium: Some Aspects of the Dialogue between Faith and Culture' in *Journal of Religious Education* 50(2), (2002), pp. 62-70.

Sharkey, Paul, 'Capacity and Commitment of Staff for New Evangelisation in Catholic Schools' in *Journal of Religious Education* 50(3), (2002), pp. 36-42.

'Matthew, Luke, John and...is it Michael?'
Reimagining the Catholic primary school

Caoimhe Máirtín

Introduction

As we experience the early years of the twenty-first century it is interesting to reflect on the significant changes that the last few decades of the twentieth century have had on education in Ireland. Not only have we experienced very significant and rapidly changing political, social, economic and cultural shifts, but the needs and the demands of, for and on Irish primary education have been unprecedented. The 1980s was a decade when primary education experienced an oversupply of teachers, an undersupply of finance, and a complete planning pause in school development, in teacher-education colleges, in curriculum. Responding to, and providing for, system, school and pupil needs was on hold, and the provision of newly-qualified primary teachers to the system dwindled to a trickle. This was followed by a period of educational reawakening in the 1990s, with some significant curricular and educational policy developments, including the publication of the White Paper, *Charting Our Education Future* (1993),[1] the introduction of the Revised Primary Curriculum (1999),[2] and the introduction of the Education Act (2000).[3] During this reawakening, teacher education colleges were preparing unprecedented numbers of young teachers for primary schools. In a primary teaching profession of just over 23,000, approximately 8,000 primary teachers have emerged from teacher-education programmes within the last ten years.[4]

The extent and the pace of change in education prompt one to question what is really happening in primary schools. Does the religious dimension to schools continue to be a guaranteed outcome of denominational education, of religious ownership and/or management of schools, of primary-teacher education programmes that include religious education and religious formation as integral to their programmes? What about ethos and values – are these dependent on school management, on school principals, on teachers, on parents, or on a partnership between some or all of these? How then do the religious dimensions and the child-centred dimensions of primary education find harmonious expression in the experiences of children's faith development in schools?

Information on primary education in Ireland is accessible – structural changes can be seen, content changes can be sourced, demographic changes can be measured. But what is *really* happening? This paper attempts to move from perception / expectation / aspiration to information. The main focus of the paper is to provide a measured view of some of the experiences, attitudes and values that emerging primary teachers bring with them to schools. It provides for a snapshot in time, focusing on the views of 450 student teachers[5] enrolled on primary-teacher education programmes who intend – given the current shortfall in primary teachers – to be appointed to full-time positions in Catholic primary schools in Ireland over the next few years.

The religious dimension to the Primary Curriculum

The inclusive nature of the curriculum, the enrolment of a growing minority of non-Catholic children to Catholic primary schools, and the significant attitudinal change of a large proportion of Catholic parents to their expectations of the religious and spiritual dimension of 'Catholic education', provide for a very interesting dialogue on 'What is "Catholic" education?' or 'How can "Catholic" education be reimagined?' What may, however, be of far more relevance at this point, is to try to understand the concerns, views, practices and aspirations of teachers who either select into, or otherwise find themselves in, Catholic schools. Providing for a Catholic education and upholding the Catholic ethos in a school are largely dependent on school management's appointment of teachers who are themselves Catholic and who aspire to provide for and to support children's religious and spiritual development.

One can, for example, cite references within the Revised Primary Curriculum that give some comfort and assurance to any concerns that religion has been removed or replaced from the curriculum of primary schools.

> The curriculum takes cognisance of the affective, aesthetic, spiritual, moral and religious dimensions of the child's experience and

development ... The importance that the curriculum attributes to the child's spiritual development is expressed through the breadth of learning experiences the curriculum offers, through the inclusion of religious education as one of the areas of the curriculum, and through the child's engagement with the affective domains of learning...'[6]

Additionally, the curriculum acknowledges the societal and cultural changes that have impacted on schools and confirms the responsibilities of curriculum, of teachers and of schools to promote tolerance and respect for diversity. 'Children come from a diversity of cultural, religious, social, environmental and ethnic backgrounds, and these engender their own beliefs, values and aspirations.'[7]

The *Alive-O* Religious Education programme for primary schools, introduced alongside the Revised Primary Curriculum, provides a refreshing, imaginative, inclusive and positive statement of the Church's commitment to children's faith development, and of the importance of parents and teachers working together in the area of faith formation.[8]

All is well... almost. But underlying the substance and content of curricula and the acknowledgement of approaching learning in a child-centred manner, some key tensions emerge. How well do home, school and parish work together? How comfortable are parents and teachers in drawing from their own experiences, beliefs and practices to support children in faith formation? The tri-partnership approach is essential, dependency is a key to success, but an over-dependency on any one of the three will probably leave children confused and unclear.

In focusing on teachers in the dialogue that follows, the objective is to attempt to clarify some of the views and attitudes that are emerging from teachers – and therefore from schools – that may inform our thinking as we attempt to reimagine Catholic primary education. This data analysis provides an initial introduction to what will, hopefully, become a far more extensive presentation of the issues that currently face primary schools regarding the role of the teacher in providing for and supporting the religious dimension of children's education. The information gathered and collated from respondents is very extensive, and should provide some clarification on fundamental issues that require urgent attention for the stakeholders of Catholic primary education.

The emerging primary teacher
Amongst the many issues that come to mind, as one tries to revisit Catholic primary education, are those that pertain to the provision of good Catholic

teachers. Primary-teacher education in Ireland remains very strictly denominational, with four of the five colleges providing exclusively for Catholic primary teachers.[9] It would, of course, be naïve to presume that all students in the colleges are 'practising Catholics'. What has, however, been difficult to establish is exactly what are the views and attitudes of emerging teachers to the 'Catholic' dimension of their profession.

A very general profile that one might sketch of emerging teachers in the 20-25-year age range would be that:

- They have come from Catholic backgrounds where religion is an important part of their parents' lives.
- They may have reflected on their responsibilities to Catholic schools and faith development when they opted for teacher education.
- They have a good 'content' knowledge of religion, which may not be supported by a faith dimension.
- They may feel obliged to, rather than aspire to, teach religion in school.
- They possibly do not attend Mass regularly or receive the sacraments, and some of the doctrinal practices that they may be imparting to children may no longer be a part of their own practice.

In truth, however, these remain only perceptions and the actual profile of the emerging primary teacher has to date rested on opinion rather than fact.

It was with a view to providing a far clearer 'teacher profile' that a survey of 450 student teachers was conducted in Spring 2002 in one of the teacher-education colleges. These students included 300 undergraduate B.E in the 18-21 age range. The remaining 150 students were post-graduates ranging in age from 23 to 53 years.[10] Of the 150 post-graduate students, 100 were surveyed on entry to their teacher-education programme, while the other 50 provided an exit-poll range of opinions, as they were just completing their course.

All students were included in the survey, and the questionnaire sought views on twenty-two aspects of their own faith dimension, their experiences of Religious Education in schools and in college, and their attitudes to, and enthusiasm for, engaging in the teaching of religion in primary schools. The questionnaire was designed in a manner that allowed students to identify with statements given on a range from 'Strongly Agreeing' with the statement to 'Strongly Disagreeing' with the statement.[11] Ten of these statements sought the personal dimension of students' faith and practice, while another twelve statements explored the students' home, school and college experiences of, or attitudes towards, religion. Students were asked one question related to content/knowledge – to name the four Gospels. They were also invited to note three things they would like to see changed regarding the Catholic primary school.[12]

After the data was compiled, follow-on interviews were conducted with a random 10 per cent of each cohort of students. The outcomes were presented to them and discussion followed in an attempt to further clarify some of the emerging trends.

Profiling the Catholic primary teacher – the personal dimension

Over 80 per cent of students indicated that traditional religious practices were still observed in their homes. Students indicated a very strong spiritual dimension in their lives and were confident that they could be described as good Christians. They attached great importance to being identified as Catholic – over 70 per cent of both graduates and undergraduates disagreeing with the statement that 'Being a Catholic is not really important to me any more'. They indicated, however, a wider range of views when asked if they could be described as a 'practising Catholic'. While most were happy to be described as such, a significant minority disagreed, and this was supported by the fact that most students suggested that their commitment to the faith now differed from that of their parents.

Being a Catholic is not really important to me any more.

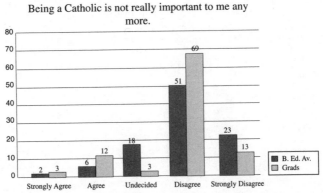

An interesting outcome of inquiring about peers was that most respondents had a much more negative opinion of their peers' religious beliefs, opinions and practices than was actually the case. This became more interesting in the dialogue that followed with a random selection of students. They were pleased that they were not alone in their faith development but disappointed that they had not had greater opportunities – particularly as future teachers – to dialogue and support each other on their faith journey. Almost 60 per cent of students agreed with the statement that 'My faith is stronger than I would like to admit in front of fellow students'. Some of the views offered in support of this position were that, if challenged by their peers, they might find it difficult to substantiate their position. In further discussion it emerged that most students felt they had been brought along the Catholic faith trail but they hadn't developed or clarified their own thinking; they cited in some cases their post-primary experiences of Religious Education whereby the pursuit of points, sometimes a lack of quality facilitation in Religious Education classes, and the absence of a structured curriculum in Religious Education in secondary schools, contributed to their inability to move forward with new confidence. They were generally disappointed that the pressure on religious methodology courses in college, and the large numbers in classes, gave them little opportunity to pursue issues and questions regarding their own faith and their possible contribution to 'Catholicism' in schools. In fact, some indicated that they found it difficult to discuss 'Reimagining the Catholic primary school' because the imagination dimension to religion was by and large absent.

The post-graduate students (averaging twenty-five years of age) were asked about their understanding and commitment to their faith at this point as against the position they held when they finished secondary school. The data below indicates a clearer sense of what their faith meant to them, but for most they considered themselves less committed now than they were at eighteen years of age.

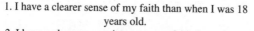

1. I have a clearer sense of my faith than when I was 18 years old.
2. I have a clearer commitment to my faith than when I was 18 years old.

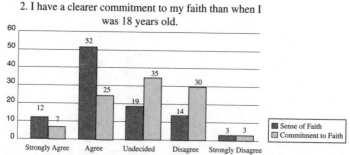

Profiling the Catholic primary teacher – the professional dimension

A wide range of opinions were sought from the emerging teachers regarding the influences that Religious Education had on them at both primary and post-primary level, and also looking to the future and their expressions of interest, of confidence, of competence in actively supporting Catholic education, and in particular taking responsibility for teaching religion and preparing children for the sacraments. There was a very strong commitment to supporting Catholic education in schools – even on behalf of students who had already declared at least some difficulties with identifying on the personal level with being a Catholic.

It was again interesting to note a more task-based reaction on behalf of those participating in the undergraduate programme, and generally a more reflective response from the post-graduates. However, a large majority of students in both groups felt they had something to offer to schools and, indeed, they were strongly opposed to any suggestion of removing Religious Education from schools.

One very heartening response was the value that students felt they got in college from Religious Education programmes, and a view expressed by most that their college experience of Religious Education had or will support and enrich their faith.[13] There was, however, a hunger for an opportunity to think, talk and explore in a 'judgement-free zone', and this was accorded a very high priority in view of the high level of responsibilities they would assume as part of a school team supporting Catholic education.

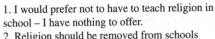

1. I would prefer not to have to teach religion in school – I have nothing to offer.
2. Religion should be removed from schools and supported elsewhere.

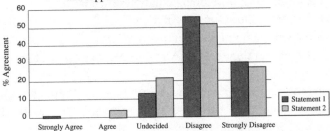

While a number of outcomes of the effort to measure the opinions, practices and intentions of newly qualified primary teachers may yield little real reimagining in terms of the primary school, some serious challenges have emerged for teacher-education colleges. The value of supporting trainee teachers in their thinking and rethinking cannot be underestimated; the outcomes of engaging in a reflective and creative process should provide schools with a more active, a more challenging, a more progressive and a less complacent approach to Catholic primary education.

Teachers talking... about rethinking and reimagining

All respondents were invited to reflect on what they would like to see changing in terms of Catholic primary education. A very wide menu emerged, but the general areas of reflection offered suggestions around creativity and flexibility in the Religious Education programme, *Alive O*: inclusiveness within schools to ensure that all children in a growing multicultural society could participate in religious formation – or at least not feel excluded; focus on connecting with the real experiences of children.

The more popular statements emerging from respondents included the following:

> 'More practical emphasis on day-to-day good living.'
> 'Make the Bible easier for children to understand.'
> 'More practical in terms of children's real experiences.'
> 'Teach about other religions – open children's minds.'
> 'Place more emphasis on day-to-day events.'
> 'More connection with church and parish – not just for sacraments.'
> 'Make it much more active.'
> 'Provide more resources – more circle-time approach.'
> 'Schools should be State Schools, not necessarily Catholic.'
> 'NCCA should have a curriculum for religion.'
> 'All teachers should reserve a minute or two for prayer each day.'
> 'Enjoy RE rather than endure it.'
> 'More interaction with the church – the priests.'
> 'More emphasis on developing children's own faith.'
> 'Make the Mass more fun for children.'
> 'Children get fed up of the routine in religion.'
> 'Less classes on religion – three lessons per week is enough.'

Students offered some very clear thoughts on how they could be supported in reflecting on their own faith and their responsibilities as teachers in Catholic schools. Some of the most frequent comments are reflected in the following:

> 'More faith exploration in college.'
> 'Need for greater enthusiasm for religious studies in general.'
> 'Non-Catholic children should not necessarily feel left out.'
> 'I'm a Catholic, but what does that really mean?'
> 'The more you study Catholicism the more you don't know what a Catholic is.'
> 'More meditation – for us as students.'
> 'Let's talk much more about our religion.'
> 'More concentration on spirituality.'
> 'Much, much more discussion.'
> 'Find out more often how we are thinking – don't be afraid of the answers.'

Religious 'knowledge'

The title of this paper 'Matthew, Luke, John and... is it Michael?' is drawn from the response of one of the students to being asked to name the four Gospels. Five per cent of student teachers failed to name the four Gospels correctly. This might cause alarm, particularly when one considers that this was the only test of content or knowledge posed. It is, therefore, very likely that if three or four more questions were asked, that many more of the emerging teachers would be found wanting. All of the respondents have had religion as integral to their education programmes at both primary and secondary schools – a very significant and costly investment of time and resources. So what does this say, and what's it all about? Well, interestingly, there was no correlation between not being able to answer this question and finding oneself on the low end of interest and enthusiasm for teaching religion in primary schools. However, primary teachers, in general, indicate a much greater commitment to, and success in, teaching subjects if they have confidence in terms of their own knowledge base. Furthermore, it is difficult to reflect on one's own faith development if there is a content-gap or content-confusion in some very basic areas. Perhaps consideration should be given to the level at which content and knowledge need to be provided for teacher educators who will span an eight-year Religious Education programme, inclusive of the preparation of children for three of the seven sacraments.

Undergraduate vs. Post-graduate profiles

One of the most interesting outcomes of this study – for those with responsibilities in teacher education – was some of the differences that emerged between the undergraduate and post-graduate groups regarding their own reflections and actions in the area of Religious Education. This paper tries to provide an overall teacher profile. However, it is important to note the following differences between the groups:

- The post-graduates appeared to have a much clearer view of their own faith dimension; the undergraduates were more attached to the 'must do' feeling, resulting either from practices at home and/or from school experiences. This emerged in a number of ways but in some instances when asked to reflect on their own faith the undergraduates often found comfort in the 'don't know' category. The post-graduates, on the other hand, had become more polarised in their views – most of them indicating strengths of interest and purpose regarding Religious Education, with a small minority clearly articulating a withdrawal from religious practice and a significant dilution in their own faith.

- The majority of post-graduates were very clear about their responsibilities to Catholic education and to the religious formation of children, and they had given consideration to this when applying for teacher education. Many of them had experience of working in schools before applying for the course and this also helped to clarify their thinking. A minority of post-graduates indicated an enthusiasm for becoming faith-leaders in primary schools and this was more apparent where their undergraduate course had either exclusively or partially provided them with the opportunity to read and reflect on religion.[14]

- The differences that emerged between the groups signalled a need to clarify course content and structures between under- and post-graduates. Their competencies – given that some of the post-graduates had studied relevant modules or courses in religion prior to opting for teaching – was in itself an indicator of a need to examine the relevancy, the breadth and the balance of the courses.

- A comparative overview of the two groups of graduates surveyed[15] – one cohort beginning the course and the other just completing the course – indicated a very positive outcome and a much greater enthusiasm for the 'Catholic school' dimension to the profession on behalf of those completing the course. However, while those who had experienced the course were happy with the formal time allocation (lectures and course work) to religion in the college, they were of the opinion that smaller groups, and follow-on opportunities – either individually or in structured and facilitated discussion groups – to dialogue and explore religion would be very desirable.

- Those who were beginning the course in general presented more anxiously and more detached in terms of their enthusiasm for teaching religion in schools.

Conclusions and recommendations

The data obtained makes for interesting reflection and prompts a hunger for extending such an information trawl at two other points: (i) to survey teachers who have been teaching for two to three years and to see whether their experiences in schools have influenced their views and practices; (ii) to compare this group, and the pre-service group already examined, to a cohort of teachers who have had a longer association with primary schools – those with over twenty years' experience, and to attempt a comparative study in terms of teacher profile, which might yield some valuable information on where, when and how Catholic primary education can be – and is being – reimagined. Another information gap that would provide for interesting reflection on Catholic primary education is to ascertain the perceptions of teachers involved in the sacramental classes in primary school regarding (i) the faith dimension they bring with them to the classroom; (ii) the influences that preparing and teaching young children for the sacraments have on them; (iii) their perceptions of faith development in schools, with particular reference to their reflections on the home and parish dimensions of partnership in sacramental preparation.

In conclusion, this attempt to profile the emerging Catholic primary-school teacher does provide for some recommendations for action:

- It is good to obtain information (in a non-intrusive manner) from teachers, both at pre-service and later on in school or school-cluster networks, and to share this information with them. Teachers feel very much alone – no matter where they are along the faith trail – and in most cases people felt that they would be judged and that their current position was probably the least accepted by their peers and by others. The experience of finding out that others are feeling just the same can, in itself, provide great support.
- It is important to establish exactly what knowledge base is required by teachers as they emerge from teacher-education courses. In recent years there has been a revision in colleges in terms of students' competency requirements in areas such as language and mathematics. The issue should now be addressed with regard to programme content (information) in religion.
- Pre-service teacher-education programmes must look beyond the course content and structures in Religious Education programmes. In order to do this successfully, resources are required that are very specific to the Catholic dimension of what teacher education is about. If the denominational aspect of teacher education is to mean anything in practice in the colleges, it should not be the case that the provision of staff to support the faith dimension in schools is measured on an equal scale with provision of other areas. Pre-service teacher educators need to think and talk through their own faith development and to the issues that present themselves.
- The position of chaplaincy and campus ministry in colleges of education should receive a much higher priority than even that already in place in third-level institutions in general. These colleges are in themselves the parishes of the future. Each teacher who remains in primary education will impact on approximately 1,000 years of faith development (twenty-five children each year for forty years). The strongest link between Church and home is the teacher.

- There is an opportunity to reimagine a Catholic partnership at primary level, which might include a small number of teachers selecting, in time, to move from general teaching responsibilities to specialised catechetical and parish responsibilities. There would be logistical implications, not least of which would be the financial responsibilities attached to such a venture. However, given the rapidly decreasing number of priests, coupled with the religious backgrounds and experiences that some of the post-graduates bring to teaching, there appears to be an untapped opportunity here.

One could cite many more opportunities for progressing the 'new look' Catholic primary school. What is important is that we begin to answer some of the urgent questions facing Catholic primary schools; that we acknowledge and value the personal experiences of children and of teachers; that we clarify where the system is going; that we are courageous enough to ask the right questions; that we set the imagination free; that we do not give up; and that we remember that it is not time but people that will bring about changes.

Appendix – Questionnaire: Profiling the Emerging Catholic Primary Teacher

1. My religion is important to me – I would fit the description 'practising Catholic'.
Strongly Agree?   Agree?   Undecided?   Disagree?   Strongly Disagree?

2. I really have very little interest in/enthusiasm for religion.
Strongly Agree?   Agree?   Undecided?   Disagree?   Strongly Disagree?

3. My opinion is that most of my college peers have little interest in religion.
Strongly Agree?   Agree?   Undecided?   Disagree?   Strongly Disagree?

4. My home is a home where traditional religious practices are observed.
Strongly Agree?   Agree?   Undecided?   Disagree?   Strongly Disagree?

5. My parents don't realise that my religious beliefs/views are different to theirs.
Strongly Agree?   Agree?   Undecided?   Disagree?   Strongly Disagree?

6. My parents really don't worry about my views on religion.
Strongly Agree?   Agree?   Undecided?   Disagree?   Strongly Disagree?

7. I would describe myself as a good Christian.
Strongly Agree?   Agree?   Undecided?   Disagree?   Strongly Disagree?

8. There is a spiritual dimension to my life which is important to me.
Strongly Agree?   Agree?   Undecided?   Disagree?   Strongly Disagree?

9. I was strongly influenced by religion through my teachers in primary school.
Strongly Agree?   Agree?   Undecided?   Disagree?   Strongly Disagree?

10. I think primary school was a greater influence on my faith than my parents at home.
Strongly Agree?   Agree?   Undecided?   Disagree?   Strongly Disagree?

11. My parents were depending on primary school to develop and sustain my faith.
Strongly Agree?   Agree?   Undecided?   Disagree?   Strongly Disagree?

12. I enjoyed the religious dimension to my primary education.
Strongly Agree?   Agree?   Undecided?   Disagree?   Strongly Disagree?

13. I think secondary school was a greater influence on my faith than parents at home.
Strongly Agree?   Agree?   Undecided?   Disagree?   Strongly Disagree?

14. My parents were depending on secondary school to develop and sustain my faith.
Strongly Agree?   Agree?   Undecided?   Disagree?   Strongly Disagree?

15. I enjoyed the religious dimension to my secondary education.
Strongly Agree?   Agree?   Undecided?   Disagree?   Strongly Disagree?

16. If I could have chosen religion as a Leaving Cert. subject I would have done so.
Strongly Agree?   Agree?   Undecided?   Disagree?   Strongly Disagree?

17. Being a Catholic is not really important to me any more.
Strongly Agree?   Agree?   Undecided?   Disagree?   Strongly Disagree?

18. I never thought about religion when I was applying for teaching.
Strongly Agree?   Agree?   Undecided?   Disagree?   Strongly Disagree?

19. I would prefer not to have to teach religion in school – I have nothing to offer.
Strongly Agree?   Agree?   Undecided?   Disagree?   Strongly Disagree?

20. I look forward to teaching religion – it's as important to me as any other subject.
Strongly Agree?   Agree?   Undecided?   Disagree?   Strongly Disagree?

21. I feel college has and/or will support and enrich my faith.
Strongly Agree?   Agree?   Undecided?   Disagree?   Strongly Disagree?

22. My faith is stronger than I would like to admit in front of fellow students.
Strongly Agree?   Agree?   Undecided?   Disagree?   Strongly Disagree?

Notes

1. Government of Ireland, *Charting Our Education Future* (Dublin: The Stationery Office, 1995).
2. NCCA (National Council for Curriculum and Assessment), *Primary School Curriculum* (Dublin: The Stationery Office, 1995).
3. Government of Ireland, *Education Act* 1998 (Department of Education and Science).
4. These teachers have been educated in the five primary-teacher education colleges in Ireland: St Patrick's College, Drumcondra; Mary Immaculate College, Limerick; Coláiste Mhuire, Marino; Froebel College, Blackrock; Church of Ireland College, Rathmines.
5. This represents the full cohort of students registered on teacher-education courses in Coláiste Mhuire, Marino during the academic year 2001-2. 100 students were registered in each of the three years of the B.Ed. programme; 50 were completing the post-graduate programme and 100 had just registered to begin this eighteen-month programme.
6. NCCA, *Revised Primary Curriculum* (1999), Introductory Book, page 27.
7. Ibid., page .
8. *Alive-O* (Series of texts and support materials for primary schools), (Dublin: Veritas Publications).
9. The Church of Ireland College in Rathmines provides a teacher-education B.Ed. course in conjunction with Trinity College for the Protestant schools. This is the smallest of the five colleges. The other four colleges provide for the education of Catholic primary teachers.
10. The average age of this cohort of students was 25.6 years.
11. See Appendix – copy of questionnaire distributed.
12. Ibid.
13. The follow-up dialogues with students confirmed that, not only was the college dimension to Religious Education a very positive and supportive one, but also a very necessary part of their preparation for the teaching of religion.
14. 12 per cent of the post-graduates had studied religion in their undergraduate programme. These were students of either Mater Dei or NUI Maynooth.
15. 100 students had just enrolled on the course, the other 50 were completing the course.

Communicating the Message:
Catholic Education and the Media

Martin Clarke

It has been observed that all work breaks down into three categories: routine, crisis and developmental. Most of us spend a lot of our time on the first two categories, but the developmental is often the most difficult to address. This applies particularly to the cultivation of a good relationship between the Catholic school and the media. It is a task that requires time, planning and resources. If we put effort into the whole area of public relations, the life of the school will be enhanced.

In Ireland, the media play a very significant role in shaping people's perceptions and influencing public opinion. Relative to the size of our population, we have a lot of media outlets on the island, both print and broadcast. Despite the enormous changes in Irish life and culture, the media (and by extension, the general public) are very interested in Church issues, religion and spirituality.

Perhaps we have underestimated the influence of media on the values, attitudes and lifestyle of our young people. I believe that the students in our Catholic schools should be encouraged, especially through Media Studies, to understand and evaluate the significance of media in all our lives.

We need to examine the nature of the relationship between Church and media in Ireland. Church and media, in the words of one commentator, 'occupy different spaces'. The agenda of the Church is significantly different to the agenda of the media. However, our agendas frequently overlap, and it is therefore important that we develop a relationship with the media that is professional and productive for both parties.

This means trying to be proactive rather than reactive when it comes to media relations. There is plenty of 'hard data' for Catholic schools to communicate, particularly the events, achievements and human-interest stories that form part of the school year. It is important to have a clear understanding of where the line is drawn between what can be made public and what should remain confidential within the school.

At a deeper level, Catholic schools have much to communicate about vision and ethos. In the public forum there is much work to be done in getting across the *raison d'être* of Catholic schools. Do the media and/or the general public really understand why we have Catholic schools today? What is the justification for Catholic education at the beginning of a new millennium? Are our Catholic schools really different or counter-cultural? And how about that debate heard so often in the context of Northern Ireland: 'If all schools were interdenominational, the problems of sectarianism would be solved....'? If I were to ask you to sum up the 'Catholic ethos' of your school in three sentences, would you be able to do so?

Catholic schools that are under the patronage of a religious congregation have an added challenge to somehow communicate the 'charism of the founder'. In doing this, it is essential to use the language that resonates with media and the general public.

Another area of need is to communicate developments in Religious Education in the school. Do the media understand the present RE curriculum? Is there sufficient clarity around the distinction between Catechetics and RE as an examination subject?

Most Catholic schools have something worthwhile to tell their local media about special liturgies, retreats and pilgrimages. And if your students are doing something worthwhile in the area of community service, why not let it be known?

At a practical level, a school should have a designated PR person. Better still, the school could establish a 'PR committee' comprising teachers, students, parents and past students to promote the school's profile and image in a positive way. That means training and resources will be needed, but money wisely invested in PR is money well spent.

Such a group could devise a three-year Communications Plan for the school. Attention could be paid to the whole area of 'branding' and 'image', ensuring that the school crest or logo is modern and attractive, and that anything published or printed by the school is of a consistent standard. The importance of newsletters and yearbooks should not be underestimated, and an attractive colour brochure containing essential information about the school is always a useful tool.

Local media are probably more important to the school than national media. In particular, there is plenty of opportunity to get good coverage from provincial newspapers and local radio. Make sure that you invite local journalists to any special functions or events in the school, and remember that simple hospitality is always worthwhile. It is also good to see a number of transition-year co-ordinators obtaining special licences to broadcast for a week on community radio.

Every school should have its own website. They are quite inexpensive to establish and run, but it is essential that they be kept up to date on a daily, weekly or monthly basis. If your school does not already have a website, perhaps it would be a good transition-year project for students.

Good communications with the 'outside world' presume that you already have good communications internally within the school. Schools, like all other institutions and organisations, need constantly to improve and strengthen their internal communications, and whenever the school is sending a press release to the media, make sure that your 'internal audience' has been informed first.

Every school should have a Crisis Management Strategy in place to deal with serious, unexpected issues or events, which can happen very quickly. For instance, what does the school do if students are involved in an accident while on a school trip? This is one particular area where a 'designated PR person' has a very important role to play.

In conclusion, I would say that the Catholic school cannot afford to be an 'island' or to be in any way inward-looking. It needs to engage with the local community through the media. Bearing in mind the theme of this conference, how can we 'reimagine' the Catholic school's identity and its public profile through the media?

Above all, we should remind ourselves that communication is central to the task of 'the new evangelisation'. Jesus Christ is at the centre of the Church and of the Catholic school. The challenge for all of us is to communicate the Good News as best we can, using all the means at our disposal.

CHALLENGING VOICES

'I can't always say what you want to hear'

Peter McVerry, SJ

When you look at the title of my talk you have to ask yourself: what idiot accepts an invitation to tell an audience what they don't want to hear? Well, you are looking at one. I am asked to say some things that may be challenging and as I do so I don't want in any way to be seen to downgrade teachers. I have the utmost respect for the enthusiasm, motivation, hard work and idealism of teachers. I myself taught for two years a long time ago and I have spent the last more than twenty-five years working with young homeless people, and sometimes people ask me how I can keep going. I say in all honesty that anytime I feel like giving up I think that they might send me back teaching.

Catholic education has failed
When I look at the last forty years of Catholic education in Ireland, I am led to the conclusion that Catholic education has completely failed. Whatever the criteria by which we judge success we have failed, especially if it's the rather narrow criterion of: are we forming young people who are committed Catholics? Well, clearly in Ireland today we are not. I live in a parish in Ballymun of 8,000 Catholics and 150 attend Mass on Sundays – and most of them, we think, are visitors. First Communion could be renamed not quite Last Communion but Second Last Communion because there is one more day in church and that is Confirmation. Confirmation is the young person's transition to adulthood, not so much by the laying on of hands as the stretching out of hands to acquire as much money as possible in the shortest time possible that is given to them. Yes children, welcome to adulthood.

If we were to use the broader definition and ask if we are forming young people who are committed to a fair, equitable and just society, I think the results are even more dismal. We have a society that is intensely divisive, intensely unfair and intensely unjust. We have a society where a young couple with two children on an income of €11,000 a year cannot receive a medical card. We have a society where the politicians argue over the National Stadium – whether it will cost €600 million or €1,000 million, and whichever it is, it is seen as money well spent. But as we talk here this afternoon the Department of the Environment and the Department of Health are arguing over 70.5 million euro, which is necessary to fund existing services for homeless people.

Something has gone very wrong with our educational system. I don't know what it is, but let's ask John and Joe and Jim. John is just eighteen and he has worked very hard for the last couple of years. He has studied late into the night, he has gone to grind school, and he has got four As and three Bs in his Leaving Certificate. He is delighted with himself, he feels he has succeeded. Joe, on the other hand, is fourteen. Joe left school last year, and he has not been back since. If you were to ask Joe why he left school, he wouldn't know. He would probably shake his shoulders and say he was bored. John and Joe actually have a lot in common; they both understand what the educational system is about. It's about jobs. John has worked very hard because education is his passport to the career of his choice, and he has succeeded. Joe has left school because he knows that the educational system is not going to make the slightest difference to his possibility of acquiring a job. He is going to be a labourer on a construction site, or he is going to be a bicycle courier, or he is going to work in security, and he doesn't see the point of learning the names of the rivers of Russia or integrating some stupid formula between the equally stupid minus infinity to plus infinity. So both John and Joe are at opposite ends of the educational system, but they are both united in the fact that they are clear that education is about jobs. If it helps you to get the job you want, you stay; if it doesn't, you get out.

Jim is a young lad who lived in our hostel. He came from a dysfunctional family, he had a rather traumatic childhood and he left school early. But Jim decided to go back to school. He went back to school, he did his Leaving Certificate and he got five passes. We at the hostel, we were thrilled, this was the first young fellow in our hostel who had ever gone back to do his Leaving Certificate, and he had passed. But Jim had a great sense of failure because he hadn't got the points he needed to get into the course in the College of Technology that he wanted to get into. Jim felt a failure, and to this day he feels that he wasted those two years. If we think that education is about developing the talents of young people we are very naïve. Education is about jobs. I would like to say to Tom Groome that I enjoyed his paper immensely, I was inspired, I was uplifted, I thought it was absolutely wonderful. But let's get real, education is about jobs.

If education is in fact about jobs, then I believe that the educational system in Ireland is the most unjust structure in our society. Why do I say that? I say that because if education is about jobs or if jobs are a primary reason for being educated, and you can't deny they are, then a just educational system would require equality of access to the educational system and equality of opportunity within the educational system. That we clearly do not have. The educational system is divisive, it is ruthlessly competitive, and it is a struggle for success. Fee-paying schools are not the most important issue in our educational system – only a tiny proportion of children attend fee-paying schools. Yet they are symbolic of the inequality that exists within the educational system. They are where parents can use their wealth to guarantee privileged access and opportunities for their children. If we seriously wanted a fair and a just and an equitable educational system we would struggle for the abolition of such opportunities in fee-paying schools. If we were to struggle for that, where would the opposition come from? The opposition would come from the parents, the parents that were taught as children in our Catholic educational system.

The educational system reflects the injustice in our society, it does not challenge it. Here our educational system is ruthless; competitors struggle for successes; you have to stand on people, not give them a hand up. Our young people are fair-minded, they desire justice passionately, but I think it is squeezed out of them by the nature of our educational system. They are taught to put number one first and justice, fairness and inequality have to wait to come in time. Sr Joan Chittister reminded us that fairness and justice never come in time, that our society is becoming more inequitable, not less, more unjust, not less, as our wealth increases.

How can we educate young people to be concerned about justice, fairness and equality if the very system within which they are educated now, is itself unfair, unjust and unequal. I mean we are fighting a losing battle, and so if the ideals we talk about, wonderful inspiring ideals, if they are to become reality we have to transform the educational system itself. You cannot do it within the individual school – we can try to do it, we can succeed perhaps a little bit in doing it, but we cannot be effective within a system that is itself pointing in the opposite direction, towards injustice, inequality and unfairness. We have got to change the system. But it is not in our interest to change the system. We are, as Sr Joan might have said, stuck with our securities: the security of the curriculum, the security of the structure, and it is difficult for us to want to change the system. That is what we have to do if we want to live the ideals that we espouse.

What about justice within the school? Yes we seek to have an inter-personal not just an educational structure that is just, but justice should also flourish within the school, and it is in the nature of schools that there will be deficiencies. It has always been a pet thought of mine that in every school we have to be encouraging young people to be elected to some sort of justice committee or justice commission. Where injustice occurs, whether from one pupil to another by way of bullying, or some other form of injustice, or from a teacher to a pupil, that those pupils would be encouraged to take up the issue, to protest, to picket the principal's office. Imagine that in a just school we are teaching children to stand up for justice, maybe we ought to be helping and encouraging them to stand up and protest and look for justice even within the school environment.

Finally, I was wondering during Tom Groome's address: is there not a contradiction in the very term 'Catholic education'? I was interested in his comments about Catholic schools in the States; how in some of them only 10 per cent of pupils are Catholics. Many Catholic schools in Ireland require at least an admission from the parents that they are practising Catholics before their children will be admitted to the school. I wonder if there is not a contradiction in terms in giving young people a respect and a reverence for the 'other' when some of those who are 'other' are excluded from participating in the community of their school. When those 'other' are excluded by religion or by ethnic background or by race or whatever, how do we communicate and give young people the example of inclusion and respect for others if we do not include them and respect them within the community we call school? In the north of Ireland where I come from we have seen the sad effects of a Catholic education that is exclusive.

So while I dream of an educational system such as that presented to us here, I think we have a long, long way to go. A long way to go in reforming the system itself, in reforming our individual schools and in asking ourselves, as Sr Joan would put it, some questions that maybe we don't want to answer.

The Pilgrim School:
From hedge to hope

Anne Looney

The purpose of this reflection is to bring to the reimagining process some of the issues that may be peculiarly Irish. It is one thing to explore the issue of Catholic education. It is another, I suggest, to explore Catholic education in Ireland. I am not going to propose that the ideas here are uniquely Irish – they may resonate with experiences in other countries. But what I am going to propose is that there is a unique set of historical, social, cultural and economic circumstances that combine in Ireland to make the process of reimagining the Catholic school here more complex and more challenging than elsewhere. In the case of each of these features, I am also going to identify an associated challenge for the reimagining process. I am not going to attempt to be comprehensive. I am just going to cover a few of the things that have struck me over the last few years and offer them to the debate. All of this I am doing as a product of an Irish Catholic education, as a former teacher in Irish Catholic education and as a student of the processes and policies of education.

I am sure, like many of you, pride of place in my primary-school bag went to my English Reader. This very particular – and very of-its-time style of textbook – was something of a treasure. In fact, the title treasury was used for many of this genre. These readers were crammed with little gems – short passages followed by written exercises designed no doubt to test very particular literacy skills, but also offering a window in unknown worlds and times and places strange and wonderful. St Patrick's misplaced crosier in the foot of Aengus – that was one that has stayed with me. As has for some reason a little piece on the canals of Venice. But the story that really made an impression on me was the story of the hedge schools. I sat in my 1970's state-of-the-art classroom – with sink and cooker mind you – and read of classrooms under hawthorn bushes (always hawthorn bushes) where raggedy children gathered to defy authorities and sit at the feet of the wise and wonderful and learn so that they could grow up and die for Ireland or become priests. Well, that's what happened in the book anyway, and believe me, it took me a while to work out that this was not necessarily the inevitable consequence of primary schooling – the options were sort of worrying if you were a girl! Of course I am exaggerating, of course there was an option for girls. They could become teachers!

Later, and somewhat more informed, research showed these schools to have peculiar curriculum combinations. In Pat Freyne's famous story of the hedge school, the school master, Kavanagh, prided himself on being able to teach forty-nine subjects. In addition to the standard fare, the curriculum included stereometry, gauging, dialling, astrology, austerity, glorification, physic (theory only) and ventilation. He was so valued as a teacher that he was kidnapped by the villagers and held until he agreed to teach in the village.

I am not the only one to have been so moved by the heroic ideal of the hedge school – in the Irish language, the *scoileanna scairte*, meaning, literally, 'the schools that call you in'. Brian Friel opens his play *Translations* in one such school in Donegal in 1833 and presents us with the heroically named Hugh O'Donnell, who turns down the invitation to take charge of the soon to be opened National School. Commenting on this scene Pádraig Hogan, in an important essay on the professional role of teaching, an essay to which I refer again later, notes the contrast between the freedom of hedge-school teachers as scholars and what he calls the puritanical restrictions placed on teachers by the National School system introduced by the British administration in 1831. He notes:

> What the utilitarian primness of the new system feared most of all was the spectre of the teacher as an imaginative adventurer, as a storyteller, as an accomplice of the seductions of song and verse, of literature and drama.

While the idea of the hedge school is one that 'calls people in' to engagement with this imaginative adventurer, it is imbued with a negative construction – as standing against certain things as much as, or even more than, for other things. It is also of note that in Ulster, Presbyterian communities also developed similar hedge schools, with an emphasis on formation in the Presbyterian traditions. The image of the hedge is an interesting one: somewhere to shelter against the chilling winds, a place to gather, to huddle. It's largely a defensive image... an education *against* something as opposed to *for* something.

I believe that when we discuss Catholic education in an Irish context especially, some of this still lingers. It may have as much to do with the historical and social construction of our Catholicism as with our vision of education. We are heirs to a Catholicism that defines itself as much by what it is not and what it is against, as by what it is in favour of. While some might argue that this is a characteristic as universal as it is Catholic, I believe that in Ireland we have a peculiar brand of it by virtue of our history. We have an education system with its roots in defiance. We have a brand of Catholicism imbued with a call, expressed in the hymn 'Faith of our Fathers', to be 'true to thee to death' in 'spite of dungeon fire and sword'. Put the two together and you have a construct of Catholic education that's perpetually on its guard, watchful and mindful of its borders and its territory.

This seems a caricature of the kind of Catholic education that is presented as something from which to recover rather than as something to celebrate. It seems to be of times past and not of times present. But echoes of this remain, and we would ignore them at our peril. If reimagining is be more than the creation of utopias, we must listen carefully to what sometimes we might rather not hear. Issues of power and control and ownership remain, and will not go away no matter how hard we reimagine.

That is the first peculiarly Irish aspect to this debate that I want to highlight – we are hedge schools no longer, but some hedging remains. Interestingly, Chambers dictionary defines 'to hedge' as 'to bet on both sides at the same time'. There is a bit of that going on in contemporary debates about Catholic education. Such hedging may be lingering precisely because of the times in which we live. As a nation, we are struggling to gain our foothold on the beach of modernity, having been tossed there by the storms of the last ten years. We have trouble articulating a sense of what it means to be Irish; all institutions, including Catholic education, are suffering as a consequence. Writing in *The Irish Times* at the end of December 1999, Fintan O'Toole observed of the Irish:

> At the moment, punch-drunk from the effects of continually having pieces of the old Ireland falling on our heads, we're happier re-furnishing our homes than re-furbishing our notion of homeland. But, if only because the one ineradicable aspect of Irishness is a perverse desire to go against the grain, that too will change.

The challenge in reimagining Catholic education is to do so in such a way that it makes a contribution to that other great project of reimagining – reimagining what it means to be Irish. We need to emerge from underneath whatever sheltering hedges may remain to say what Catholic schools are for, and what kind of nation they can be Catholic schools in.

The second characteristic feature of Irish Catholic education is the teaching profession that is its powerhouse. Pádraig Hogan in the piece previously mentioned talks about the priority given in teaching in Ireland to the cultural qualities of the teacher. Hogan suggests that the great majority of Irish teachers understand their purposes as lying within the cultural and personal domain and, as he says, helping young people to achieve through their learning a progressive realisation of their own inmost potentials and an unforced disclosure of their ever-emergent sense of identity.

Research by Ciaran Sugrue into the motivation for taking up a teaching career, conducted among pre-service primary teachers, found a high association between teacher identity and a sense of care. Andy Hargreaves' assertion that teachers become teachers because they want to make a difference seems to be particularly the case in Ireland. We don't talk about this much. We seem to talk about it less and less. In these contentious times even the teaching profession itself is becoming quieter and quieter about this. I would suggest that current debates about Catholic education are not helping to raise these voices. Why? Because while we talk a lot about Catholic schools in Ireland, and about Catholic education, we are largely silent on Catholic classrooms. Perhaps it is because echoes of power and control still linger, but we seem to be very reluctant to get the heart of the matter. Engage with teachers on school ethos and hidden curriculum, pastoral-care structures and student councils – all will be addressed with enthusiasm. But levering open the classroom door is a different matter. And yet, for children and young people, THE site of engagement with Catholic education is not the school, but the classroom. THE critical transaction is not at the macro level of the whole school but in the micro interactions that take place in that mysterious process of teaching and learning. In Ireland, we don't talk enough about this. Most worryingly of all, teachers don't talk enough about this.

A challenge must be to focus on classrooms, to enable teachers to voice their own practice, to articulate the challenges they face and to support them. One of the basic tenets of Catholic theology is the sacrament of the encounter. If this is so, then the most sacred place in the school might be the classroom rather than the chapel or oratory, for it is in the classroom that human potential is nurtured and the grace of self is discovered.

I note that one of the other papers in this conference focuses on the question of relationships. The connectedness or lack of it that is forged in classrooms is central to how students experience their education. And it's not about methods alone. Parker Palmer, who writes on the theme of spirituality in education, recounts how students describe their good teachers. Some of them describe people who lecture all the time, some of them describe people who do little other than facilitate group process, and others describe everything in between. But all of them describe people who have some sort of connective capacity, who connect themselves to their students, their students to each other, and everyone to the subject matter. He summarises that people have difficulty describing what good teachers do, because they are so different. They have no problem describing bad teachers, because they are all the same; they do not connect.

In summary, we have a teaching profession that, we are told, is underpinned by a strong sense of personal commitment. At a time when the teaching profession feels itself to be somewhat under siege, when it is losing the emotional energy, the 'heart' to forge connections, the Catholic education debate here in Ireland is largely silent on the contribution of teachers, not to schools, about which we have much to say, but in classrooms where their profession is enacted. We all need to start talking about classrooms.

The third particular feature of the Irish context that has implications for how we engage in reimagining Catholic education is our ambivalent attitude to what is generally referred to as the marketisation of education. In education markets, an education becomes a product, parents and students become consumers or clients, and teachers become service providers. Parental choice becomes a central driver for school development, and the most important education change for a school is the one that is going on in the school down the road.

The Irish attitude to this feature of education in the developed world is decidedly ambivalent. We tut tut at the excessiveness of this Thatcherite view of things, but set SMART targets for our schools. Marketspeak. It sneaks up on you when you are least aware of it and suddenly you are churning out mission statements promising quality and high standards and effective strategies to achieve them! Do you remember the moment when you were asked if this was the way you wanted to talk about education? Do you remember when you first started talking about effective strategies? No? That's the power of the market. It is all-pervasive and powerfully seductive. Because if the paradigm is market driven, then to be in with a chance of parity of esteem we must 'market' ourselves. It is such an inadequate paradigm for the richness of education. It is ultimately self-defeating, but, more than any other, the educational enterprise leads to large numbers of unmeasurable outcomes. But how else is education being described, and by whom? It's back to the silence again. Alternative and credible voices are few and far between. The reimagining process must engage with education on its own terms and not be seduced by the market.

A further characteristic of the Irish education system is its approach to partnership. Although it can seem fragile, recent education legislation has sought to give it a stronger base. My own organisation – the National Council for Curriculum and Assessment – is the only one of the curriculum and assessment bodies on these islands to have a representative structure, a structure now protected by the Education Act. That same act requires that all schools put student councils in place. We all realise that the journey from rhetoric to reality in the construction of meaningful partnerships is fraught with difficulty. To paraphrase George Orwell, some partners are more partners than others. Nonetheless, this is a feature of our education system, indeed of social and economic institutions generally, that is much treasured and much admired elsewhere. It is striking in international settings, in gatherings and conferences, how the language of partnership stands out against the language of edict and control. I heard an official from an Asian country present how, in response to the economic crisis in her country, on 1 January 2001 the school system introduced differentiated group-work, to what had traditionally been a system built on whole-class teaching. On 2 January the change was in place. I was aghast and asked her what work had been done with teachers to enable them to make this enormous change. She was taken aback by the question. They were told to do it, she said, and they did. Now while we look at this from the high moral ground of partnership, don't for a second try to hide the tiny feeling of envy that you now feel – especially any of you involved in policy-making. The appeal of this approach to educational change – just do it – is very real! But so are its dangers. Colleagues in education systems nearer to home who work in this dynamic, speak of the de-professionalisation that is wrought by being at the receiving end of endless initiatives in which they played no part, and by being subject to political whim, and endless public criticism for not responding fast enough to those whims.

Partnership is precious and must be nurtured and protected against those who argue that it slows things down, that it hinders real development, who would have us 'just do it', and what they mean is 'just do it my way'.

There are consequences for the reimagining process; the vision of Catholic education cannot be shared with parents and students and teachers – it has to be created with them. Great strides are being made in this direction by those who work in Irish Catholic education, not least among the organisers of this conference. More work is needed. Especially among those who do not find it easy to have their voices heard, who are silent in the process – those who are the discussed rather than the participants in the discussion. Particular work is needed with parents who may, like many Irish adults, find that they have trouble working out what it means to be an Irish Catholic, let alone what it means to participate in an Irish Catholic education.

When such uncertainty reigns, the power of the default setting is unleashed. You know the default setting – if you have a computer you can reset the margins, change the font and the paper size, but the next time you turn it on, it's still at Times New Roman. There is a default setting for Irish Catholic education: created under hedges in times of persecution, a place of protection and order, against lots of things, keeping certain things out.

We have an education system characterised by partnership – the challenge is to continue to bring this to the reimagining process, which will mean engaging with all the uncertainty over being Irish as well as the uncertainty over being Catholic. Not an easy task, but an enormous challenge for Irish Catholic education.

All of which makes me a little worried about some of the suggestions on the role for the future of religious congregations in Irish education published last year by the Conference of Religious of Ireland. This reflection paper is a wonderful overview of the commitment and involvement of religious in the creation of the education system in Ireland and it holds that involvement up for analysis against the light of the founding charisms of the congregations. It is a timely and important publication – for the congregations and the challenges they face and for the education system as a whole.

The report notes that congregational involvement in schools is marked in the twenty-first century by the transfer of trusteeship to lay people. Many here today are involved in that process in creative and constructive ways. The emerging education mission is mapped out for the congregations and involves three strands – trailblazing initiatives, public debate and advocacy, and forming alliances. These three features of the proposed work of the congregations are discussed at length in the document and related back to the founding charisms. It is an exciting and challenging vision and the three strands proposed are to be welcomed.

The report presents a rather bleak view of Catholic schools. The education system comes in for strong criticism in the document – essentially conservative, of benefit to the well off, narrow, academically focused, and in the grip of consumerist values. Education, the report notes, will never be a transformative force. What is needed, especially for the marginalised, is a different kind of educational experience inspired by gospel values. An option set out for the congregations is to work with poor and marginalised and to take on a public advocacy role for the counter-cultural voice.

In the scenario presented in the report, are Catholic schools being left under the hedges? Are teachers, who wanted to make a difference, being left to an impossible and fruitless task? – you may want to make a difference but if you work in a classroom you will never change anything! Are the education partners being told that theirs is not gospel work, not good news, but bad news?

The CORI document suggests that the energies of congregations should be focused on unmet needs. But some of the greatest unmet needs are in the schools founded by religious congregations. Schools are the construction site of future generations. Consideration is needed for religious congregations to be more – not less – engaged in that process. Some have already developed creative and exciting ways of supporting schools and classrooms. But others need to send a strong message to their partners in the schools – schools have the potential to be gospel-filled; they can be places where a difference is made.

When that partnership is maintained, the Catholic school is not abandoned to the market, to the vice-like grip of the points system. Instead, it can become a pilgrim school – a symbol of possibility, a beacon of the meaningful, in a world seduced by the lure of the superficial and meaningless. Pilgrims engage, but set themselves apart. Pilgrims journey, but theirs is not an aimless wander. A pilgrim is a visible witness that some things matter more than others, and gives that witness in a public way. There is no hedging, no hiding here. The symbol for this conference, the growing tree, is a powerful call to rebirth and renewal. But it must be a place of departure, not a shelter from icy winds. It must allow for branches to be taken from it and forged into the pilgrim schoolroom. It must allow for seeds to be scattered, and not simply gathered under its shade.

Above all else, the pilgrim school offers hope; it would be tempting to suggest that a pilgrim school would be a sign of hope to the world. It is far more difficult to look inside, at how the pilgrim school offers hope to its students, in its classrooms. And I don't mean hope of success, hope in life chances. I mean the hope that is born in the foundation of Christian faith, that the human is graced beyond measure and that life can be transformed. We stand in need of such hope. We stand in need of such education.

'The Past is Not What it Used to Be'

Brenda Power

At the time that Alice Taylor's book, *To School Through the Fields*, was published some years ago, I recall being much amused by the public curiosity at the novelty of her basic concept. To school through the fields – what a quaint notion, ran the general response, how charming an idea; what an idyllic existence it conjured up. Imagine walking through fields to get to your school. Even the choice of title itself presupposed an element of wonder amongst the modern book-buying public at the very thought.

For younger readers, I imagine the suggestion must have seemed even more fanciful and remote – what! no school buses, no micro-scooters, no four-by-four jeeps complete with bull bars to ferry young Fachtna and Sibeal to the local multidenominational high school, along with their lacrosse sticks and their playstations and their mobile phones? Worse still, no handy newsagents *en route* where you might nip in for the twenty Silk Cut and a Ready-to-Go top-up card?

What tickled me most of all, though, about the response to Alice Taylor's fine memoir, was what it illustrated about the very selective, customised, purpose-built nature of our own schoolday memories. Because I, like, I suspect, quite a lot of people here, walked to school through the fields. But for a while I was so busy being charmed by Alice's recollections, and envying her the pastoral simplicity of those early experiences, I forgot that completely.

After all, large sprawling cities, like two-car families, are a very recent innovation – it is not so long since the suburbs that are now considered part of central Dublin were outlying villages. Much as it might make Liam

Lawlor's teeth water to recall those times, these villages had many large green areas of unspoilt woodland or pasture, with farmers still running their dairy operations within a few miles of the GPO until surprisingly recently.

Walking to school through the fields was not always the enchanting experience the phrase evokes, although it had its moments. It is more than a quarter of a century since I last walked that route to my own rural school in south Kilkenny, and yet even today I could step every foot of it in my imagination. I remember the field sometimes inhabited by a wicked auburn bull, the stile where we stopped to polish off the blackened remains of the lunchtime banana sandwiches, fearful of the repercussions if they survived the day. I remember the ditches of bluebells that heralded the arrival of the summer holidays far more reliably than the calendar ever did, and the heart-sinking mornings when I forgot my school shoes and had to sit through the whole school day in my big black wellingtons, providing the nastier village girls with taunting fodder they didn't really need.

It is, of course, as impossible to be objective about your school days as it is about your childhood itself. You have to rely for the narrative, after all, on a very biased, inexperienced, impressionable historian – yourself, aged five or ten or fourteen. That imperfect chronicler tends to remember all teachers as towering autocrats, given to capricious bursts of kindness or unpredictable harshness, all winter school days wet and cold, all summer holidays endlessly sunny.

I know objectively speaking that one teacher of mine was no more than twenty-one when she first taught me and yet, try as I might even today, I cannot imagine her as a young person, because teachers remain in your memory as stern, didactic adults to your perpetual child, and never as what they were – ordinary, fallible, well-intentioned human beings trying to do a job, and a hard job, as best they could, often, in the past, with school rooms and facilities and – let's face it – raw material that left a lot to be desired. The truth is that your school days were never either quite as good or quite as bad as you remember them – and I suspect that our own children will take away memories from their own current school days, that will be just as dappled with fact and perception and flawed memory.

The Irish school system of Alice Taylor's day was probably no better or worse than mine or yours, given whatever limitations that particular generation worked through. My own father, who would be of a similar vintage and would certainly have walked to school through the fields, remembers going barefoot in summer, carrying the slates that predated our neatly lined copybooks and, in winter, bringing to school a sod of turf to fuel the only source of heating in a big draughty building – the open fire behind the master's desk, the meager heat from which, he rather ruefully noted, the master's ample bottom absorbed in full.

Many of us here came of a time – unimaginable to contemporary children – when corporal punishment was allowed. One of the nuns in my school, a kindly old dear well into her seventies by the time I crossed her path, kept in her desk a short stumpy knuckle of a furze bush – no doubt lovingly collected on one of the nature walks with her students she enjoyed so much on sunny early summer days – which she used to dispense punishment. In fact, it didn't hurt nearly as much as the flat ruler favoured by the other nuns, it was completely shorn of any thorny bits, but it still looked a lot scarier.

Yet it clearly never occurred to that nice, gentle old lady that there was anything at all amiss in lining up seven-year-old girls, who really wouldn't have been the most unruly pupils you could imagine, and slapping their hands with a lump of wood. Modern schoolchildren really have difficulty with the notion of teachers who might have slapped you for talking in class or staining a schoolbook, and, in the retelling, it is not easy to convince them that these were by no means violent or cruel or frightening people. But they were not.

What some children knew then, though, and what most of us accept now is that there certainly were a lot of teachers who abused the corporal punishment rule and employed it to mask their own disturbed, dysfunctional, sadistic urges. They relied on the fear and silence of the children they harmed, and traded on the fact that they didn't have parents to go home to or, if they did, these parents would be so deferential to the teacher's role in society that they would be slow to credit a child's account of excessive cruelty or sexual abuse, slower still to act upon a report and, all round, far more likely to punish the child for being naughty enough to anger a religious brother or a respected schoolmaster.

But still, very many children of those years have positive memories of their schooldays. Discipline might have been, sometimes, harshly imposed, but it certainly defined the boundaries and the certainties that growing young minds need. Good and bad, right and wrong were clearly determinable within a rigid value system that served a purpose in its day. Just as in the school context, you knew that society would also punish bad, unsocial, disruptive or dishonest behaviour, and your parents' reluctance to gainsay the teacher's authority confirmed your faith in a solid, respected, unambiguous social order.

We have, in recent decades of curriculum review, dispensed with many of the teaching methods that drummed the poetry and the Irish grammar and the arithmetic tables into the most resistant of brains. Indeed, a controversial new polemic on the matter of compulsory Irish even goes so far as to suggest that the very practice of teaching Irish to young children was a mistake, that it did more harm to the language than centuries of British suppression, and that it constrained them academically by absorbing such a great portion of their schooldays at a formative stage. I don't know if this is true – I know I feared and hated Irish as a child, I still have nightmares in which Peig Sayers features prominently, and I'd quite like to learn to speak it now, though the scars left by the *Tuiseal Ginideach* make that very unlikely. I'm not sure, though, that all of these curricular reviews and modifications are necessarily an improvement.

Children don't seem to learn the alphabet in order any more, because of the Letterland system used by most schools, so they have to rely on Barney and Sesame Street if they're ever to hope to read a phone book. I can't figure out my eight-year-old daughter's method of multiplication, and keep reverting to my 'times tables' to check that her homework is right. I am sure there is sound psychological and educational reasoning behind these changes.

But most of all, I wonder if an equally progressive and enlightened approach to school discipline really is providing children with the certainties they need. Many will gratefully remember being gently and sensitively dealt with when they transgressed – no more knobbly stumps of furze bushes on display – but they will also see others, who have behaved in a genuinely unacceptable way, being just as mildly reproached, if at all. A recent case, that made headlines, highlighted this development. A teenage boy, in a County Wicklow school, was found to be – better be careful here – making cannabis available to his schoolmates on a trip to the west of Ireland. The head teacher investigated the matter, formed a view as to who the ringleaders were, and tried to take action that he believed appropriate. The parents of the boy, who had certainly been caught in possession of drugs, whatever his purposes were, took High Court action to prevent the school expelling him. They subsequently said, on radio, that they would discipline their child in their own way – what they succeeded in doing, of course, was to make himself and his enterprise into a household name. What they also did, though, was chip a further chunk out of the disciplinary authority of the school system, and suggest that education and discipline were entirely distinguishable ends. I wrote a piece in the *Sunday Tribune* at the time, suggesting that most parents might have thought it more appropriate to take their child out of the school, apologise to the head and the rest of the pupils, and quietly move him to another place, where his drug dabbling would not be public knowledge, in order to give him a fresh start, and a firm lesson. Those parents sent me a solicitor's letter for my temerity as well.

In the main case, though, the headmaster lost the legal battle, and substantial legal costs as well; the young lad is back in the school with the full support of his litigious parents, and it is really hard to imagine that other impressionable youngsters could view him as anything other than a hero in the schoolyard. Clearly, the revelations of recent years, and the general trend towards more relaxed discipline, have undermined the authority of the teachers, even in cases that seem absolutely black and white. All parents know that it is a bad idea to disagree, in front of the children, on a matter of discipline or rules: when youngsters see those in authority do precisely that, it's hardly any wonder that we have, for example, the public-order offences, the casual violence and vandalism, the vicious and unprovoked late-night attacks on our streets, some of it seemingly carried out by 'decent' youngsters from good schools.

Bullying has always been a schoolyard problem. It is not a recent consequence of inadequate discipline or affluence or material competitiveness, or whatever you want to blame. I was teased, as I said, on those days that I had to come to school in my wellies – nowadays youngsters are belittled and isolated by their peers if they don't have the right Nike or Adidas runners at 100 euros a pair – in that instance, only the nature of the footwear has changed. But the bullies seem to have adopted far more insidious and destructive tactics – my brother, who teaches primary children in Clondalkin, told me how he saw a six-year-old reduced to miserable tears by a bunch of classmates chanting Zinger at him; when he asked the child what was the matter he was too embarrassed to tell, but another pupil explained that this was the brand name on his Dunnes Stores runners. Bullying seems far more difficult to counter these days than in the times when the teacher, even if it required the aid of a knobbly furze stump, exerted some authority. And its consequences are truly terrifying – every year we read of more than one inquest into the death of a child who chose suicide as the only way to escape the most hurtful schoolyard taunts.

We are certainly raising a generation of more secure and more assertive children. Far removed from the more meek, timid, submissive schoolchildren we were ourselves. That has to be a good thing, and I doubt that we would have seen the economic success of the past few years if it wasn't for the strength and confidence and self-esteem of the generation who came of age in the early nineties and set a high value on their own worth and talent.

The title of this part of the day's proceedings is, 'The past is not what it used to be' – a bit ambiguous, perhaps, appropriate to a revisiting of the recent history of our Catholic education. There has been an understandable tendency, I suppose, in recent years to come down on one side or the other – to lay claim to the idyllic childhood, the 'To school through the fields' template, or else to relay horrific recollections of chilling cruelty and insensitivity, incompetence and frustration. I went to school through those fields, they could be mucky and cold, you might sometimes stumble and lose your footing, snag your best socks on a lurking thorn bush, spend a whole day in chilly misery; but they could also be glorious, full of sunlight and laughter and the scent of wild flowers in an endless springtime. I guess my schooldays were much the same, and I can hope my children will have similar memories.

Catholic Education
and the Future

Don Herron

The millennium prompted scenario-building for many aspects of human endeavour. Sketching in future scenarios is a regular aspect of strategic planning in both private and public sectors. Attempting to forecast the future, whether population, road usage or style, defies accurate prediction. The future of Catholic schools has not been ignored. This has been accentuated by the changes taking place since Vatican II, decades that have been paralleled by major economic, social, political and cultural changes for societies, ours included. The changes that have significant implications for education include the increased secularisation of societies, the importance of education in economic development and the resulting impact on purposes of education, the marketisation of schooling and the role of parents in education. There are fewer religious personnel to teach and manage Catholic schools and there is evidence of changing attitudes towards denominational schools.

Catholic schools exist in different circumstances depending on the country or part of the world, the size and social position of the Catholic community, the experience of the Church there, the constitutional framework and the historic development of the educational system. Scenarios outlining the future of Catholic schools will differ in each country. Several authors have outlined the types or models of Catholic school likely to emerge in the next decades (Treston, 1997; Arthur, 1995; Feheny, 1998; Boeve, 2001; Youoniss and Convey, 2000) and these range from the traditional Catholic school and alternatives that reflect Catholic schools' responses to the emerging environments described above (cf. McCann in this volume). Some broad patterns emerge from these writings:

- The importance and influence of the social and cultural environment in which the Catholic schools operate and the interaction between the school and that environment (CORI, 1997a).
- The differences in direction have a basis in different philosophical, theological and sociological perspectives of the Church and of Catholic education (Youniss and McLennan, 1999).
- The development of liberal or procedural states is leading to participation of Catholic education in State/public education systems, with the constraints this imposes on curricular, intake and other policies (Sacks, 2000).

The contemporary Catholic school does not appear to be in as strong a position as its predecessor. In places where there was support by the State and society, the Church could exert high levels of influence on matters external as well as internal to the schools (Williams, 1999). In other contexts the Church and the schools were set apart from the society and they supported and sustained their own system. Prevailing societies today are increasingly apathetic to religious beliefs, values and leadership. Parental choice of schools is influenced by many factors, not least the career and vocational needs of their children. The students themselves actively participate in society as consumers, workers and groups. The realisation that the school climate or ethos 'is constituted by the interaction and collaboration of its various components: students, parents, teachers, directors and non-teaching staff' (Congregation for Catholic Education, 1998: par 18) rather than imposed from above, marks out the twenty-first-century Catholic school from its predecessor of say fifty years ago. The future shape and profile of the local communities that the schools serve will be an influence on the manner in which Catholic schools engage with their community. The identity of the school will be shaped by the interaction with this external environment and the intentions of Catholic community; the making of this identity will be the interactions and collaboration of the parties concerned.

The position in Ireland

The development of the Education Commission of CORI [then the CMRS] led to and stimulated research, review, appraisal and critique of the many aspects of the religious congregations' involvement in and commitment to education and of the education system itself. In CORI's documents one can discern articulation of the role and the characteristics of the Catholic school (CMRS, 1988a; 1988b; 1989a; 1989b) and the proposals for educational reform in the Republic of Ireland in the 1990s.

Their conference on the *Catholic School in Contemporary Society* (1991) pointed to several interlinked shifts in understanding and position and the way forward for education was elaborated in key CORI publications (CORI, 1996; McCormack, 1998, 2001) [cf. Maxwell this volume]. These documents are futuristic in so far as they point to possible ways to progress: on trusteeship, partnership and the Catholic community's responsibility for education, school leadership, the school community and the rationalisation of schools. If 'vision' is partly about creating signposts, the CORI documents have done so in a measurable manner.

Dr Dermot Lane's paper at this conference was widely disseminated after the conference as a separate publication (Lane, 1991). Lane highlighted the challenges facing the Catholic school in 1991. It is illustrative to list and record them for comparison with those challenges that seem to be emerging for the next decade. Lane highlighted:

- agreeing an underlying philosophy and creating a distinctive ethos in Irish schools (p.12);
- schools as Christian communities (p.24);
- the role of the chaplain;
- lay ownership, responsibility and leadership for Catholic schools (p.25);
- the balance of responsibility between home, school and parish (p.27);
- the need for a 'new image, new story' to empower Catholic education and the Catholic school (p.28).

There is a growing level of research into Catholic education elsewhere and in Ireland. McDonnell (1995) examined ethos in Catholic voluntary secondary schools. He concluded that the schools, in many ways, worked out of a traditional model of Catholic school and, as a result, there were significant differences in the perspectives of the participants. There was 'confusion surrounding the question of the existence of a distinct philosophy of education underpinning the work of Catholic voluntary schools'. In this situation the fundamental tenets of such a philosophy seemed to have very little influence on the ways schools operate (vol. II, p.521). Norman (2000) also examined ethos and recommended the need for the Church to increase the effort it puts into the pastoral dimension of life in Catholic schools through an analysis of the merits of chaplaincy (cf. Norman, 2002).

Tuohy, Maume and Maxwell (2000) interviewed principals and RE teachers in secondary schools and pointed up the positive current reality of schools where the schools all had elements of the traditional Catholic school. However, many of the catechists felt that the faith development aspects of the schools took second place in the competition with points, and others felt that they were absorbed into a State system that controlled the real ethos of the school (ibid. p.63). The Christian Brothers' action-research project (O'Brien and Coyle, 2001a, 2001b) found relatively high, but by no means unanimous, levels of endorsement for core characteristics of the Christian Brothers' schools. As no real debate on the aims of Catholic education had taken place they may have been displaced by a more functional, utilitarian role, quite similar to many non-religious schools (p.28). Reports of young adults' schooling also highlighted the dominance of school purposes such as achievement in exams and preparation for work (Brennan, 2001; Fulton et al., 2000; Tuohy and Cairns, 2000). They highlighted the future faith-formation work of the Church in supporting parents and the challenge of continuing the work of school among young adults (Tuohy and Cairns, 2000: 198-200; McDonnell, 1995: 520; Codd, this volume).

The Education Act 1998 provides the legal framework for future education administration in Ireland. Demographic change will provide some of the impetus for structural change. Political and parental attitudes have a determining influence on the levels of support and resources for schools. Increasing diversity (of lifestyle, values, beliefs, language, etc.) within communities will necessitate channels of representation, choice and decision-making in schools to reflect these viewpoints. Economic developments will have a significant impact on curriculum and assessment. This is the developing framework in which Catholic schools will operate in the future. The integration of the Catholic schools into public education systems generally is a recent phenomenon. The Catholic position was recently reiterated in *The Catholic School on the Threshold of the Third Millennium* (Congregation for Catholic Education, 1998): as Catholic schools are at the service of society 'the Catholic school willingly occupies its place within the school system of the different countries and in the legislation of the individual states, when the latter respect the fundamental rights of the human person, starting with the respect for life and religious liberty' (para. 16).

What then are the priorities facing Catholic education in Ireland in the next couple of decades? Where does Lane's (1991) agenda stand a decade later? What challenges need addressing in the next number of years? The Catholic School Project is based in Marino Institute of Education and was set up to support and resource Catholic schools. Its conference, 'Reimagining the Catholic School', was supplemented by this research – the identification of the future challenges. The results would be of use in various ways but mainly to support the bodies involved in the future of Catholic education.

Methodology

The Delphi and Delphi-inspired techniques are a form of structured, qualitative and indirect interaction futures methodology. Other methods include 'future issues scanning' reports and use of focused group discussions using relevant experts. The Delphi technique has been applied to policy formation, education and training, and marketing (cf. Adler and Ziglio, 1996; Clayton, 1997; Critcher and Gladstone, 1998). Its use of several rounds: opinion – feedback – refining opinion, is considered more reliable than individual statements and may be more objective in its final outcomes and lead towards greater clarification of or agreement (Linstone and Turoff, 1975).

The assumptions underpinning this approach are that the relevant experts are the best sources of the information and that these expert opinions are better if given anonymously. Hence the use of post, fax or e-mail to send and receive opinion and feedback. It is also assumed that opinions are better if the participants are allowed modify their opinion in the light of others' [anonymous] opinions. This process requires more than one round of responses.

The advantages mentioned in the literature (cf. Sproule, 1995) are its speed and cost-effectiveness and the informed consensus, avoiding contention because of the built-in anonymity. It may also elicit innovative or risk-taking thinking or responses. The method also has strong, though contested, claims to validity (Adler and Ziglio, 1996; Clayton, 1997; Critcher and Gladstone, 1998). However, there is a lack of sample independence after the initial choice. The group will usually diminish as there is a drop-out factor (Critcher and Gladstone, 1998). A critical feature in futures research is that it may not be exhaustive in considering all aspects (Clayton, 1997). A methodological difficulty is the tendency to judge future events as isolated rather than interdependent and interrelated events (Alder and Ziglio, 1996). Finally, the process may be vulnerable to researcher bias in assessing incoming opinions and framing the questionnaire rounds.

A Delphi-inspired technique was used in this project and it accessed a number of experts in the area of education and religion. The responses formed the basis for a subsequent questionnaire, for a more considered response from the group. It was conducted by mail and e-mail. A panel comprising people involved in planning was drawn up and included people from the sectors outlined in Table 1 below. This led to an invited group agreeing to participate in the manner outlined in this table. Phase One took place in late 2001 and Phase Two in early 2002.

TABLE 1 SAMPLE DETAILS AND PARTICIPATION

Respondent Category	Agreed	Round 1	Round 2
Trustee / Education Office	9	8	7
Educator / academic	8	8	6
Diocesan / managerial administration	6	4	1
Principals	3	2	1
Parent representative	2	1	1
Totals	**28**	**23**	**16**

The initial instrument was constructed around a key focus: the view of Catholic education and the challenges facing it in 2010 and beyond. This identifies the decisions or tasks ahead in a concrete way. The initial instrument:

> The environment for Catholic education in Ireland will be different in 2010 and beyond. Major changes will occur in such areas as culture, religious belief and practice, the economy, social conditions, technology and education.

1. Describe what this environment will be for Irish Catholic education in 2010 and beyond by describing the significant changes and events that will have occurred by then. Please be specific.
2. Describe your view of what Catholic education will look like in 2010 and beyond.
3. For the vision of Catholic education that you have provided for the year 2010 and beyond, what are the challenges that must be met?
4. In order to meet these challenges, what are the major developments that are needed, changes that are required?

The responses to the questions were summarised and returned to the panel for refinement. In the case of questions three and four, the panel were also asked to prioritise the challenges and comment on the responses that were summarised using *essential, very important, important but other needs may take priority, not immediately important,* to *unimportant,* in their responses. These priorities were scored and aggregated. The process, therefore, collected and organised opinion and judgements in a systematic way. The drop-off rates were within the usual range for Delphi research. In respect of the general environment in Ireland in 2010 and beyond, the picture drawn was by a panel selected for expertise related to education and Catholic education rather than for economic, cultural or social forecasting *per se*. The environment emerging may reflect that.

Respondents' view of environment for Catholic education

The respondents see that Ireland will be a multi-cultural and multi-ethnic society to some extent, particularly in the larger urban areas. This will mean being, to some extent, multi-denominational, and an increase, from its small base, in the numbers seeing themselves as non-denominational. Linguistic diversity will increase. These developments will add to the trend towards pluralism.

The workforce will reflect various societal changes: immigration and increased female participation. Young people's [part-time] participation will continue. Many people's identity will be allied to their occupation. A growing interest in lifelong learning will mirror changes in occupational mobility and promotion. There will be a changing age structure, with effects on the school-age population. There will be less time given to voluntary or community activity. There will be increases in social isolation, some the result of social exclusion. This phenomenon will be contrasted with a public concern for sustaining or regenerating community.

The population will be generally more educated and travelled. It will have developed various external international reference points (for example, the EU, media, etc.) for choices in lifestyle, interests, leisure and values. There will be a continuing income gap and the resulting marginalisation of various groups. There will be increasing urbanisation and this will be accompanied by rural, small farm and western population decline.

In the area of values and religion, Ireland will be an increasingly secular society, and this will be seen in social, political and institutional structures. There will be greater separation of Church and State in policy and decision-making. A large percentage of the population will be nominally Catholic, accompanied by lower church attendances and religiosity. For a large proportion of the population there will be less identification with or influence by the institutional Church. Relativist moral thinking and decision-making will increase. Religion will become a private matter, with religion less evident in the public sphere. This is paralleled by the adoption of a neutral position of the State towards denominational groups. Its position will be one of religious tolerance and pluralism. There will be, however, no upsurge in anti-Church sentiment.

There will be a dynamic lay Church with a smaller number of committed members. They will be more informed in their belief, of their values. Their theology will inform their views of social justice in society. Lay people, alongside a smaller number of clergy, will exercise their gifts for the common good and will come to feel and to exercise adult ownership of the faith community to which they belong. There will be enhanced roles for women and for young people. The pastoral focus of this community will be on the values of truth, caring and social justice and it will be appreciative of spirituality. It will be participative and there will be voluntary commitment. There will be, however, some tension as a result of a polarisation among believers as this process progresses.

The educational environment forecast is for a mixed, generally competitive educational landscape, with Catholic-denominational, community, public inter- or non-denominational and private [for and non-profit] schools. Location and population will determine the range of choice. Each system will be managed, at all levels, by lay/professionals. Schools will be settings for other social, welfare and healthcare services, sometimes on the campus [more often primary schools]. Many will attend to adult and community education [usually second-level locations]. Some parents will opt for home education.

With a reduced pool of pupils there will be less emphasis on competitive results and more on an appreciation of and demand for places based on school quality and service. Respect for rights, students and parents, and communication with parents, will be a key element in this service. Schools will also respect the lifestyle choices and beliefs of parents. However, society will place greater student social and personal development demands on schools.

The curriculum will become economically driven to maintain Ireland's international competitiveness. This will involve greater innovation in delivery and assessment. This will be complemented by greater use of ICTs, which will be more integrated into home, work and school and with other forms of information and knowledge acquisition. There will be a growing critique of educational and curriculum policies, including that from a Catholic perspective.

Respondents' view of the challenges facing Catholic education in 2010 and beyond

Catholic schools will exist in a competitive **environment** of different types of school: denominational, public-community and private (both non- and for-profit) schools. Inevitably, this will have an impact on school 'ethos'. Through rationalisation there will be fewer Catholic schools. Some rationalisations will be of existing Catholic voluntary schools while others will be rationalisations between them and VEC schools. These will result in new community schools or colleges with Catholic representation on management. Most of the Catholic schools will be under lay forms of group trusts, either covering schools of one congregation together, or regional or diocesan-based, covering schools of several congregations. All schools would have active parent and student participation. Equitable State financial support would be provided.

The transition to alternative ownership structures was a very important challenge in the survey responses (rating was 2.1 and standard deviation [sd]1.1). The development of the structures should continue to involve strategic planning so that a long-term structure will be in place. Not all models of trusteeship adopted need be the same but they will differ according to circumstances, including distinctive congregational charisms.

Catholic thinking on education **philosophy** and **ethos** will have evolved to the point where it will be meaningful to think of a distinctive philosophy of Catholic education. Respondents foresaw that the cultivation and transmission of a distinctive culture or ethos would have been worked out (cf. Catholic Bishops of Northern Ireland, n.d.). It would be possible to define and benchmark educational practices in Catholic schools against it. These two items received the highest rating of all the challenges identified in the survey.

TABLE 2 THE PHILOSOPHY AND ETHOS CHALLENGE

Score	Sd	Challenge	Response
1.3	0.9	To clarify, agree and articulate **a philosophy** and **shared vision** of Catholic education.	Define the philosophy and agree aims of Catholic education in Ireland. Support process of articulation and dissemination.
		Clarify the issues surrounding **ethos** and	School community **reviews** and develops its culture, [ethos] and
1.23	0.3	outline the implications for the schools.	promotes it through charter/mission statement.

Scoring

Essential	Very important	Important, but other needs may take priority	Not immediately important	Unimportant
1.0 – 1.75	1.76 – 2.49	2.5 – 3.49	3.5 – 4.25	4.26 – 5.0

This distinctive profile or identity will inform and be informed by the school planning and evaluation processes, and management and educational practice. These corporate practices will lead to better-organised, accountable and effective Catholic schools. These developments will stimulate curricular, pastoral, pedagogic and organisational innovation, which were hallmarks of the Catholic school sector. Catholic schools will be positioned to be a leading sector in Irish education innovation.

The process of clarifying Catholic philosophy and ethos and their impact on school curriculum and organisation at the schools' level will be matched by greater sophistication in parental **choice of school**. Differences between the two sets of expectations will emerge that will present dilemmas for school leadership – at both board and school levels. Alternatively, this may move, with less competition for third-level places, towards greater discernment in parental choice, one based on quality of education, emphasising values, religious commitment, cultural, social and personal development as well as academic attainment. Implicit in this scenario are a variety of schools available locally to reflect parental choices. Where this is not the case it will pose a challenge for Catholic schools and, in particular, those Catholic schools exclusively serving a local community.

TABLE 3 THE IN-SCHOOL CHALLENGES

Score	Sd	Challenge	Possible Response
2.0	1.1	To develop **curriculum, pedagogy** and **school organisation** to reflect Catholic educational and moral values; in all aspects of school, from management to classrooms; to contribute to State curriculum and education innovation.	Develop research and literature in Irish Catholic education and leadership, based on innovation in education, presenting a critique of State and other innovation, journal for Catholic education.

Score	Sd	Challenge	Possible Response
2.9	1.2	Respond to varying levels of **religious commitment** among staff members and students. induction policy.	Staff [development] programmes. Recruitment and A culture to support staff to contribute to and support the ethos of the school.
			Minority view highlights selection issues, and consequent organisational issues.

Scoring system

Essential	Very important	Important, but other needs may take priority	Not immediately important	Unimportant
1.0 – 1.75	1.76 – 2.49	2.5 – 3.49	3.5 – 4.25	4.26 – 5.0

TABLE 4 THE CHALLENGE OF CHOICE

Score	sd	Challenge	Possible Response
2.6	1.0	To cope with increasing tendency of parents and pupils to approach education as **consumers** or a **product** rather than a Catholic education perspective.	Research parental choice and school marketing strategies. School reviews its own priorities.

Scoring system

Essential	Very important	Important, but other needs may take priority	Not immediately important	Unimportant
1.0 – 1.75	1.76 – 2.49	2.5 – 3.49	3.5 – 4.25	4.26 – 5.0

There was no one voice on a future Catholic school **profile** or **identity** but there were several emphases. The following scenarios depict the range of possible developments. They are not mutually exclusive.

(1) The Catholic school will be *open to all faiths and none* in community settings. This scenario represents an education for the Catholic students who attend the school as compared to a Catholic education for all in the school.

(2) A Catholic school whose direction will emphasise the Church's *mission to the marginalised* who are, or are included in, the student body.

(3) Schools that will serve the needs of an *identifiable faith community* and place reasonable limits on the intake of others. They will retain a definite Catholic character and expect partners to participate in worship and religious culture of the school.

(4) Schools will continue as *Catholic in name* and demand for places will continue to be high. The demand will depend to a large extent on the school's success in examination achievement. The parents' and students' commitment to a Catholic purpose of education will be nominal, symbolic or pragmatic.

(5) Catholic schools will remain within the publicly funded sector and will be fully integrated into the State's curriculum and management structures. There will be recognition of their distinct ethos. There will be tensions with the direction or emphases of State education policy or practice. There will be tensions where this school is the sole school serving a community.

Identities or profiles will take shape over time. This will be in response to the emerging environment inside and outside the schools, the school's tradition and its understanding of its role. It will result also from the various proactive decisions taken and how these work themselves out over time. The decisions and events are dynamic in that they interact with one another and within the wider framework of society and economy. The panel saw the need for monitoring and research as critical.

The **role of the parish** in education and faith formation and development will continue to evolve. The links with the school will depend increasingly on the role, person and function of chaplains, more often specific to schools. The role of the school will be clarified within this context.

TABLE 5 THE CHALLENGE OF FAITH FORMATION

Score	sd	Challenge	Possible Response
1.9	1.1	Debate the issues surrounding **faith formation / development** roles of home, school and parish and ensure that the school faith community links appropriately with local parishes.	Develop a broad-based support for and among Catholic parents to meet the challenges of catechesis / faith formation and schooling [*Alternative minority response: is this feasible in the future?*] Develop a framework for schools and parish(es) and explore support of full-time, trained, chaplains and trained adult educators.

Scoring system

Essential	Very important	Important, but other needs may take priority	Not immediately important	Unimportant
1.0 – 1.75	1.76 – 2.49	2.5 – 3.49	3.5 – 4.25	4.26 – 5.0

The source of support to the home in faith formation is uncertain for the moment: is it the school or the parish? This challenge takes place also in a context where parish and community will weaken as social institutions with which people identify. It is, moreover, bound up with the type of Church that will exist in 2010 and beyond.

This challenge was placed in a wider context of the future of the institutional Church that has been accepted for generations. Could this uncertainty about the future development of the Catholic Church also impinge on the Catholic school of the future? The future shape emerging in the data in this survey (bearing in mind its focus was the Catholic school) is of a more informed Church membership, whose commitment informs their work and who adopt various roles within the community of believers. There is a critical dimension to their world view and in their engagement with society and education. The Catholic school will reflect its community just as a nation's schools reflect its society.

TABLE 6 THE CHALLENGES FOR THE CHURCH

Score	sd	Challenge	Proposed Response
2.0	1.03	Develop **spirituality, values** and **theology** of those involved in Catholic education.	Develop adult / community education: in faith formation, theology, etc. and in education. [*This is not specifically a school/education community responsibility.*]
1.9	1.0	The 'dialogue' of Christian **faith** with modern and youth cultures; implications for the Catholic school.	The dialogue will influence /reflect the Catholic school profile; Have implications for managing, staff and curriculum policies.
1.9	1.14	To form lay Catholics in **leadership, management** and other **key roles** to enable involvement in schools and parishes.	Prepare/educate and train people for leadership in Catholic education; Create development opportunities; Develop the local Catholic communities where clergy and laity all exercise their gifts for the community.

Scoring system

Essential	Very important	Important, but other needs may take priority	Not immediately important	Unimportant
1.0 – 1.75	1.76 – 2.49	2.5 – 3.49	3.5 – 4.25	4.26 – 5.0

There were different expectations regarding the future position of **religious education**, instruction and faith formation in schools. This area was described less certainly and clear pointers could not be identified. Religious Education as an exam subject was both an opportunity and a threat depending on the Catholic identity of the school, timetabling issues, levels of teacher expertise, the student mix and expectations related to this. Alternatively, religious instruction / faith formation could become separate from Religious Education and this could impair the shared Catholic school, home and parish responsibilities.

TABLE 7 CHALLENGE OF RELIGIOUS INSTRUCTION AND FAITH FORMATION

Score	Sd	Challenge	Response
2.7	1.4	Balance the **school's responsibilities** for faith formation/instruction with the pressures of RE as an examination subject.	Develop the role for faith formation within the school also with trained teachers; with the support of staff; in a whole-school context. [*Assumes a specific school profile?*]

Scoring system

Essential	Very important	Important, but other needs may take priority	Not immediately important	Unimportant
1.0 – 1.75	1.76 – 2.49	2.5 – 3.49	3.5 – 4.25	4.26 – 5.0

Finally, the panellists in this survey foresaw that there would be more **informed debate** with and among Catholics on religious, moral and cultural issues generally and on educational issues in that context. This debate will emphasise policy and practice more than ownership and control. It may facilitate also a forum for open discussion on emerging concerns of Catholic education. It will enhance the Catholic school's current capacity to respond to contemporary and youth cultures. The challenges in this debate are in Table 8.

TABLE 8 THE CHALLENGE OF EQUITY

Score	Sd	Challenge	Response
2.8	1.4	Address the dilemmas raised by **State recognition, regulation** and **funding** of schools.	Adequate protection in Education Act?

Score	Sd	Challenge	Response
3.1	1.2	Ensure **equity** of resource allocation to Catholic schools.	Advocacy role developed to pursue equity for all schools. [Equal funding basis announced on 14 December 2001]
3.3	1.4	To address the issue of **fee-paying** Catholic schools that become the preserve of a select minority and the impact of this on a vision of Catholic education.	

Conclusion

It is hard to aim effectively at a fast-changing target. Lane identified the targets for the future of Catholic education in 1991. The intervening years have been challenging for everybody in Irish education and the reform and legislative programmes of the State set the pace and demanded attention. Now that the future direction of Irish education has been agreed, the ways forward for Catholic education can be mapped out based on the research and reflection that took place in the intervening years. The research and debate here and elsewhere on the efficacy of Catholic education enriches the reservoir of shared resources. Ireland can both draw on as well as contribute to this as it faces the challenges outlined.

Bibliography

Adler, M. and Ziglio, E. [eds], (1996), *Gazing into the Oracle: the Delphi Method and its Application to Social Policy and Public Health* (London: Jessica Kingsley).

Arthur, James (1995), *The Ebbing Tide: Policy and Principles of Catholic Education* (Leominster, Herts: Gracewing).

Baker, D. and Riordan, C. (1998), 'The 'Eliting' of the Common American Catholic School and the National Education Crisis', in *Phi Delta Kappan*, September, 16-21.

Boeve, Lieven (2001), 'Giving a Soul to Education in Europe: a Challenge for Catholic Schools'. www.katolirus.hu.hu/kpszti/magyar/kulugy/AGBudaEN.rtf

Brennan, O.J. (2001), *Cultures Apart: the Catholic Church and Contemporary Irish Youth* (Dublin: Veritas).

Catholic Bishops of Northern Ireland, (2001), *Proclaiming the Mission: The Distinctive Philosophy and Values of Catholic Education* (Armagh).

Clayton, M.J. (1997), 'Delphi: a technique to harness expert opinion for critical decision-making tasks in education' in *Educational Psychology*, vol. 17, no. 4, pp 373-86.

Congregation for Catholic Education (1998), *The Catholic School on the Threshold of the Third Millennium*, (Rome).

Conference of Major Religious Superiors [CMRS] (1988a), *Inequality in Schooling in Ireland* (Dublin: CMRS).

CMRS (1988b), *Staff/School Development* (Dublin: CMRS).

CMRS (1989a), *Inequality in Schooling in Ireland: The role of Selective Entry and Placement* (Dublin: CMRS).

CMRS (1989b), *Staff Meeting Reflections: New Syllabi, New Learning?* (Dublin: CMRS).

Conference of Religious in Ireland [CORI] (1996), *Trusteeship of Catholic Voluntary Schools: a Handbook* (Dublin: CORI).

CORI (1997a), *Religious Congregations in Irish Education: a Role for the Future?*, a reflection paper (Dublin CORI).

CORI (1997b), *The Future of Trusteeship: a Review of Some Options for the Way Forward* (Dublin: CORI).

Critcher, C. and Gladstone, B. (1998), 'Utilizing the Delphi techniques in policy discussion: a case of a privatised utility in Britain' in *Public Administration*, vol. 76, pp.431-49.

Doyle, E. (2000), *Leading the Way: Managing Voluntary Secondary Schools* (Dublin: Secretariat of Secondary Schools).

Feheny, J.M. [ed], (1998), *From Ideal to Action: The Inner Nature of a Catholic School Today*, (Dublin: Veritas).

Feheny J.M. (1998), 'The future of the Catholic school: an Irish perspective' in J.M. Feheny [ed] *Fulton* (2000).

Grace, G. (1995), *School Leadership: Beyond Education Management* (London: Falmer).

Grace, G. (2002), *Catholic Schools: Mission, Markets and Morality* (London: Routledge).

Hogan, P. (1984), 'The question of ethos in schools' in *The Furrow*, vol. 35, pp.693-703.

Lane, D. (1991), *Catholic Education and the School: Some Theological Reflections* (Dublin: Veritas) and also CMRS (1991), *The Catholic School in Contemporary Society* (Dublin: author).

Linstone, H.L. and Turoff, M. [eds], (1975), *The Delphi Method: Techniques and Applications* (Reading MA: Addison-Wesley).

McCormack, Sr T. (1998), 'The changing role of Trustees and Boards of management' in J.M. Feheny [ed], *From Ideal to Action: the Inner Nature of a Catholic School Today* (Dublin: Veritas), pp.145-55.

McCormack, Sr T. (2001), 'Arriving where we started and knowing the place for the first time' in Breen, M. and Weafer, J. [eds], *A Fire in the Forest: Religious life in Ireland* (Dublin: Veritas), pp.105-19.

McDonnell, M. (1995), The Ethos of Catholic Voluntary Secondary Schools, unpublished PhD thesis, UCD, 2 vols.

Norman, J. (2001), 'Ethos and the Catholic School' in *Oideas* 47, pp.66-79.

Norman, J. (2002,) *Pastoral Care in Second Level Schools: the Chaplain – a Research Report* (Dublin: Centre for Research in Religion and Education [CRRE]).

O'Brien, S. and Coyle, T. (2001a), *Towards an Identity and a Contribution: findings from the Identity Project – Final Report* (Dublin: Christian Brother Network of Schools/Marino Institute of Education).

O'Brien, S. and Coyle, T. (2001b), *Towards an Identity and a Contribution: findings from the Identity Project – Summary Report* (Dublin: Christian Brother Network of Schools/Marino Institute of Education).

OECD (1991), *Reviews of National Policies for Education: Ireland* (Paris: OECD).

OECD (2001), *What Schools for the Future?* (Paris: OECD).

Sproule, N. (1995), [2nd ed], *Handbook of Research Methods* (Metuchen NJ / London: Scarecrow Press), pp.242-44.

Treston, K. (1997), 'Ethos and Identity: foundational concerns for Catholic schools' in R. Keane and D. Reilly [eds], *Quality Catholic Schools* (Brisbane: Brisbane Catholic Education Office), pp. 9-18.

Touhy, D. and Cairns, P. (1999), *Youth 2K: Threat or Promise to a Religious Culture?* (Dublin: Marino Institute of Education).

Tuohy, D., Maume, M. & Maxwell, R. (2000), *Beyond Nostalgia: Issues in Trusteeship with regard to the Catholic Ethos of Post-Primary Schools* (Portarlington: Presentation Ministries Office).

Williams, K. (1992), 'School ethos, values and the nature of society' in *Doctrine and Life*, pp. 561-70.

Williams, K. (1999), 'Faith and the Nation: education and religious identity in the Republic of Ireland' in *British Journal of Educational Studies*, vol. 47, no. 4, pp. 317-31.

Youoniss, J. and Convey, J. [eds], (2000), *Catholic Schools at the Crossroads: Survival and Transformation* (New York: Teachers College Press).

Leadership at the Edge

Martin Daly

Browsing in bookshops is a favourite hobby of mine. Most of the time I am struck by how many books I want to read and have to resist buying them, knowing that they will in all likelihood lie on my shelf gathering dust. If I start reading a book, I feel I ought to finish it, but it is then that I remember Doris Lessing's advice in her introduction to *The Golden Notebook* (Flamingo, 1993, pp.17-18), to read only what interests you and if you start a book and it does nothing for you, then leave it and pick up something else.

In a perfect world I would be able to do so. Unfortunately, I am obliged, in order to 'keep up with the literature', to browse through the management sections of bookstores. One could not fail to see the proliferation of titles on how to run organisations and the number of people who have opinions on what makes a good leader of an organisation. I am filled with envy when I pick up one of these 'bestsellers' and realise, on quickly leafing through it, that one could summarise in three lines what the main idea is and then leave it aside, having got the picture, well, having got most of it. I just wish I had thought of those three lines! The unspoken truth that anyone who has been in a leadership position knows, is that no 'how to' manual can actually tell you *how to exercise leadership in the moment*. So be assured, reader, if you have got this far – and are still interested – that you will not be told the 'three tenets' or the 'seven secrets' of good leadership! Instead, I invite you to think about how you *actually* lead and about how you follow. What kind of leading do you follow and what kind of following does your leading evoke? A trusted friend once asked me: 'Martin, how do you think you would like having to work for someone like you?' You may surmise from this that my way of talking about leadership grated on my friend! Seriously though, I have always found this to be a very useful question to keep in mind in order to help me observe how I am leading and how my style of leadership is being experienced by others. I would like to invite you to appraise your leadership – as it is and as it might be – not in order to assess how grating it is, but, more positively, to appraise whether or not it has an *edge*.

Positive and negative edges

Think for a moment about what the word 'edge' evokes for you. I notice how pupils in school react to that 'edge' in a teacher's voice when they take it to mean that he or she has it in for them. It is then that one's edge grates on people. The edge is hostile. Most of us react to that felt sense of hostility, and possibly with good reason. We pick up a sharpness, a hint of danger, a threat. We become uncomfortable and wary, and feel afraid and intimidated. In the long term and, perhaps, even in the short term, this is not going to be conducive to creating relationships that support the task and purpose of our organisation. On the other hand, does there not have to be some edge to a leader, or even the belief among others in the organisation that he or she could develop an edge if the need arose? Doesn't a leader need teeth? What is it like for others when you are edgy? Does your edginess keep them on their toes or wear them out? When are you at risk of burning others out? Burnout is the systemic interplay between the temperament and issues of the individual and the peculiar demands of the profession itself. When are you bringing others to a creative, learning 'edge' and when are you bringing them to the edge of their stress, beyond which there is nothing but a steep drop? When are you doing it to yourself?

A cutting edge

Does your edginess keep you and your organisation at the cutting edge? Are you at the cutting edge in any aspect of your work? How would you know whether you are or not? What is it like when you sense you are? Think about the energy you felt in that moment or experience and about the conditions and contexts that created that sense of 'edge'. Or do you tell yourself that you are not really that kind of person? Have you or your organisation lost your edge? *'When salt has lost its taste, it is good for nothing.'* Are you bland? I believe the most damning judgement of a leader is that he or she has lost their edge.

Positioned on the edge

Supposing you were to think of 'edge' in terms of position or location in an organisation. What thoughts might the following questions evoke? How is it for you to be on the edge of your organisation or association or profession? Is this a place you would be more or less inclined to choose? What might motivate you to choose the margins or the edge rather than the comfort of the fold? Is it more comfortable on the margins and might it be more difficult for you to be 'in' the group rather than marginalising yourself? Perhaps the edge is the centre. Where do you locate yourself in your particular working context or organisation? How does your positioning of yourself or your being positioned affect how you exercise leadership? Perhaps those on the edge could become new centres. What as a leader might you do to make this possible? Perhaps you need to change your thinking about where the centre and the edges are.

Discourses about leadership
I suspect many people are ambivalent about leadership, whether they or others are exercising it. In Ireland there are immense cultural constraints that discourage one from exercising leadership. These constraints are internalised as voices that are powerful dissuaders and give rise to many questions for us.

- Who am I to take my authority and exercise leadership?
- What will 'they' say or think if I do?
- What happens if I get it wrong and fall flat on my face?
- What happens if I fail?

All these voices disempower and dissuade one from taking the risk of going to the edge and bringing others to the edge of their learning and experience, the edge where all lasting and deep change occurs. 'The risks during such times are especially high because change that truly transforms an organisation demands that people give up things they hold dear: daily habits, loyalties, ways of thinking. In return for these sacrifices, they may be offered nothing more than the possibility of a better future' (Heifetz and Linsky, June 2002, p.65). Such leadership may evoke the madness and hostility of the group. Groups and institutions often serve the function of carrying the infantile tendencies and dependencies of individuals.[1] These individuals will not thank you for asking them to grow up and for making life less secure. People get very edgy around someone who is likely to push the boat out a bit, someone who cannot be relied upon to place the comfort of the group as the highest context informing the decisions that person might make. People join and stay in organisations for a whole range of reasons that may or may not have a lot to do with the purpose of the organisation. They can become very dependent on things remaining as they are because the way things and relationships are configured, meets their needs. Issues from an earlier period in their lives, in particular unresolved issues of autonomy/dependency in relation to parental figures, of separation anxiety/abandonment may resurface when they are faced with the threat of change or especially when they have to engage with a leader who appears to place the purpose of the organisation as the highest context for any discussion or interaction with the staff.

People can become enraged, and disproportionately so, when they hear the word no. Parents whose children do not get selected for a particular team or event may present as traumatised! – certainly much more upset than their children. Staff may feel, if they have put their case for a particular change of schedule, for additional resources or for how you should arbitrate in a situation of conflict, that you as leader will automatically agree to their request because your job is to meet their needs. They may find it extraordinarily difficult to handle that you could understand their situation or position or opinion and yet still choose not to accede to their request or to go along with their point of view. In order to resolve this for themselves, they may personalise it and tell all and sundry: listen until I tell you what *he did on me*. When you find, as a leader, that you are becoming the object of hostility, you need to stand back and ask yourself: how much has this actually to do with the incident or situation that the other person claims gave rise to their extreme reaction? You need to bear in mind that institutions and organisations meet a whole range of emotional needs for people and that a leader may be the subject of a plethora of emotions and feelings that the leader may well have triggered, but that ultimately may have very little to do with him or her. Initiating a process of change in an organisation, placing the purpose of the organisation as the highest context for decision-making, and consistently engaging people around the task of the organisation, may evoke extreme reactions in some individuals.

Authority

'Authority' in Ireland has been synonymous with control and authoritarianism. The predominant discourse of authority has made people reluctant to claim or exercise their authority for fear of being labelled authoritarian or autocratic. Those who do, in my experience, can become the object of others' resentment if they trigger associations with past authority figures, be they familial or institutional. Taking authority in the face of such powerful constraints *is refusing to be limited by the stories others tell about you or to be constituted by them*. In doing so, we become authors in our own right. In my experience, it is a real struggle to do so consistently, particularly in the context of our culture, which so discourages the taking of authority. It is particularly difficult to manage the isolation and hostility that anyone who is in a position of responsibility, who takes their authority and exercises leadership, may have to face. Anyone who has not been in a position of leadership cannot understand the isolation that one must face if as the leader one is prepared to bring people to the edge of their learning and to ask them to change, to unlearn present skills, habits and attitudes. Of course, leaders more than most are vulnerable to blind spots. My friend's question to which I referred earlier has always to be kept to the fore of my mind. Many people are adept at intuitively analysing the lacks in others and extraordinarily inept at analysing their own shortcomings. You risk becoming grandiose, imagining you are 'the big fellow'. You risk cutting yourself off from an awareness of your own and others' human realities and limitations. You can become immersed in your 'project' and carried away by your fantasies.

In short, you risk narcissism. Others become pawns in your desire to 'get the results', to turn the organisation around. People sense the narcissism sooner or later and begin to feel used. There is a very thin line between being committed to the task and being driven to succeed whatever the consequences may be for others. There is an even thinner line between bringing an edge to an organisation and undermining people's confidence in their ability to do their work. Any good manager must strike the balance between challenging people, putting it up to them, being ruthless if necessary, and on the other hand being sensitive.

I recall speaking to a group of principals some time ago and outlining what I thought needed to happen in order for a school to have a sustained edge. In attempting to be 'challenging', I overstepped the mark. I could feel that people were beginning to get uneasy. Remarks were fed back that people found my suggestions too confrontational. What I was suggesting wouldn't work in their context. Some said that they didn't feel able to implement the kinds of strategies I was suggesting. They felt they did not have the resources in the school or did not feel competent to act in the ways I proposed. The effect of my addressing them as I did, was to undermine them and leave them feeling worse off than if I had said nothing! It was a painful illustration for me of my 'challenging' being overly challenging and my desire to introduce a bit of an edge into my address backfiring on me. It only evoked stories of deficit among them and left them convinced that my 'style' was not for them. It may have allowed some to 'opt out' from engaging with what I was proposing to them because of how I was coming across in proposing it.

Professional supervision

If you are to exercise leadership that brings an edge to an organisation without forsaking the humanity people need to sense, so that they feel able to follow, and without committing the cardinal error I did in that case of undermining their sense of self-confidence, then you have to open up your motivations, feelings and actions to someone suitably qualified to hold you and to enable you to question yourself. In my own struggle to lead with some integrity without forsaking my humanity, and to lead with an edge, I have found the space that supervision offers invaluable, particularly in the ways illustrated below.

Firstly, in helping me to articulate for myself the 'why' informing my work, i.e. the deep values that drive my sense of purpose in my work context. In connecting with what matters on a very personal level to me, that deeply personal motivation is available to me as a leader and I am then able to offer those whys to others. If people can hear my heartfelt convictions – what I really believe in – and how these convictions are connected to what I am asking of them in terms of deep and fundamental changes, they are more likely to follow. I have never felt more vulnerable and at the same time that I had most authority than when I have spoken from that place of conviction, and I think in those most vulnerable moments people have been most persuaded. I forget so often that people are working in the hope of finding purpose and meaning, and in my experience teachers at the moment need to be built up and reminded of how much they matter and why they matter. Crucially, in asking people to change, they need to know that while you are intent on seeing this through, you are not indifferent to the pain this may cause them. People need to hear that you understand the loss you are asking them to accept. You need to name that loss and explicitly acknowledge what this may cost them and to connect this with the convictions you have about why these changes are so important and what they are for. People may be afraid of where you are leading them and you need to offer them the hope that these changes will make the future possible.

Secondly, I have found supervision has helped me to deal with my own anxiety about leading and, in particular, helped me to have the courage of my convictions and, thus, consistently to act out of them in the school. The more I kept making the connections and remaking them between what I was doing and why I was doing it, the more I was able to call on this when I most felt like giving up or when I met overt hostility or passive resistance.

Thirdly, it has helped me to manage my reactions to difficult people and situations so that I didn't react to them, but began to develop the ability to observe my participation in those situations and relationships. This 'reflexive' awareness gave me the crucial ability to stand back and ask myself: what is the highest context here? In doing so, I am more able to remain in role and remain mindful of the primary purpose of the organisation.

Fourthly, it helped me to monitor the stress people were experiencing as a result of the edge I introduced. You need to create some tension and anxiety. Without this there is no incentive to change. People need to see how the changes are connected to the survival of the organisation, but they need to know that this is about survival. However, this can very easily become counterproductive if the anxiety is incessant and there appears to be no relief. The best way I have found to manage what Edgar Schein calls 'survival anxiety' (*Harvard Business Review*, March 2002, p.100ff.) is to mark achievements as soon as possible after changes have been made, so that people can see some tangible signs of success, and to connect this achievement with the changes made, thus reinforcing them and allaying some of the anxiety people are feeling.

Finally, it helped me realise that I need help and to get into the habit of asking for help and not acting impulsively, but waiting until I have talked with someone else about the possible courses of actions and their meanings for the people involved.

Conclusion

Learning to examine my motivations, my actions and reactions critically has in the long run helped me to keep myself on some learning edge. We can only ask of others what we are willing to undertake ourselves. In the final analysis, we can only take people as far as we have ventured ourselves. To manage them in that process, we must above all manage ourselves. Leadership with an edge ultimately asks as much of the leader as it does of the led.

Notes

1.   Stokes, Jon, 'Institutional chaos and personal stress' in *The Unconscious at Work*, Chapter 13, (ed.) Obholzer, Anton and Zagier Roberts, Vega (London: Routledge 1994).

Conversations...
Beginning and Continuing

Various Contributors

This chapter contains the reflections, responses and challenges of some of those who took the time to write to the Catholic School Project team in Marino after the March 2001 conference

THE BAIT OF POSSIBILITY *(Tony Hanna)*

Conferences fall into two categories: the 'been there, done that, got the T-shirt' variety, which soon becomes a faded memory, and then there is the other kind, a much rarer species altogether; it is the sort that disturbs and provokes and surprisingly surpasses all our expectations.

Imagination can be dangerous, even subversive, because it lures one away from the tried and tested, away from the staid and mediocre, and it dangles the bait of dream and possibility. Imagination excites!

W. B. Yeats wrote about the difficulty of writing poetry in 'The Song of the Wandering Aengus'. Imagination fired him to go apart to think: 'I went out to the hazel wood because a fire was in my head'. The process of constructing the poem is then explained: 'and cut and peeled a hazel wand and hooked a berry to a thread'; these allude to the method of fashioning the poem and how from this there emerges 'a little silver trout'... the first draft so to speak.

I see this conference as the first step in fashioning a new vision, a poem for Catholic education. There has been some peeling and some connecting of various facets. Something new is being enfleshed although its shape is still somewhat uncertain.

Initially it required prophetic/poetic mind, the visionaries to call us apart to engage in a work of the imagination. The next step requires other skills of pruning and linking to help shape the future.

With Yeats the imaginative spark fuelled the search and the passion, but later a sharper, more precise intellect was needed to create the concrete shape of the poem. The conference was a prophetic work of the imagination; the next phase will require different skills and focus, but it too is obligatory to the process. The shape of the Catholic school of tomorrow will depend on how we make concrete the vision that is emerging, one that not only treasures the legacy of the past but also welcomes the freshness of the new and the different.

CLARITY OF VISION – ESSENTIAL *(Matthew Feheny)*

This conference was one of the notable achievements in Catholic school studies in Ireland in recent years. It was an intellectual *tour de force* and was for many their first introduction to scholars in the forefront of research in Catholic schooling, such as Joseph O'Keefe, SJ and Thomas Groome.

While the vast majority of those attending appeared to be on the same wavelength as speakers such as O'Keefe and Groome, there was at least one moment when the need to bridge the gap between researcher and consumer became apparent. The occasion I have in mind was during a question from the floor session when a parent made a plea for more 'practical' efforts to support teachers in Catholic schools in their work of evangelisation and catechesis.

It seemed to me that the questioner was not clear on the purpose of the conference, which was to help leaders in Catholic education to clarify their vision of Catholic education in a changing society at the present time. If leaders are clear on the task facing them and know how to access the necessary literature and supports, then the fruits of conferences like the reimaging one will surely percolate down to the teachers and parents. But we must keep emphasising the old saying, 'Where there is no vision, the people perish'. In times of difficulty and confusion, many people will opt for the immediate solution of shooting the crocodiles in preference to starting the onerous and long-term task of draining the swamp.

So, let us make sure that the workers at the pit face appreciate the importance of up-to-date research in Catholic education. The most practical solutions often come from the most theoretical research. Just think of the work of Piaget, Skinner, Friere or Gardner!

REIGNITING THE PASSION *(Oona Stannard)*

I write simply to congratulate you on an absolutely stunning conference in Dublin. I can hardly put into words my appreciation both professionally and personally for the insights and growth opportunities that were offered to me at City West.

It was a great privilege to have been invited to the conference and I learnt an enormous amount both from the formal inputs and, of course, from the informal networking opportunities. I truly met many very impressive people from whom I gained a great deal. The conference also offered me a splendid opportunity to reignite my passions for issues of social justice and equality (particularly gender!) and to be reminded of how I need always to ensure that they are at the heart of my policy work for Catholic education.

SEEDS OF HOPE *(Siobhán Foster-Ryan)*

Being honest, I have to say I was very surprised at the turnout to the conference. For me that was a huge boost in itself – that so many would choose to take time out to attend this event, especially given the particular circumstances of those days. I wondered why they were there – what answers they were looking for, or new directions, or was it for some inspiration, or to have their voice heard, or perhaps a measure of solidarity? What were my reasons? I'm a mother, a teacher, a trainer of teachers … I came with a concern for the future of the Catholic school in Ireland.

I have an enormous gratitude for the education I received from the Sisters of Mercy – thirteen years in their schools in Dundalk. I am concerned that while it can never be the same into the future, I want something of that spirit, that character formation, that investment in every aspect of our development, that strong spiritual dimension, not to be lost but to be made available in new ways to the next generation – to my daughters. This conference – this gathering – gave me real hope that this is possible. I listened to the vibrancy, conviction and vision of Joan Chittister and was delighted at how she both related so well to the Irish context and inspired us with the importance of what our schools can offer. She set high standards for the contribution Catholic schools could and should make. She argued that there need be no hiding in corners, that the purpose for Catholic schools was still very evident, and she also pointed out the joy there was to be found in being part of such a mission in the context of a fast-changing country such as our own. She was clear and challenging in stating that we must stand for justice, respect and equality – she did not mince her words and it is this clarity that we need.

Over the few days of the conference my sense of the preciousness of our Catholic school legacy grew stronger – that while there are many mistakes to learn from, there are many values that need to be preserved and rearticulated for the context of contemporary Ireland.

The conference also was heartening from the point of view of the range of contributors; while questions were raised we were also given some new directions to explore. It is clear that this is a time of great transition in Irish education, and especially so in the Catholic sector. The conference pointed out that there is a very committed group interested in creating a future for the sector. This is a crucial time of opportunity; let us not let the next generation down, and let us, to borrow one of the words from the conference title, reimagine together what our Catholic schools can offer to education in Ireland.

HIGHLIGHTS TO REMEMBER *(Finola Cunnane)*

'What a fabulous conference.' 'This is the beginning of a great conversation.' 'I can't wait to tell others about this.' 'This conference has whetted my appetite for more.' 'I feel so enriched after these few days.' These are some of the comments that I overheard as I was leaving the City West Conference Centre on 5 March, 2002. As a national and international group of educators, we had been journeying together over three days, exploring the role and heart of Catholic education, as well as imagining the future for this endeavour. Conscious that 'without a vision, the people perish', the importance of developing richer forms of community, together with the necessity to re-engage the religious imagination, were highlighted. The result was an invitation to a future filled with hope.

Reminding us that 'now is the time', the Opening Ritual set the scene by inviting us to begin the journey of reimagining surrounded by the care of God. 'This is the time to take new life', Ned Prendergast stated in his welcome speech, while John Quinn reminded us of the great power in uncertainty. In her presentation, 'A New Century in need of Catholic Educators', Joan Chittister, OSB began by suggesting that 'the map we use to explore this new world will be the path by which the next world walks'. Our first task, therefore, as spiritual leaders in Catholic schools today, is to ask 'On what roads should we lead them now?' The answer to that question, she states, has been clear for over two thousand years. In leading them to the One who said 'I am the Way', our role as Catholic educators is to teach our young people to question what is obstructing the coming of God's kingdom in our world today. It is to lead them to envision a better way. It is to take them to where there are no roads so that new paths may be explored. Aware that it is only the Spirit that can do the impossible, we are fired with a passion to do what is possible.

It is helpful when our attempts to do what is possible are nourished by the principle of sacramentality. In his presentation, 'Education for Life: The Heart of Catholic Education', Dr Thomas H. Groome explains that the sacramental principle is far broader than what goes on in our churches in relation to the seven sacraments. The principle of sacramentality, rather, is to see God in all things. It is to notice God's presence in the ordinary and in the everyday. A God with us, Emmanuel – we are invited to encounter God in the 'bits and pieces of everyday'. Incorporating the sacramental principle into our schools would be to engage in shared Christian praxis, a praxis where we bring faith to life and life to faith. Such a conversation is created by the questions we raise. The task of Catholic educators, therefore, is to nourish our own souls. In this way, we will be enabled to sharpen the questions that create conversation.

The questions that create conversation are being sharpened by the United States' experience of Catholic schools as communities of service. In his presentation, Fr Joseph M. O'Keefe, SJ painted a panoramic picture of Catholic schools from their meagre beginnings to their contemporary conversations. Outlining the early stages of the Catholic school, Fr O'Keefe talked about their humble beginnings, the challenge of the immigrant era, and the search for a new rationale. Despite shifting populations and lack of financial resources, their conversations have led the Catholic school to become a centre of participation and multi-culturalism, with an emphasis on ecumenism, option for the poor, justice and service.

Maureen Gaffney's contribution concerned the heart of relationships. The role of the Catholic school, she believes, is to help young people become more and more authentic, i.e. more and more themselves. This is particularly urgent in an era when individualism has become the benchmark of society. It is particularly crucial when the spiritual hunger of young people is prompting them to question the meaning of life and their contribution to it. Wondering who they are in relation to other people, young people think about such issues as their appearance, their future, how to get people to like them, and intimacy. In forging a new identity, they re-examine relationships and search for glimpses of a perfect world. Their answers can leave them feeling very vulnerable, while adults can feel rather exposed. But these, Dr Gaffney assures us, are authentic sacramental moments.

Recognising the authentic sacramental moments facing contemporary Western society, Jacques Janssen in 'Re-Engaging the Adolescent Religious Imagination' acknowledges the young person's dislike of power, history and institutions. While we are not the first generation to experience this dilemma, religion as an institution is fading and the Churches are losing contact with the younger generation. Despite the fall off in church attendance, there has been little or no growth in humanistic and agnostic institutions. This is because young people are still interested in religion, with a survey revealing that 61 per cent engage in prayer and meditation. A new age is rampant. Spiritual books, candles and oils enrich our homes. Our task, therefore, is to captivate rather than to capture. It is to create interest and wait – on a wing and a prayer!

Two workshops

During the conference, each participant had the opportunity to attend two workshops. The two I attended were *Partnership: Towards a Richer Model of Catholic School as Inclusive Community* presented by Ned Prendergast and *What will be the Issues for Catholic Education in 2010? Preliminary Research Findings: Marino Catholic School Project* by Don Herron.

Ned Prendergast's workshop *Partnership: Towards a Richer Model of Catholic School as Inclusive Community* suggested that partnership be approached through getting relationships right, through a more enlivened model of community and through the engagement of mind, heart and soul. Engaging in the Partnership Way enables everyone to be welcomed and recognised, asked, told and heard, included and involved, and, therefore, happy. This leads to a more enlivened model of community where people share vision and aims, are recognised and invited to contribute. The result is growth and empowerment. People feel they are cared for and that their needs are met. They are responsible towards and accountable to each other. They trust each other and feel they belong. In this way, right relationships are established, institutions become more just, morale is higher, genuine democracy flourishes, richer forms of community ensue and Christianity is evident.

Don Herron's workshop looked at the issues that Catholic education may be facing in 2010. The environment for Catholic education in 2010 was examined under the following headings: demographic; values, culture and religion; and education. In 2010 it is projected that our society will be multi-cultural, multi-ethnic, multi-lingual and multi- and non-denominational. As a result, we will have a socially, politically and institutionally secular society with a separation between Church and State. Schooling, therefore, will be mixed and generally competitive, with the curriculum becoming more economically driven. There will be a distinctive Catholic philosophy of education, together with the cultivation and transmission of a Catholic ethos. This will lead to better organised, accountable and effective Catholic schools and may further lead to curricular, pastoral, pedagogic and organisational innovation.

Conclusion

In conclusion, this conference provided an opportunity to appreciate, question and envision a landscape for Catholic schools. The stories we told, the faith memories we shared, gave us a fresh language with which to weave a new garment. I came away with a renewed sense of meaning and identity, together with a passion for mission. But I am not alone. Together we are a pilgrim people. We are a people invited to respond to the hunger for meaning, to the hunger for community. Let us continue the conversation. Let us continue to explore new roadmaps in order to reshape the vision for Catholic schools and, perhaps, like T.S. Eliot, we will '... arrive where we started and know the place for the first time'.

A PARENT PERSPECTIVE (*Veronica Cluxton-Corley*)

So often I attend a conference and only come away with what I have learned for myself. The main idea of the conference has been forgotten or shelved or has taken off on a road that does not realy involve me.

It is difficult to put any ideas to use unless there is back-up, follow-up or support. The conference itself opened up a Pandora's box for me. As a parent I am concerned about the future of Catholic education. I came away with more than twenty questions! Ultimately, it is my responsibility as a parent to look after my children's needs in this area. Historically, the Church did not trust parents with this responsibility because of their lack of education. Parents were not considered equipped to do so. To an extent I would agree with this. We (ordinary parents) are unsure of our role, we do not feel we know enough about it, so we entrust the responsibility to the teachers – perhaps we even lack the conviction or have questions ourselves. Things have not really improved. Each of the past few years I have had a child receive a sacrament. I felt very much excluded from the preparation and only invited to rubberstamp the event – I am aware that each school is different. At the end of the day it is at home and through living that the knowledge we acquire at school is put to use – 'Do as I do, not as I say'.

The conference was excellent, but I felt some people who would have seriously benefited were unable to attend. Especially parents who are not in the education field but just send their children to school.

If I may, I would like to comment on the speakers. I was so taken with all the experts and their contributions. I was particularly impressed with Anne Looney: 'Unless we look at the classroom situation nothing is going to change.' That is where a lot of it really happens. Much as we would like it to come from the home, a lot of influence is there in the classroom. That is why as a parent I am concerned that our culture and ethos from home is reflected in the classroom! We must have communication between parents, teacher and students if it is going to happen and we must all play our part. We must be clear in our intent and our roles and how we intend to fulfil them. Parents need to realise their responsibilities and be educated. Sorry, but a lot have no interest or are not concerned and do not even feel it to be their 'job'.

Jacques Janssen was very impressive too. He was at the heart of the situation and very familiar with the way youth think today. He was pure excellent. His method of presentation was excellent too.

Thomas Groome is obviously an expert in his field, but I felt he did not offer much in the way we might move forward. Sorry! Maybe I missed something! Maybe I am wrong, but although how our mothers did it is important, parents today are different, home life is different and some kids have so much more of a questioning nature and do not necessarily ask Mom and Dad anymore! – or parents do not have the time! They work out life philosophies in their own way but they need foundations to work from. Can we create areas for them to bounce these enquiries off?

I would love to be in a working group with Joan Chittister and work through her ideas. You nearly had an expectation that there would be thunder before long – she is not afraid to rattle cages and that is a quality I admire.

The workshops

As I was participating in one workshop, I only got to attend one other, which was the Identity Project run by Marino in the Christian Brother network of schools. This work is excellent – I feel it could be brought to every school in Ireland, every workplace, so that people get a sense of purpose and belonging.

To be quite honest, my head was reeling with ideas when I came home, and you really need time out with someone who was there to bounce it all off, but that was not to be. Again at the end of the day I have a responsibility. I am lucky that Jimmy and I try our best together to give example. It is very difficult sometimes. Now I am not just a parent of seven children, I am a parent of three adults. 'If I knew then what I know now', but even with my younger gang I can only do so much and maybe try harder. But time, time, time.

SACRED EXPERIENCE (*Eithne McKenna*)

The conference was great and left all with lots to muse about in the months ahead. I think we all need such thought-provoking days to keep us going and challenge us to take on the future – whatever that might bring!

The one thing that strikes me about such a gathering is the level of conversation it provokes among complete strangers – but all with common goals and questions to ask. We may not have got any answers but the debate and sheer fun will remain for a long time. I can still remember the 'high' I was on as I left after the final liturgy and it was a difficult thing to describe to someone who was not there but I felt the sacred experience all the way down the dual carriageway!

PARADIGM SHIFTS – A PERSPECTIVE FROM THE USA (*Dale McDonald*)

As a colleague from the National Catholic Education Association in the United States, I was delighted to have the opportunity to attend the Catholic school conference and participate with so many colleagues in the task of 'Reimagining the Catholic School'.

Several things made a strong impression on me:

a) The hospitality of the participants to the few 'foreign' colleagues among the group was so welcoming and inclusive. It was good to share experiences and identify the similarities and differences in the Irish and US educational systems, and their developments over the course of the last century, and learn from one another what might be effective future strategies as both of our nations deal with diversity in unprecedented ways.

b) The willingness of the Irish educational community to confront the reality of the changing cultural and religious ethos of the country and to be proactive rather than reactive is a sign of the vitality of Catholic education in Ireland and bodes well for its future.

c) The paradigm shifts in Ireland are phenomenal – moving from a monolithic religious and cultural society to one that is becoming increasingly multi-cultural, multi-lingual and multi-denominational. This reality presents unprecedented challenges for educational institutions. It will require attention and intense strategising efforts to adapt structures without abandoning principles. Conferences such as this one can do much to educate the educators about how to comprehend and effectively direct new trends toward desired and effective outcomes.

OUR DEEPEST CONVICTIONS (*Jim O'Connor*)

I found the experience to be very enriching in that it surfaced and helped put into words some of our deepest convictions about our identity as learning communities. The conference was timely in that it helped many of us to be more confident about this identity of Catholic schools, and to be willing to proclaim in a humble way what this means for the way we run our schools and classrooms.

I felt a need at times during the programme for space to absorb and discern what 'spirits' were being stirred – in myself, and also in the group at large.

I suggest that there would be merit in a selection of people getting together soon to 'read the signs of the times' in light of the conference and the state of things in our culture.

It seems to me that we may need to look at more serious and creative networking of people who are all working 'in their own boxes', but towards similar ends.

In any case I believe it would be worth gathering together the crumbs... and who knows... Just a thought.

A selection of thoughts from some other letters and cards received...
'I returned to school with renewed spring in my step. I felt all the better for being there.'
Sr Christina Greene, DP, chaplain

'We are both challenged and invigorated by it (if that's possible).'
Education Secretariat, Archbishop's House, Dublin

'I would see *networking* on all levels as one of the key areas for the growth and development of Catholic Education.'
Sr Clare Hanly

'You and your friends have put us all in your debt. What a contribution the Christian Brothers are now making to Catholic education. *Prospir Procede et Unfia!*'
Aidan Lehane, CSSp

It's the Purpose First and Last

Luke Monahan

Baton passing

As a person not especially known for his sporting prowess or indeed for a great interest in same, nonetheless it is from this sphere that I have drawn a key image that has helped me in the struggle to characterise what is occurring in Irish Catholic education. The image is that of the passing of a baton in a relay race. We know that this is a vital moment in the race – how that baton is passed is utterly crucial to the eventual outcome. I believe that this is precisely the moment we are witnessing in Catholic education in this country; a time when the lay Church will be centre stage, when new forms of trusteeship will be implemented, when clerical and religious involvement will end, when Catholic schools will stand alongside others in the marketplace, when the purpose of the Catholic school will have to be effectively articulated and enacted. So how will baton passing go? I invite you to reflect on this image in relation to your role or interest in Catholic education.

- Will the baton be dropped at the moment of passing?
- Will it be effectively taken up?
- Will it be fumbled and badly handed over?
- Who is doing the handing over?
- Who is taking the baton?
- How prepared are they?
- What is the reaction of those on the sidelines?

It is a daunting task to explore how to enable the Catholic contribution to education become more visible and accessible – how the next lap on the relay can be one that makes a significant difference. There are compelling reasons to avoid the task, chief among them being the deepening disenchantment with the Catholic Church at this time in Ireland. Many would advocate a break from the past, suggesting the future of education is a State concern, a humanistic endeavour, a socialising and vocational enterprise. This direction would, I believe, be a lost opportunity to contribute to the next generation, an enormous disservice to the work of past generations, in summary, a betrayal of our responsibilies to the new and emerging Ireland.

A contribution

Among other choices, each deserves the option of an education influenced by the Catholic perspective. Those of us concerned about Catholic education need really to think about this statement, because unless we are passionately convinced about the purpose of Catholic education then we have already dropped the baton. It could be said that until very recently it was only possible to have a Catholic-directed education in Ireland. With the advent of a choice of school types, the possibility of choosing a clear ethos is becoming ever more available. This allows for a greater richness in the educational system and for a greater challenge to each school type to clarify its character. One of the drawbacks of a predominant approach such as we have had in Ireland is that it can become in many instances dulled, presumptuous, shallow and complacent. There is now a new opportunity for the Catholic tradition to outline what it offers to education – the qualitative contribution it can make by reconnecting with fundamental purposes and by reimagining new responses for new times.

If Catholic education is worth fighting for, our first task is to be able to answer cogently, coherently, comprehensively and compellingly the question why – because the why question gets us to the fundamental purpose of a Catholic school and it is our conviction around purpose that will determine how the baton is passed. In order to make a viable contribution, the school with a Catholic characteristic spirit needs to be clear regarding its ethos and character and how its policies, practices and programmes are influenced by that ethos.

Each school is distinctive. The questions the school community needs to ask are:

- What is distinctive about our school – ethos, policies, practices, people?

- What contributes to this distinctiveness?
- Is our present particular distinctiveness what we are striving for?

A vision that directs

Having a compelling purpose for our schools needs to impinge at every level. In theory, a Catholic school has a living and vibrant core ethos that guides and directs everything that occurs in the school community. In practice, the reality might be very different, with the Catholic dimension being at best peripheral or patchy. A school wishing to take seriously the Catholic approach needs to place this approach at the centre of its activities. This is not to recommend a reliance on control or imposition – history has shown the cul-de-sac of that strategy; rather, it is to encourage dialogue, appropriate influence and the making of a contribution. If the school declares it is Catholic, the associated values and practices must be in dialogue with those of the syllabus, Government requirements, school policies, students, teachers, parents, management, for the optimum environment to emerge. This is not a paper exercise but a fundamental and ongoing series of conversations. At the core of these conversations must be a form of 'ethos charter' that encapsulates the Catholic character of the school. This ethos charter is a vital document as the school community daily attempts to negotiate the variety of pressures, expectations and differing value systems.

An urgency

If the contribution of the Catholic perspective is to be experienced in Irish education, there needs to be a consolidated and comprehensive approach taken to the issue in the immediate future. For many, it is the eleventh hour – for some, that is a generous reading of the timing. There can be, in my view, no underestimating the task ahead. If we believe in the transforming contribution the Catholic vision can have, the radical nature of its comment on values, its commitment to the dignity of the person, the centrality of justice and compassion, then there can be no shirking of the responsibility to proclaim its message. The positive element of such a challenge is that it can often bring out the most creative side in people, it can break through defences, it can offer new possibilities only hinted at previously.

It is in this context that Marino, with others, is making its contribution; we have developed effective processes and practical resources to work with staffs, parents, students, management and trustees around articulating and enacting characteristic spirit in a real and visible manner. No longer can it be said that it cannot be done – yes it can… if there is the willingness and the commitment.

As a way to conclude my remarks I want to offer the text of a homily I gave to the General Assembly of European Committee for Catholic Education shortly after the Marino conference on reimagining the Catholic school in City West. It captures my sense of the challenge and the opportunity of this *kairos* moment in Catholic education in Ireland – the baton is being passed...

Readings: Friday Week Four of Lent [Jerusalem Version]
Wisdom 2:1, 12-22
The godless say to themselves, with their misguided reasoning:

> 'Let us lie in wait for the virtuous man,
> since he annoys us and opposes our way of life,
> reproaches us for our breaches of the law
> and accuses us of playing false to our upbringing.
> He claims to have knowledge of God,
> and calls himself a son of the Lord.
> Before us he stands, a reproof to our way of thinking,
> the very sight of him weighs our spirits down;
> his way of life is not like other men's,
> the paths he treads are unfamiliar.
> In his opinion we are counterfeit;
> he holds aloof from our doings as though from filth;
> he proclaims the final end of the virtuous as happy
> and boasts of having God for his father.
> Let us see if what he says is true,
> let us observe what kind of end he himself will have.
> If the virtuous man is God's son, God will take his part
> and rescue him from the clutches of his enemies.
> Let us test him with cruelty and with torture,
> and thus explore this gentleness of his
> and put his endurance to the proof.
> Let us condemn him to a shameful death
> since he will be looked after – we have his word for it.'

This is the way they reason, but they are mislead,
their malice makes them blind.
They do not know the hidden things of God,
they have no hope that holiness will be rewarded,
they can see no reward for blameless souls.

John 7:1-2, 10, 25-30

Jesus stayed in Galilee; he could not stay in Judaea, because the Jews were out to kill him.

As the Jewish feast of Tabernacles drew near, after his brothers had left for the festival, Jesus went up as well, but quite privately, without drawing attention to himself.

Meanwhile some of the people of Jerusalem were saying, 'Isn't this the man they want to kill? And here he is, speaking freely, and they have nothing to say to him! Can it be true that the authorities have made up their minds that he is the Christ? Yet we all know where he comes from, but when the Christ appears no one will know where he comes from.'

Then, as Jesus taught in the Temple, he cried out:

> *'Yes, you know me and you know where I came from.*
> *Yet I have not come of myself:*
> *no, there is one who sent me and I really come from him,*
> *and you do not know him,*
> *because I have come from him*
> *and it was he who sent me.'*

They would have arrested him then, but because his time had not yet come no one laid a hand on him.

'Yes, you know me and you know where I came from.' A powerful line from this Gospel passage – one that has so much to offer us as Catholic educators and supporters of the Catholic school. It offers us so much because it challenges us to be rooted in Christ in all that we do, as, to know Christ is to be rooted in him. Do we know Christ?... and more crucially, do we act out of that knowledge? That is the question I believe the scriptures put to us through these passages.

To act out of this knowledge means clearly to take up a stance, to be a witness to clear values. From this point let me bring us back to the passage from Wisdom where it says: *'Let us lie in wait for the virtuous man, since he annoys us and opposes our way of life...he claims to have knowledge of God...'* The clear link is that the knowledge of God transforms our lives, even to the extent of disturbing those around us, challenging the very society we live in.

To move to our Catholic schools, how does our network of schools show that distinctiveness, that clear identifiable character? My great fear is that we suffer in our network from a blandness, a safe lowest-common-denominator approach that rather too easily fits into society and often gets lost within it.

To what extent are our schools asking disturbing questions of our culture, how are they unashamedly standing for the values that:

- respect life
- celebrate community
- promote reconciliation
- witness to the Jesus of the Gospel in the Catholic tradition?

As those with responsibility in Catholic education we are challenged when, so clearly, the signs of the times tell us that our network is in danger, where in the words of the Book of Wisdom '...*our endurance is being put to the proof...*'

I believe we are in the darkest hour but this is the best time because it is at the cusp of a new day, a new beginning, a time when people become most creative, when the urgency is so evident, when denial of reality no longer shields us. So what will we bring to this end time? We know surely now, and especially in the Europe of this new millennium, that the answers of yesterday will not suffice for today, and certainly not for tomorrow. We are, rather, called to build on our tradition and we bring that quality that the Holy Father, Pope John Paul, proposed to this very gathering when you met him in April last year, and I quote: '*creative faithfulness*' – what a wonderfully rich phrase that captures the challenge, the opportunity of this time. It's in this context we look for the signs of hope, and there are some here in Ireland in terms of Catholic education: the work of the Association of Management of Catholic Secondary Schools (AMCSS) on the Catholic nature of schools, and the very positive contribution the Conference of Religious of Ireland (CORI) is making in the area of trusteeship. Another sign was the conference we in Marino organised, titled *Reimagining the Catholic School*. So many said don't do it, there will be little support, it is yesterday's issue, it is already too late. We enjoyed the support of AMCSS, CORI and many others. It was a great and inspiring gathering, where people from all levels in our Catholic schools' network came together and declared by their engagement that we have something worth fighting for, we have a contribution to make, we have a role to play in the new emerging Ireland.

So how do we go forward? We look to the scriptures again for hints; we look to the virtuous one in the Wisdom passage and we ask what qualities will we need to carry on our mission. I summarise them as follows:

Conviction – the conviction of our common faith, a conviction that we have a contribution to make, a compelling conviction around the purpose of Catholic education.

Communion – we are a gathering of believers, we are strong together, we gather around the Lord, we are rooted in him – he is our strength in the face of trials. We must all work together, drawing on each other's gifts to do the Lord's work.

Creative – as the Holy Father has proposed, we are called to be creative in how we enable our Catholic tradition to be accessible. New approaches for new times to enable the age-old gospel message of love, justice and peace to be heard anew.

And finally **Courage** – we will face opposition – *'people will lie in wait, we will annoy, we will oppose the way of life of others'*. So with the courage that comes from our knowledge of God let us be in communion, creatively responding to the needs of our time, doing so out of our conviction in the gospel. Let us stand with Christ because we know him and earnestly wish others to know the precious, transforming love of God.